LA CUCINA DI
LIDIA

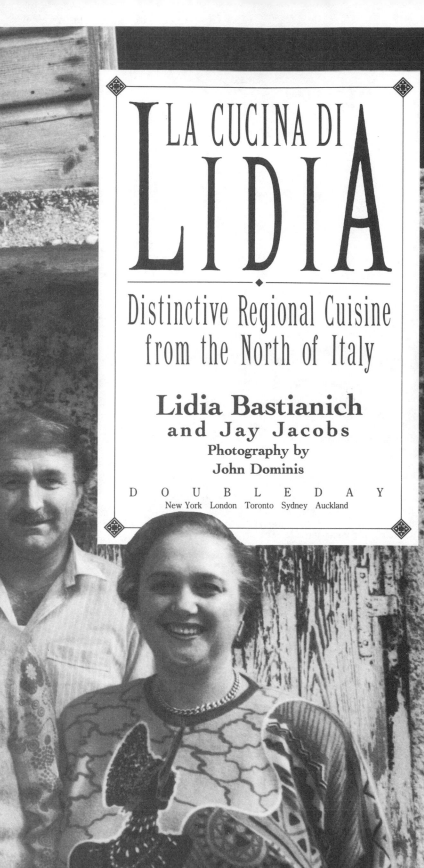

LA CUCINA DI LIDIA

Distinctive Regional Cuisine from the North of Italy

Lidia Bastianich
and Jay Jacobs

Photography by
John Dominis

D O U B L E D A Y
New York   London   Toronto   Sydney   Auckland

The families of Lidia and
Felice, Busoler.

PUBLISHED BY DOUBLEDAY
a division of Bantam Doubleday Dell Publishing
Group, Inc.
1540 Broadway, New York, New York 10036

DOUBLEDAY and the portrayal of an anchor
with a dolphin are trademarks of Doubleday,
a division of Bantam Doubleday Dell
Publishing Group, Inc.

One portion of this volume, "The Anatomy of a
Dinner," originally was published in slightly different
form as an article in *Connoisseur,* under the title
"Memories of the Feast." A second, "Coming
Beautiful," first was published in *Gourmet,* almost
identically but under the title "The Art of
Prosciutto."

Some photographs courtesy of Lidia Bastianich.
Additional photographs copyright © 1990 by John
Dominis.

Library of Congress Cataloging-in-Publication Data

Bastianich, Lidia.
     La cucina di Lidia: Distinctive regional cuisine
from the north of Italy / by Lidia Bastianich and Jay
Jacobs.—1st ed.
        p.   cm.
     1. Cookery, Italian—Northern style.   2. Cook-
ery, Yugoslav.
3. Felidia (Restaurant)   I. Jacobs, Jay.   II. Title.
    TX723.2.N65B37   1990
641.5945′3—dc20   89-49470
ISBN 0-385-24511-4   CIP

DESIGNED BY JOEL AVIROM

To Tanya and Joseph

Thank you for your love,
support, and understanding of a mother very much
dedicated to her passion: food.

———

ACKNOWLEDGMENTS

TINA UJLAKI

*For the patience and knowledge of testing
all the recipes*

———

ELEONORE SERRA
ISA BERNOCCO
GRACE DUMICIC

*For transforming all my scribbles into
legible material*

———

FRANCO MOTIKA

For helping me to organize my book

———

ERMINIA MOTIKA

For being my mother

———

GIANNOLA NONINO
BRUNO VESNAVER
BRANKO CENDAK

For helping me with the character pictures

———

*The whole staff of Felidia for contributing
and being supportive*

CONTENTS

◆

A Few Words from the Authors

Why this book? Of course, it's nice to see one's name in print and to share one's recipes with others, but, for me, much more is involved.

I was raised in a world where food was the center of life, where everyone's labor and activity centered on the feeding of the family. I remember great feelings of contentment and gratification at each meal. We would sit around the table, and an overwhelming feeling of security, love, and belonging would blanket me. Usually there were three generations of my family at the table: myself and my older brother, Franco, our parents and our grandparents. Stories were told, and words of wisdom spoken, by the family elders; my parents discussed plans and projects for our future. But the principal ingredient of those meals was love and security: the certainty that we were cherished, wanted, and needed right there, at the table; the feeling that we all would gather there forever.

Today, in another place and another time, mealtime remains very special for me, both at home and in the restaurant that my husband, Felice, and I opened twelve years ago. It's a time to express and receive love and to celebrate life through the sharing of food. It's a time of giving.

With this book, I want to share my recipes, of course, but recipes cannot exist in a vacuum. To live and resonate—simply to make sense—they require a larger, more meaningful context. For this reason, I also want to share my life and experiences and my reasons for cooking particular dishes at particular times, or in particular circumstances. To write "Do this, do that, add this, stir that" is not to share knowledge but to impose it dictatorially, and that is not the purpose of this book. As you cook the foods that are intimately connected to my heritage, background, and personal experiences, I want you to know not just how, but why you are preparing a particular dish in a particular context and selecting a particular wine as its accompaniment. I want you to feel what I feel and sense what I sense.

My goal cannot be achieved without mutual trust and unless you accept this book and its recipes as a catalyst for the expression of your own personality, taste, traditions, and sensibilities. All the recipes are simple and straightforward. I know that you will be able to reproduce them without difficulty, and if your finished products are a bit different from mine, if you add a spice or herb that I normally wouldn't use, it's perfectly OK. It's wonderful. It's an expression of yourself, and if you can achieve this with my guidance, we will have accomplished the sort of sharing that makes me very happy.

Lidia, Pula ca. 1953.

How did this union of coauthors between Jay and myself come about? Well, twelve years ago, when Felice and I opened our third restaurant, Felidia, Jay was one of the first reviewers to write about us. His review, in *Gourmet,* went much deeper than the menu. It captured our culture, our food, and what we were all about. I asked myself, Who is this man who understands us so well through our food? Well, we've been friends ever since, and it is through his prose that you will get to know Felice and myself.

—Lidia

Saliently, among a good many other things, Lidia Bastianich is a restaurateur and chef. A naturalized American citizen who learned English as a third language (after Italian and Croatian) and went on to learn two others, she is not a writer by profession. Lacking both her talent and good sense, I am. Because Lidia is this book's protagonist and *raison d'être,* she appears in Part One of this book as the third-person star of the show, while the first-person narrator functions as straight man and occasional chorus. Early in our discussions of the book's ultimate purpose, style, content, and format, Lidia and I agreed that neither a ghostwritten first-person approach nor unequal billing with an interposed "with" or "as told to" would suit our mutual purposes. Hence, while I may be the writer of record, Lidia is much the more indispensable of the book's coauthors.

I met Lidia and her husband Felice in 1981, not long after they opened Felidia, an Italian restaurant on the Upper East Side of Manhattan. On opening day I knew

nothing about the place except that its name—which, as it turned out later, telescoped the couple's given names—suggested something having to do with cats, and that, after months of mysterious goings-on behind plywood hoardings on East Fifty-eighth Street, it had supplanted a modest establishment called Puerta Real. I entered the expanded, distinctively remodeled premises for the first time in a thoroughly skeptical frame of mind; I had been partial to Puerta Real, one of the city's very few reasonably authentic sources of Spanish cooking, and resented its replacement by still another Italian venture in a block already crammed with presentable examples of its genre.

I was then the New York restaurant critic for a national food and travel magazine and had dropped in only to case the joint for future reference while having a quick nip at the bar. While absorbing a dry Martini unequaled anywhere in my considerable experience, I gradually became aware of a medley of altogether beguiling aromas—stimuli that had a salutary effect on my own and my companion's appetency. We decided to stay for dinner.

Half an hour later, my tablemate, a tidy size three but a relentless predator of small birds, basked blissfully in the afterglow of a portion of *fuzi con quaglie*, having put herself on the outside of a well-browned brace of rosemary-scented quail, the unfamiliar pasta whereon the birds had nested, and the last vestiges of a sauce compounded largely of their drippings and spare parts.

Thanks in no small measure to Felidia and a handful of other pioneering ventures, today's Italian restaurants in New York (and, by extension, in North America) are a far cry from what they were a mere decade and a half ago, when their menus were virtually interchangeable and utterly predictable. Although what loosely is termed Northern Italian cooking had by then become the Italian cuisine of choice (having shouldered aside the bastardized pseudo-Neapolitan clichés that generations of Americans had mistaken not only for Italian cookery, but for Italian cookery in its entirety), the food served in most Italian restaurants might be said to have had a generalized Italian accent but a largely American vocabulary.

To be sure, arugula and radicchio had begun to supplant the more prosaic American greens in salads, and a few big-ticket enterprises even featured Piedmont white truffles in season, but soup choices remained pathetically underrepresentative of Italy's rich diversity, pastas still were pushed as main courses (profitably enough for the restaurateur willing to prostitute his heritage), and beef—a relative rarity throughout most of Italy—remained a best-seller in this country. Polenta and risotto continued to be slighted, the sauté pan reigned supreme among kitchen utensils, grated cheese still could be found on seafoods, and most mushroom dishes were made with cellar-grown produce that would have been deemed unacceptable anywhere in Italy. All in all, what was acceptable at the close of the 1970s was a marked improvement on what had preceded it, but Americans who had traveled in Italy had little reason to celebrate what they found on their plates back home.

Hundreds of dishes after the fact, I don't recall what followed the quail preparation that first evening at Felidia, but I do remember remarking that, for the first time in this country, I'd eaten an Italian meal that actually might have been prepared on Italian soil. But where, precisely? A good-sized town on or near the Adriatic in all likelihood, but I wasn't then familiar enough with the east coast of Italy to pinpoint the provenance of a style I found quintessentially Italian, but otherwise geographically uncertain.

In my dubious capacity as an accredited restaurant pundit, my policy was to maintain as much anonymity as possible while scouting prospective subjects. During the few days that followed, I managed to visit Felidia incognito two or three times, before my cover was blown by a colleague who operates with all the discretion of a rhinoceros in rut. My identity thus established, I was approached by a rather large, big-boned, well-upholstered woman who introduced herself simply as Lidia. "Well," she said, "now that I know who you are, I know why you've been here so often in the space of just a few days." With that, she withdrew, leaving an altogether smitten couple in her wake. Although she was then still in her early thirties, she was, my consort and I agreed, the radiant personification of Mama-in-the-Kitchen, the paradigmatic earth mother. Although we had eaten a succession of dishes of great refinement and sophistication, along with several transcendentally gratifying rustic offerings, we assumed she had been born cooking expertly and *con amore;* that she was an untutored immensely gifted natural whose talent was no less a product of genetic happenstance than were her sturdy good looks.

Only as our friendship with Lidia developed did I begin to realize that the woman we had taken for a Douanier Rousseau or Grandma Moses of the kitchen is perhaps the most scholarly and analytical of the hundreds of professional chefs I've known; that, far from being the immensely gifted naïf she had seemed at first blush, she was someone who had undertaken intensive studies in food-related chemistry, physiology, anthropology, and the effects of weather and climate on eating and drinking, and in several other subjects of little or no concern to most professional chefs. But at the end of that first brief meeting, I still was uncertain about the regional origins of her style and repertory.

—J.J.

LA CUCINA DI
LIDIA

PART ONE

Origins: A Courtyard in Busoler

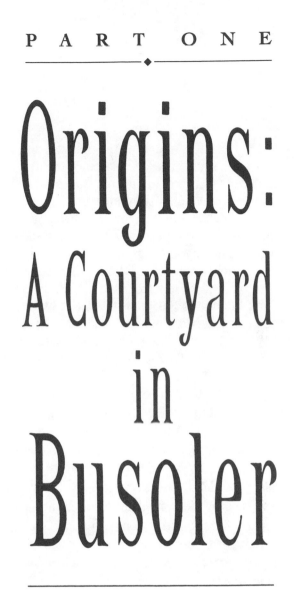

As seen on maps of the Adriatic and its environs, the Istrian peninsula is a somewhat suggestive appendate of the crotch formed by the Gulf of Trieste at the juncture of Italy and the former Yugoslavia. No farther than ninety miles from Venice at any point along its sixty-mile length, Istria's west coast historically has maintained stronger cultural ties to the Venetians than to the more insular Slavic cultures that commence in the Istrian interior and sweep eastward across the Gulf of Veliki Kvarner and beyond what was formerly eastern Yugoslavia.

The region was settled during the late Bronze and early Iron ages by the Illyrians, a proto-Slavic people from the Carpathian mountains, and Mesopotamians from the Tigris-Euphrates Basic. In the course of a long, remarkably unstable political history, the peninsula has been controlled wholly or in part by the Romans, the Franks, the Duchy of Bavaria, the patriarchs of Aquileia, Venice, Hapsburg Austria, Italy, and, after World War II, Yugoslavia.

To one extent or another, influences of these disparate cultures can be found throughout Istria today, but an even richer mix obtains on the Adriatic coast, where the influence of Venice, with its own eclectic influences from the domains of the Saracens and points east, is most strongly felt.

Lidia Motika was born of ethnic Italian parentage in Pula, a fortified seaport at the southwestern tip of the peninsula, in the immediate aftermath of World War II. As part of the Italian region of Venezia Giulia since 1920, the city had been called Pola, but along with Lidia's maiden name, Matticchio, and her future husband's surname, Bastiani, the place name was Slavicized by law when Istria was annexed by Yugoslavia.

Lidia and Franco in Pula. The tree is a *nespola*, or medlar, which yields fruit somewhat similar to the kumquat.

"We were Italian, except for a dash of Rumanian on my mother's maternal grandmother's side," Lidia explains. "But I was born in 1947, the year after Istria became part of Yugoslavia." Such have been the vagaries of Istrian history that, although the Matticchio and Bastiani families remained in place, the last three generations born on Istrian soil successively were born subjects of the Austro-Hungarian Empire, Italy, and Yugoslavia.

By Lidia's estimate, the ethnic breakdown of her native region during her childhood worked out roughly to sixty-five Italians and thirty-five Slavs per hundred, a ratio imperfectly reflected by the cookery of Istria in general, which she assesses as "fifty percent Italian, thirty-five percent Yugoslavian, and the rest mixed German and Hungarian."

Writing specifically of Trieste, which lies some sixty-five miles up the coast from Pula but shares a common culinary heritage, Waverley Root described "a mixed cuisine, englobing reminiscences of the Austro-Hungarian Empire . . . and seepages from the basically Byzantine cooking to the east, Hungarian, Greek, Slavic and Jewish." Root went on to note, however, that "the cooking . . . is much more Italian than that of the Alto Adige, which after all is not surprising, since the Latin character of this region was established long be-fore there was a Yugoslavia or a Serbia or an Austria."

The Latin character of Pula was established in 178 B.C., when the Romans, who called the sea-port Pietas Julia, positioned a military and naval base there. The town was destroyed in 39 B.C., during a war against the Illyrians and Dalmatians, and rebuilt four years later. As a small, bilingual child, Lidia played amidst Roman ruins and Byzan-tine architecture and in a remarkably well-pre-served Roman amphitheater. "All the cultural influences of the region were reflected in the food

Market, Pula.

we ate," she says. "Our family meals were basically Italian, but we also made Hungarian *gulyas*, Slavic sauerkraut, *palacinke*, and a Germanic dish of gnocchi with plums."

Polenta, the corn-based descendant of an Etruscan grain mush known to the Roman legions as *pulmentum*, was a mainstay of the Istrian kitchen, as was risotto, a legacy of the Saracens. As in most of Italy proper, however, pasta remained the starch of choice, although variations on more popular forms bore such designations as *pasutice, fuzi, krafi*, and *parenci*.

Times were hard and shortages prevalent in Istria, as elsewhere in Europe, during Lidia's early childhood. As Felice, her husband, who was born in Albona (now Labin, about twenty miles northeast of Pula), recalls, "Whenever anyone in a village got hold of a prosciutto bone, it would be passed from one family's pot to another's, until there wasn't a trace of its flavor left. Sometimes, the last ones to get it only imagined they could taste it in a soup."

Seafood was plentiful along the coast, but went largely unharvested for lack of boats and fishing gear. Mountains thrust up behind a rocky littoral with, as Lidia puts it, "not much in between," except for small family kitchen gardens. The region depended on game for much of its meat, but, with guns and shot in short supply, a single small bird more often than not had to be stretched far enough to allow every member of a large family to get, in Lidia's words, "at least the taste, if not much of the substance." The family menu was augmented whenever possible with foraged mushrooms, wild greens, roots, and the like.

Lidia's hardscrabble formative years of make-do cookery had a lasting effect on her personal culinary style, bringing into sharp individualized focus a regional cuisine that, for all its richly textured polygenetic tradition, lacked clear definition in its generic manifestations. Unlike, say, Venetian cooking, which itself has absorbed all manner of alien influences, Istrian cooking resists easy identification, even in its most Italianate guises. Root's "reminiscences and seepages" are less thoroughly assimilated in Istria than anywhere in Italy proper, and without the imprint of a highly developed personal style, the provenance of many Istrian dishes remains somewhat conjectural, at least for outsiders.

The distinctive characteristics of Lidia's cooking, at her restaurant and at home, are intense flavor and heady aroma, both attributable to the exigencies of a postwar childhood during which the most had to be extracted from the least. As she has remarked during the course of our many conversations on her early life in food and vice versa, "From a single scrawny chicken, we had a satisfying soup, a complex sauce, and a festive pasta. I learned, first from my grandmother and mother and later from a great-aunt, Nina, in Trieste, to bring out the fullest potential of a basic ingredient through the judicious use of herbs and spices."

The chicken inspectors are Joseph and his sister Tanya during a visit to Busoler ca. 1974.

Although her parents lived in the center of Pula and she attended grade school there, Lidia spent her free time—vacations, weekends, even after-school hours—at her maternal grandmother's house in the village of Busoler, two kilometers outside the Pula city limits. She began to describe the place as we sat together in the rear dining room of her restaurant one morning, about an hour before the arrival of the lunch crowd, but interrupted herself to place half a dozen fresh figs on a plate, which she positioned between us: a gesture, I realized a few minutes later, that may have been a calculated equivalent of Marcel Proust's involuntary epiphanic encounter with the celebrated *madeleine.* Although there are now a good many new buildings there, Lidia explained, "Busoler hasn't changed much since my childhood, when it was a small, typical Istrian coastal village of about twenty-two houses lined up along a road. My grandparents came down there from a predominantly Slavic village called Tuplijak, underneath a mountain called Ucka, and a number of their relatives settled there in Busoler, in houses grouped around a communal courtyard."

"That courtyard was the center of activity for the whole tribe. There were always children and animals there, especially during the summer, when all the grandchildren gathered from wherever they lived the rest of the year. There were fig trees lined up in the courtyard, and when the fruit was ripe, we kids would pick them and eat them right there, while the chickens ran between our legs, eating whatever had fallen to the ground." With a faraway look in her eyes, Lidia seemed to savor a particular sensation in retrospect, but I couldn't tell whether it was the taste of the figs or the fig-fattened chickens. I picked up a small green fig and crushed it between my teeth. As figs available in New York in season go, it wasn't at all bad, but my own memories of the sun-warmed, insidiously pudendal figs of Provence and Apulia and Catalonia, eaten in situ and out of hand, lay dormant, sluggishly incapable of transporting me to other places and times.

As Lidia warmed to her subject, it became increasingly apparent that just about all her early childhood activities, formal schooling excepted, were tied one way or another to the production, procurement, and preparation of food; that even her games, playthings, and daydreams derived from comestibles and their by-products. It also became increasingly apparent that, contrary to what logically might be inferred and certain shortages notwithstanding, it was anything but an unhappy or deprived childhood.

"We may have lacked some things," Lidia explained, "but we always had wonderful meals. My grandmother kept a kitchen garden and sold or bartered the surplus for whatever she couldn't

Nonna Rosa tying grapevines.

raise herself. Nothing was wasted. When we harvested the corn, we'd save the husks for mattress filling, and the children would dress up in corn-silk wigs. The mattresses would be freshly filled each year, and I loved to lie in bed, listening to the crackling of the husks and imagining that I could hear songs and the sounds of animals. In the mornings, my skin would smell of corn. Then, when I'd dress, I'd smell of quince, because we'd put green quinces in the closets to perfume the clothes as they ripened in the dark."

Lidia and her family weren't the only inhabitants of Busoler who smelled of good things to eat: "We had olive groves, and we would stone-grind the ripe fruit for our oil, using hot water so the oil would float up from the stone. There was one kid who dunked his head in the oil."

His head?

"Yes. Some of the men used a little oil as brilliantine, and one in particular was very handsome, a real lady-killer. Well, this one boy thought he would grow up to be even more handsome than the real lady-killer if he put enough oil on his hair. We kept the olive oil in stone troughs, and one day this kid leaned over our trough and ducked his whole head into it."

The lunch crowd, made up in large part of upper-echelon business and communications executives, began trickling in as Lidia elaborated on the "single scrawny chicken" mentioned earlier, a progenitor of the elegant but intensely savory pheasant and partridge preparations featured on the day's menu. "When we had chicken, we used every bit of it," she said. "The feet and head and wings for soup, the rest for *sugo,* and the innards for a dish we ate at *merenda* (elevenses), which was made with the intestines, the giblets, and the eggs we found inside the bird, all fried together. One of my first chores in the kitchen was to split and wash the intestines." A dreamy expression came over Lidia's face as she summoned up the dish in her memory. I mourned both its noninclusion on the menu and the alienation from their own, similarly frugal culinary heritage of a couple of generations of increasingly prosperous but gastronomically deprived Americans.

"We were better off than many people in the region," Lidia continued, "but meat was scarce for everyone." To illustrate her point, she went on to tell a story, popular around Busoler at the time, about a man who regularly managed to extract for himself what little meat was to be found in a communal stew by dramatically enacting the fate he purported to have in store for his shrewish wife. "The farm women would cook for the land help," she explained, "and they'd serve them their meals in a single bowl set in the center of the table. The dish would be garnished with a little meat, as much as could be spared, and in this story six men would gather around the bowl. Well, as soon as they sat down each day, this one guy would start complaining about his wife while he gobbled up the meat from the part of the bowl nearest him. He'd pretend to get more and more agitated, and he'd say, 'Someday, I'm gonna wring her neck like a chicken's—like this.' Then he'd grab the bowl and twist it around far enough to get at someone else's share of the meat. Five times at every meal, he'd twist the bowl to show how he'd wring his wife's neck, and all the meat would be gone before anyone else got a scrap." The story didn't elicit much more than a small smile from me, but I supposed you had to be there to appreciate it.

Given comparable talent, there remains a difference of sensibility between the cook who knows food from the ground up and the cook whose familiarity with raw ingredients is based on the purchase of what others have raised or harvested. Many a renowned chef takes pride in and receives kudos for trudging through the market each morning to make personal hands-on selections from the cream of the day's crop. Commendable as the effort may be, it's undertaken at the final phase of the food-production chain and in no way reflects an intimate familiarity with the entire growth cycle, from seed to harvest. To put it another way, the city-raised, restaurant-educated three-star chef may have a perfect idea of how a market tomato should smell, look, feel, and taste, but won't necessarily know how it tasted, smelled, looked, and felt as it contended for early survival and ripened in the fullness of its season; how it would have tasted while still suffused with the languorous heat of a high-summer sun and the spicy, nicotinic pungency of the vine leaves, as it was picked by green-smudged fingers and eaten before the virtually immediate onset of chemical breakdown and change.

From her earliest girlhood on, Lidia has lived intimately with foodstuffs throughout their life cycles. As a consequence, her culinary style today is rooted in a thorough understanding not just of how market produce is best prepared for the table, but of how the natural essence of a given ingredient is optimally preserved in the finished dish. "My earliest memories are of helping my grandmother in the garden," she says. "As a little girl, I'd walk behind her as she hoed up the potatoes, and for the next planting I'd cut up the seed potatoes we stored over the winter.

Growing cabbages, Istria.

As soon as our vegetables were picked, I'd help to clean and wash them in the courtyard, where the beans were shelled, the garlic was braided, and the next spring's seeds were flailed out on mats. We dried vegetables, too, for use during the year, and in the fall the whole courtyard would be festooned with drying vegetables.

"On market days, I'd help pick vegetables very early in the morning, wash them in the courtyard, and load them into my grandmother's handcart. Then, on the way to the market, I'd ride in the cart on downhill stretches and get out and help push when we had to go uphill. We had a stall at the market, with scales and stacks of old newspapers. I'd weigh the vegetables and put them into paper cones for the customers. On the way home, we'd barter whatever we hadn't sold for old restaurant bread, which we fed to our animals.

"Most business at that time was done by barter, and the barter system created a network of interdependency and closeness. There was a community mill, for example, and the miller was given one bag out of every ten in exchange for milling our grain. When the grain was harvested and threshed [by flailing], we'd spread it out in the courtyard to dry and ripen, and we'd scatter Seckel pears and quinces through it, to ripen with the grain. When the grain was fully dried, we'd load it onto a horse cart and take it to the mill as needed."

Although relatively few New York restaurants bake their own breads, Felidia does. I haven't yet detected the bouquet of pear or quince in the dinner rolls or *focaccia*, possibly because wheat doesn't grow very well within the city limits and there isn't a community mill in town. Nonetheless, the breads at Felidia are first-rate.

Lidia interrupted our discussion to greet a regular lunchtime customer, a reigning advertising genius and his retinue. Returning to our table, she nibbled a fig and Prousted back to postwar Istria. "What I loved most as a child was the *samanj*," she said. "The *samanj* was the equivalent of an American country fair. My grandmother, grandfather, and I would load our produce and animals onto a donkey cart and set off on a two- or three-hour journey to the fair. As we traveled, we'd pick up the local specialties at the towns and villages along the way—distinctive olive oils, *speck* [which Waverley Root defined as bacon or boned ham, "smoked slowly and intermittently" over a period of three months], cheeses, and whatever else our own village didn't specialize in. We ate at the fair after business was concluded, and there would be music—including bagpipe music—and dancing." (Both Lidia and Felice are accomplished singers and astonishingly graceful, versatile dancers. Lidia's signature rendition of "Summertime," from *Porgy and Bess,* rendered in a lusty, creamy contralto, is a show-stopper at Italo-Istrian picnics and weddings, and Felice's virtuosity on the accordion is legendary in New York's surprisingly large Istrian community.)

In Istria, the elderly have lived under Austrian, Italian, and Yugoslavian rule.

As the years of Lidia's early childhood passed, it became increasingly obvious to a great many ethnic Italians in Istria, including her parents, that, in a geopolitical sense, they were displaced persons. Although Tito's Yugoslavia wasn't toeing the line precisely as Moscow had drawn it, the Istrian ethos had undergone a politically imposed change, and the peninsula's ethnic Italians, although they may have constituted a numerical majority, became in effect a social minority. As was not the case within the more rigorous Soviet sphere of influence, however, they were given the option of emigrating, and Lidia's parents elected to "return" to Italy.

Fortunately or not, as it would later turn out, so many others sought to exercise the same option that Italy, unable to absorb them all, was forced to impose a quota, and the Motikas found themselves in Campo Profughi Sansaba, a staging area for prospective repatriates. The camp, on the outskirts of Trieste, consisted of no-frills barracks divided into family cubicles that afforded little comfort and less privacy. "We had a bed and a chest," Lidia recalls, "and that was it. I was ten years old by then, and I remember it very clearly. Everyone ate communally in the *mensa,* a sort of mess hall, and the food was nothing like what I was used to."

Lidia's gastronomic and culinary fortunes took a marked upturn after some months at the camp, when an aunt of her mother's, who had an apartment in Trieste, took her grandniece in. As Lidia describes the situation, "Aunt Nina already had two tenants who shared the kitchen, so it would get pretty crowded in there, but that's where most of my time was spent. Aunt Nina had worked as a cook for a rich family before the war. She was a sensitive cook with sophisticated tastes, and it was from her that I learned refinements that I hadn't known about in Pula or Busoler. Trieste was a cosmopolitan city and, although the cooking there was basically the same as it was farther down the coast, it had more finesse. Among other things, I was introduced to dried pasta in Trieste. At home, we had used mostly fresh."

In a snapshot taken during the family's stay in Trieste, Lidia poses with her mother Erminia, father Vittorio, and older brother Franco. Behind them, a family friend, Inez, is flanked by Lidia's great-aunt and uncle, Zia Nina and Zio Nicola Rapetti.

To many recent American converts to the cult of so-called Northern Italian cuisine (which is not one but many disparate cuisines), the association of dried pasta with finesse may come as a seeming reversal of form. As it happens, however, factory-made pasta today is highly esteemed throughout Italy, a few insular Germanic pockets of resistance in the high north excepted, and is considered more suitable for many purposes than the softer, generally richer fresh pastas. To prepare, for example, *Spaghetti alle vongole* with fresh pasta would be to diminish rather than enhance the harmony of the dish. At Felidia, as at most better Italian restaurants, both the kitchen's own fresh and factory-produced dried pasta are used, depending on the respective appropriateness to a given dish.

Lidia's parents were able to quit Campo Profughi when they were taken on by a well-to-do Trieste family as live-in domestics: her mother, who had been a school-teacher in Pula, as cook-housekeeper, and her father, an erstwhile automotive mechanic, as chauffeur. Lidia herself by then was enrolled in a convent school. "It was there, at school," she says, "that I saw my first professional kitchen." It was there, too, that she put in her first stint, at age eleven, as a professional kitchen hand: "I worked for about a year to supplement my tuition, and had learned something about volume cooking by the time we were accepted for relocation in the United States. Actually, we had expected to go to Australia, but the American quota opened up a few days before the Australian. We boarded a KLM plane in Rome and, after a refueling stop at Reykjavik, we landed in New York. That was in April 1958.

"Naturally, my parents had mixed feelings about cutting themselves off from Istria and their families and traditions for an uncertain future in a strange place, but we kids—my elder brother by three years and I—were very excited about the trip. We stayed in New York under Catholic Charities sponsorship, and were put up for two weeks at the Woollcott Hotel. There was a Horn & Hardart Automat on the corner, and we had most of our meals there. I ate mostly bananas and milk. And American white bread, which was like nothing I ever tasted."

That last observation seemed to me to be open to more than one interpretation. I asked Lidia whether she could recall what she thought of American white bread at the time. "I loved it," she replied. "And I loved the Automat. To a little kid from Istria, it was magic." Not just to a little kid from Istria: Today there isn't an Automat left in the city, but when I, a native New Yorker, was a little kid, there were thirty-odd scattered around Manhattan, and they were all magic. To the child-me, the most magical thing about them was neither the coin-operated food dispensers

nor the nickel-activated beverage spigots, which filled your cup with hairbreadth precision, but the human money changers, more machinelike than machines, who infallibly thumbed the requisite number of nickels— five, ten, fifteen, or twenty—from their cupped hands in instants, lining the coins out across hollowed marble countertops in tight, precisely counted rows. Even today, decades later, the unique, indelible aromas of the Automat's baked beans, hot chocolate, and macaroni casserole are reactivated vividly for me when . . . but this is Lidia's story.

At age eleven, Lidia attended a convent school in Trieste.

After a couple of weeks at the hotel, Lidia's father landed a job as a mechanic with a Chevrolet plant in New Jersey, and the Motikas found an apartment in nearby North Bergen. "Our neighbors were Canadians," Lidia recalls. "We couldn't communicate, but we played with their kids anyway. And we had lots of fun. Sometimes their parents would give us fresh fish, and my mother would try to express her gratitude by inviting them for drinks." Signora Motika's good intentions might have been undermined to some extent by her minimal command of English. "She would say, 'Go home, have beer,' " Lidia explained, giggling.

At that time, most Istrian expatriates (and Yugoslavian émigrés in general) in the New York area gravitated to the Astoria section of the borough of Queens, which today remains the social and mercantile hub of an Istrian community now nearly half a million strong, first-generation Americans included. With the urging and assistance of relatives, Louis and Marie Matticchio, who had taken up residence there earlier, the Motikas followed suit, although Lidia's parents continued to work in New Jersey. Within a year, Lidia and her brother were fluent enough in English to make sense of their courses at a junior high school in a nearby neighborhood, where, as Lidia puts it, "I became intensely interested in home economics." The interest wasn't merely theoretical: "During this period, my mother wouldn't get home from New Jersey until eight o'clock in the evening, and it was my responsibility to prepare dinner for the family. I loved it. We had three-course meals every night."

Lidia Motika met Felice Bastianich, seven years her senior, while she was attending Bryant High School in Queens. Felice, an erstwhile journalist who filed his copy in rhyming verse, then was working as a waiter in Manhattan. They married in 1966, when Lidia was nineteen, thereby derailing her plans for a college education. As Lidia describes their early life together, Felice "always talked about opening his own restaurant. We shared this intense interest in food, and I also began to work in restaurants."

Lidia's restaurant work was put on hold temporarily in 1968, with the birth of the couple's first child, Joseph, but Felice's longing to open a place of his own was realized three years later, with the launching of Buonavia, a thirty-seat establishment in the Forest Hills section of Queens. Then in Lidia's words, "I became pregnant again with our daughter, Tanya, who I think was the product of our opening night celebration. My pregnancy and all, we both worked very hard, and the restaurant was a big success, right from the

Felice as a young man.

start. We still had a lot to learn, but we made an honest effort that our customers seemed to appreciate. We had a line at the door every night."

By 1977, two enlargements later, Buonavia seated a hundred and twenty diners, with people still lining up at the door every night. Two years later, the couple opened a second venture, Villa Secondo, in the Fresh Meadows section of Queens. In Lidia's description, "It had been a small, unsuccessful restaurant which had closed, but a few months after we reopened it, we had lines at the door again."

Although Felice Bastianich cheerfully admits that some concessions to popular taste were made during the couple's ownership of the restaurants, he himself is one of the most discriminating eaters I've ever known, and one of the more exploratory—far more so in the latter respect than Lidia, who doesn't share his enthusiasm for unfamiliar cuisines and foodstuffs that lack close counterparts in her own culinary heritage. She abstains from the caviar orgies Felice stages on occasion, and had evinced little more than mild academic interest in gravlax, which Felice tasted for the first time at one of my New Year's Eve parties and has been addicted to since. A few years ago, I left a batch of infant whelk, the size of escargots, at the restaurant. A day or two later, I asked Felice what he and Lidia had thought of them. "I ate them all," he replied. "They were delicious." The clear implication was that the minuscule *scungilli* would have been wasted on Lidia.

Accommodations to the taste of the regular clientele notwithstanding, both Queens establishments attracted more than just local notice. A good deal of favorable ink was shed on the restaurants' behalf by Manhattan-based food writers, and a good many other Manhattanites (for the most part, people who wouldn't otherwise be found dead in the infra-dig "outer boroughs") frequented both places.

Taking up the thread of the Bastianich saga, Lidia confided, "By that time, we had our eyes on Manhattan. Like a show, we had gone through our out-of-town tryouts and were ready for Broadway. In 1980, we began to build Felidia and, after some delay, we opened in the spring of 1981, after selling Buonavia and Villa Secondo the previous fall."

Felidia opened to initially mixed notices, but people again began to line up at the door, and have been doing so ever since.

As Lidia and I concluded the day's working conversation, she observed that the move to Manhattan had entailed enormous risk, but that she and Felice had been sustained by their faith in the innate rightness of putting good, honest food on the table. "All this is the outgrowth of our childhood experiences," she said. "For me, it goes straight back to that courtyard at Busoler and the struggle to live decently in the aftermath of a war, when food was scarce and there was a reverence attached to its production, its preparation, and its consumption. Whatever else a meal may be, it's first of all an act of communion."

Just then, Felice joined us at the table, and Lidia said, "What shall we have for lunch?"

"Let's have a steak," Felice replied. "I'm going to cook it." A superb cook, he disappeared into the kitchen as it occurred to me that I never had eaten beef in any form at the restaurant. Although the menu contains a perfunctory selection of steaks, I had assumed they were included as an unenthusiastic accommodation for single-minded carnivores, and couldn't recall ever hearing a captain spontaneously recommend them. For that matter, I seldom had eaten beef in any Italian restaurant. The Florentines excepted, Italians are neither notable cooks nor consumers of beef. Although several of the better New York steak houses are run by Italians, I'd always operated on the theory that there was no point in bucking the odds elsewhere.

Felice rejoined us after ten minutes or so, followed by a waiter who served what looked like a textbook reading of France's most popular meal: *steak aux pommes frites* with a tossed salad on the side. It was a meal I had shared scores of times with French chefs in this country, including several vaunted exponents of haute cuisine, and had eaten in scores of bistros in France. Felice's version was easily the best I've been served anywhere. When I remarked that I hadn't expected him to produce something so typically French, he replied, "Why not? They can cook, too." Lidia returned my quizzical glance with the luminous equanimity of a nun, and the three of us fell to.

If pasta with chicken sauce has ever turned up on an Italian menu, I've missed it. Nor can I recall ever having seen a recipe for such a dish in a legitimate Italian cookbook. For some weeks after Lidia's discussion of her Istrian childhood, I found myself puzzling over her frequent references to the "festive pasta" that supposedly derived from "a single scrawny chicken." I had more or less concluded that her childhood memories had undergone some distortion over the years; that what may have seemed festive in a time of scarcity might not seem worth cooking or eating today. Certainly no such dish had appeared on the Felidia menu, and in all likelihood, not a single portion would have sold if it had. I intended to question Lidia more closely on the matter, but Felice cleared up the mystery before I got the chance.

It was fairly well along on a Friday evening, and Lidia already was on her way home, when I dropped into the restaurant for a nightcap. As he often does once the dinner crowd has thinned, Felice joined me at the bar to compare notes on what we'd eaten since we last chatted. It was late autumn. I had just harvested the last of the fennel and bok choy from my garden, and I nattered on at some length about the delicately aromatic soup the two vegetables had produced in combination. Felice had attended a benefit buffet earlier in the evening and, by his account, had outeaten then Mayor Edward I. Koch, the city's most renowned trencherman. "I ate three dozen oysters, at least," he recounted, "and just as many clams, and salmon prepared three different ways." As he warmed to his itemization, Felice began to work up an appetite. "Let's eat some *Fuzi*," he said. "You'll never be able to guess from what I made the sauce." Unlike Lidia's, Felice's diction and syntax betray his relatively late acquisition of English.

Twenty minutes later, Felice emerged from the kitchen, a waiter trailing in his wake. A couple of pasta-laden dishes were set before us. I inspected the sauce, a meaty, mellow-looking, mahogany-colored piece of work with a heady, decidedly gamey aroma, and with lots of small bone in evidence. "*Coniglio* [rabbit] or *lepre* [hare]," I declared. I was instructed to taste the sauce before making rash pronouncements. Dutifully, I tasted the sauce. It was as intensely flavorsome as any I'd ever tasted, and full of resonance. "Definitely *coniglio*—or possibly *lepre*," I hedged, once I could speak.

"No," I was corrected. "That sauce I made from chicken. Free-range chicken. An old stewing bird that I cooked four hours and fifteen minutes. It was tough like hell when I put it into the pot, but now the meat falls off the bones."

As I tucked into the dish, I found myself drifting back to my own childhood, part of which was spent on a Pennsylvania farm in a time of general deprivation, when a large household salivated all week long in anticipation of the fresh-killed chicken to be served on Sunday. Conditioned by decades of flavorless, immature, factory-packed poultry, I had forgotten the depths that can be plumbed by real birds: birds allowed to mature as nature intended them to, scratching for a living in open air and taking on the profoundly sapid cussedness of advanced age in the process. Lidia's memory, I concluded, had not betrayed her. If anything, her case had been understated. After decades of marginal commercial survival, the free-range chicken had made a comeback of sorts during the past few years, at least in circles where cooking and eating are regarded as art forms. Raised by small growers for the delectation of the so-called gourmet market, the free-range fowl purveyed to the more progressive restaurants and retailed to the fancy food trade unquestionably are superior to the standard supermarket product. Still, they're a far cry from the "live" (which is to say, killed-to-order) birds favored by foreign-born Americans and sold mostly in the urban enclaves of various ethnic minorities. Free-range or not, the relatively costly birds raised for recent converts to the food faith are marketed when no more mature than their mass-produced counterparts, and, like the latter, are sold minus the accessories—notably the feet—deemed essential to the making of a proper soup or sauce by untold generations of foreign-born home cooks.

Felice had picked up the makings of his *fuzi* sauce in the Astoria section of Queens, a neighborhood populated for the most part by immigrants: Istrians and prewar Yugoslavians, Greeks, Latin Americans, West Indians, and, among more recent arrivals, Southeast Asians and émigrés from the Indian subcontinent. Dependent on local taste and custom, the Astorian markets offer a much wider range of raw materials—including the elderly live stewing birds demanded by a tradition-bound foreign clientele—than can be found anywhere else in the city. Although Lidia has developed a highly sophisticated, far-flung network of off-beat suppliers who fly all manner of esoteric delicacies to the restaurant at various seasons (during the winter, for example, a huge bag of *mesclun* arrives daily from California, along with an assortment of edible flowers, elk from Texas, wild mushrooms from the Pacific Northwest, and the like), Felice scours the markets of Astoria each morning, searching out the basic stuffs of traditional Istrian cookery.

As noted earlier, Felice is an adventurous eater with a cosmopolitan palate. Nonetheless, he seems most in his element when he has found something in the day's market that relates directly to his formative eating experiences. "Look at these," he'll say, lugging into the restaurant a carton that leaks a blend of melted ice and diluted juices onto his costly, impeccable Italian haberdashery. "Have you ever seen such beautiful *polipetti* [octopus] or *triglie* [red mullet]?" Significantly, neither *polipetti* nor *triglie* are big sellers in this country, where the octopus generally is thought to be a creature of science fiction and red mullet (a superb little fish with a distinctly nutlike flavor) suffers because of its boniness.

Another view of Trieste's Mercato Centrale.

A day or two after the *fuzi* supper, Lidia and I got together to talk about her first years in this country. As we sat down, I asked whether she had tasted Felice's creation. "I tasted it long before I even met Felix," she replied. "That's exactly the way we cooked it when I was a little girl in Busoler, and Felix and I still make it often at home on Sundays, or in the restaurant for the family."

Ever since I'd known Lidia, she had collectively referred to, and treated, her employees as "family," and her fifty-two-person staff is indeed the most familial crew of restaurant workers, possibly including those made up of actual kinfolk, that I know of. In a métier infamous for temperamental outbursts, intramural blood feuds, petty deceit, and open boss-hatred, the manifest mutual affection of all members of the Felidian operation is deeply touching. "You're the best" is a house shibboleth heard constantly as scullions deliver ice to the bar, waiters pick up orders in the kitchen, cashiers make change for table captains, and various workers delay their departures at the end of their shifts, waiting for colleagues to share their rides home.

Although a good deal of badinage is exchanged among a polyglot crew composed predominantly of Italians, Istrians, and Dalmatians, along with a scattering of Mexican and Peruvian Indians, various Latinos, the odd WASP, and a Botticelli Venus of Irish-Scandinavian parentage, it has never been tinged with the merest bit of rancor in my hearing. Nor has frequent raillery betwen the sexes or the often hilarious double entendres traded by waiters in passing. Aside from the replacement of voluntary retirees, employee turnover has been minimal since the restaurant's opening, and, on the rare occasions when outright dismissal has been unavoidable, Lidia, Felice, and the rest of the "family" have mourned the departed as they would a child or sibling strayed from the fold. "Goddammit, all he had to do was ask for another chance to change his habits," Felice lamented, after a problem drinker was given his walking papers. "But no, he was too stubborn to do it. Just one word from him and we would have welcomed him back with our arms open, but the son of a bitch wouldn't let us do it." It was the only time I'd heard a voice crack as someone was referred to as a son of a bitch.

My flicker of reaction to Lidia's "the family" didn't escape her notice. "I run a very tight ship here, and I demand a lot from my people," she said, "but I do try to cultivate a family feeling among all of us. Everyone is encouraged to contribute, to participate creatively, and to take pride in what they do. I take pride in people like Dante and Nino [brothers, and the upstairs and late downstairs headwaiters, who doubled voluntarily as the restaurant's *salumiere* and wine steward, respectively], and I'm proud of the fact that Šime [Šime Peroš, the nonpareil mixologist whose legendary dry Martinis attract connoisseurs from as far afield as Japan and Australia], who grew up speaking Serbo-Croatian, has made an effort to learn Spanish in order to communicate with a Mexican busboy and make him feel valued. Felice personally selects our fish every morning at the market, while most restaurateurs just phone in their orders. All these little details add up. Our customers may not know or care that I've studied the chemistry and physical characteristics of pasta dough, but they recognize that there's a difference between what we and some other restaurants serve them."

Somewhat taken aback by her own volubility, Lidia paused, said, "Where were we?" and answered her own question: "Oh, yes, the *fuzi*.

Joseph, Felice, Lidia, and Tanya Bastianich, with their faithful kitchen staff.

For the sauce, we buy three-year-old chickens. You have to get an old hen that's no good for laying anymore, or an old rooster that's no good for anything but the pot. You just can't get the right flavor and texture with most ordinary commercial chickens. You know, during the first few years after I came to this country, I was seduced by anything American, any food that came in a package. I was fascinated by Jell-O, which had a texture I had never experienced before, and I'd try anything that was advertised on television. I explored frozen foods and instant mixes, and thought they were exciting. For a while, I even managed to convince myself that they were better tasting than what I'd known at home in Istria. It was the same with supermarket chickens for a while; they were young and fat and so tender that I ignored the fact that they had none of the flavor of a tough old bird, that they had almost no flavor at all."

By the time she enrolled in Junior High School 204 at age twelve, Lidia "still wasn't speaking much English, but was able to keep up with the class work." Just how well she was able to keep abreast of her studies is indicated by her election, at the end of the ninth grade, to the presidency of her school's chapter of the national scholastic organization Arista. At fifteen, she applied for a part-time job at Walken's Bakery, operated by the family of the actor Christopher Walken, and was taken on as a salesgirl. "My job was up front, at the sales counter," she says. But every chance I got, I'd end up in the back, decorating cakes, and I spent whatever free time I had in the kitchen, baking."

As became abundantly evident one morning in the kitchen of her restaurant, Lidia's experience at Walken's has stood her in good stead. By the time I arrived there to witness a demonstration of gnocchi and *fuzi* making, Lidia had changed from her dining room garb to her kitchen togs (white chef's jacket and apron, houndstooth pants). As I watched her pummel a mass of pasta dough into submission (an exercise I'd conducted often enough in the privacy of my own kitchen, but couldn't begin to explicate with any authority), I realized that for her the stuff was a living presence with a decided temperament whose mood swings were conditioned by a host of variables apprehensible only to the most sensitive of adepts.

"The temperature and humidity on a given morning have a definite effect on the character of the dough," Lidia said, as she pounded the hell out of a sluggish five-pound mass of sifted flour, beaten eggs, olive oil, salt, and warm water. "Not every batch of flour is the same, either, and you have to be able to sense the differences."

Putting her full weight into the work, Lidia stretched the dough (which had begun to take on a decided muscularity of its own) this way and that with the heels of her hands. "You have to stretch it to break up the glutens," she explained. "The glutens are like clusters of rough wool, and you want to bring out their elasticity. When the dough has been properly worked, it takes on a sort of sheen—a smooth, elastic texture that's unmistakably recognizable when you've done this often enough." She scooped up the blob and flung it back down onto the marble work surface with jarring vehemence. "The glutens are still fighting," she said, running a rolling pin over the dough.

Lidia worked the dough a while longer, until the combative glutens were subdued, then divided it into halves—one for *fuzi* and the other for *pasutice,* which might be termed *fuzi* in a state of arrested development. *Fuzi* takes a short, tubular configuration, similar to that of the more familiar, machine-extruded penne, a dried factory product that retains more resiliency when cooked. After first rolling out the *fuzi* dough by hand, Lidia cut it into broad lasagnelike strips, which she then fed between the rollers of a motorized pasta machine about twice the size of the standard hand-cranked model designed for home use. "At home, for just the family, I'd do the whole thing by hand," she said. "Here in the restaurant, though, the machine saves a lot of time when you're producing in volume." The conclusion was inescapable that use of the machine represented a reluctant concession to practicality and that the mechanical intervention minutely diminished the end result: a diminution discernible to nobody but herself, but one that troubles her sensibilities.

Rapidly plying a chef's knife, Lidia sliced the parchment-thin sheets of dough into inch-wide strips, which she then cut diagonally to form lozenges. "What we have now is *pasutice,*" she said. "A delicate pasta that lends itself well to vegetable and fish sauces." *(Pasutice all'istriana* [recipe page 153], served with shellfish sauce, has been a steady best-seller at Felidia since the restaurant's opening.) "For *fuzi,*" she continued, "I roll the *pasutice* around my little finger, like this, overlapping the corners. Why don't you try a few?" Why not? Years earlier, without benefit of a demonstration, I had turned out a creditable batch of tortellini on my first try, and *fuzi* take a much simpler form than tortellini. With Lidia looking on, I botched three or four efforts before getting the hang of the thing. "Personally, I prefer *fuzi* this size and a little uneven," Lidia said (perhaps in deference to my own ragged handiwork), "but the customers like a more dainty, more uniform product." At that juncture, a *sous-chef* appeared, bearing a dowel three-sixteenths of an inch in diameter, around which he proceeded to wrap little tetrahedrons of dough at dizzying speed, turning out pieces of precise uniformity in fractions of seconds.

Lidia turned her attention to the day's gnocchi (recipe page 117). A kitchen assistant already had delivered a batch of riced boiled potatoes to the pasta counter, where the boss-lady formed them into a sort of mesa with a crater at its center. After filling the well with beaten eggs, she quickly incorporated the elements, adding flour in regular increments. "For gnocchi," she said, "the potatoes have to be completely cooled, so that the egg remains raw, and the dough has to be worked fast. The longer you work a potato dough, the more flour it requires, and the more flour you use, the heavier the dough gets. You want to keep your gnocchi as light as possible."

Continually dusting the dough, the work surface, and her hands with small amounts of flour, Lidia brought the incipient gnocchi to a stage she deemed optimal in less than ten minutes, then cut it into segments, each of which she hand-rolled into a foot-long rope about half an inch thick. The strands were then hacked into half-inch lengths, whereupon each piece was indented on one side with her thumb and, on the other, with the tines of a fork, for maximum adhesion of the day's sauce. The various fresh dough-based foundation foodstuffs in which the cuisines of Italy abound entail more intimate manual involvement—more "hands-on" attention, in current terminology—than anything else in the repertory except homemade bread. Lidia's pasta and gnocchi demonstrations convinced me that she's happiest in the kitchen when, as the French culinary maxim has it, *"il faut mettre la main à la pâte."*

During Lidia's midteens, her social activities were restricted for the most part to Astoria's Istrian community, a good many of whose male members, Felice included, were restaurant workers. "At that age, we weren't allowed to run around," Lidia recalled at lunch one day. "My best friends were Wanda Radetti and Graziella Dumicic. Graziella came from Felice's part of Istria. After Mass on Sundays, the young people would visit at one another's houses, especially at Grace's, where the young men used to congregate, and—"

"—and there came the victim, Felice," Felice put in, in mock-rueful tones.

The "victim" had been singled out for his sacrificial role by Grace, who sensed some interest on Lidia's part. "I pretended I didn't know who she was talking about when Grace said she was inviting Felice," Lidia recalled, "but she said, 'You know exactly who I mean—the guy who plays the accordion.' Well, I couldn't pretend not to have noticed the accordion player, but I *did* pretend I wasn't interested in him." As is the case with any serious undertakings between Istrians, the ensuing courtship was conducted at table. "Felice was a very shrewd operator," Lidia said. "He didn't play up to me, but to my parents. He'd send my mother flowers, and she'd invite him to our Sunday dinners."

"They stuffed me like a pig," Felice interjected. "They were fattening me for the slaughter."

Just how smoothly the course of true love might have run had Lidia cooked all those Sunday dinners is open to conjecture. "I was still doing the cooking during the week," she said, "and I was still experimenting with American products—frozen stuff, packaged baked goods, and things like that. I was still fascinated with apple pie, pumpkin pie—even mince pie, although I could never figure out why anyone would eat mince pie. To me, it was the most distasteful food in the world.

"Of course, not everything I cooked in those days was American. My father needed good soups, and I'd make them with chicken necks and beef bones—

"The guy who plays the accordion," ca. age twenty.

The Motika family, Trieste ca. 1956.

healthy things like that. What may have saved me was that my father would eat only traditional Istrian foods—*baccalà* [recipe page 58], *yota* [page 77], sauerkraut, homemade pastas, *brodetto* [page 153], and similar dishes. I made *gulyas* with potatoes, too, and there were good Greek butchers in Astoria, where I got lots of organ meats, but most of the weekend meals were cooked by my mother."

"Chicken," Felice muttered. "Always chicken. I would say, 'Next Sunday, *fuzi*.' "

The intensity of the courtship can be gauged by Felice's demand: When Istrians get serious about potential future relationships they begin lining out menus. "Felice also liked steaks," Lidia said. "So we used to buy sirloin with the bone in, and grill it and slice it. We were frugal, but we were impressed by the abundance of beef in America. Mostly, however, we ate chicken, because it was good and inexpensive. We'd have it roasted with potatoes, and then we'd have gnocchi with plums [page 121], and *palacinke* [page 246] for dessert."

Lidia was a full-scholarship student in her freshman year at Hunter College when her marriage to Felice temporarily interrupted her formal education (but not her involvement with academia: She since has taught university courses in food-related anthropology, lectured extensively, and participated in various seminars). The groom was then working as a waiter in Manhattan and making a decent living, but the couple's decision to embark on a two-month honeymoon tour of Europe would have been out of the question had it not been for traditional Istrian folkways.

Two or three years ago, when I was invited for the first time to a wedding of two adherents of Lidia's and Felice's ethnic heritage, I asked Šime Peroš, Felidia's non-pareil bartender, a native Dalmatian, what sort of wedding gifts were expected. "Cash," he replied, succinctly and definitively. As I discovered the following weekend, several hundred expatriate compatriots routinely turn up on such occasions, all bearing envelopes stuffed with legal tender, thereby producing a gross revenue that these days easily can run to the high five figures and would have been proportionately significant in the 1960s, when Lidia and Felice exchanged their wedding vows.

Among other things, the honeymoon put an end to Lidia's fascination with American foods. "We went to Paris, Germany, Austria, and Italy," she recalled over a recent lunch. "Then we went back to Istria and spent a month there with Felice's family while I reacquainted myself with my heritage after a lapse of seven years. In France, we ate simple meals in simple restaurants, where dinner for two came to about ten dollars, a liter of wine included. We'd have *steak aux pommes frites* and salad, just like the lunch Felice cooked for the three of us a couple of weeks ago, and I was impressed by the genuineness of the ingredients. In Austria, I found echoes of dishes I had eaten and cooked at home in Pula and Busoler. I remember one dish in particular, oxtails and *Nockerln,* at one Austrian restaurant, which seemed typically Istrian although I had never eaten a dish precisely like it in Istria. I bribed the chef with two dollars for the recipe. Up in the mountains near the Yugoslavian border, we got cold cuts with dark bread, which I found very disappointing at the time."

Different circumstances produce different reactions. Two or three years ago, Lidia, a couple of fellow travelers, and I drove up into the Italian Alps above Lake Garda. It was midspring, and the ski season had ended, although a late storm had blanketed the landscape in snow, and all but one of a few scattered restaurants were closed. The *padrone* of the single operative place we found apologetically confessed that he could offer us nothing but an assortment of cold meats, some beans, a salad, and coarse home-baked bread. Perhaps because none of us was romantically involved with another, and certainly we weren't honeymooning, the meal suited everyone, Lidia included, right down to the ground.

In Italy, the couple visited various relatives, including an aunt who had access to a source of uncommonly small clams and cooked what Lidia remembers as "the best linguine with clam sauce I've ever had." In Rome, Lidia went on to say, "We stayed with Felice's aunt Lucia, who was an exceptional cook. She had left Istria early, for lack of work, and was taken on as a cook by a Roman family. She prepared an absolutely delicious *coniglio alla salvia* for us, with potatoes [recipe page 221]. Even though they lived in the city, she and her husband maintained the country traditions she had grown up with in Istria. They canned their own tomatoes, and would go out to the country to buy their olive oil fresh from the farmers.

A *salumeria*, or pork store, on Via Carducci, Trieste.

"With Felice's family in Istria, we ate *raznjici* and *cevapcici*—dishes with a much more pronounced Slavic influence than what my own family had cooked. *Raznjici* was pork, cut in bits and grilled on skewers over an open fire. *Cevapcici* was a blend of pork, lamb, and beef, formed into cork shapes and broiled on the grill, with minced onion and pureed roast peppers served with the meat. My mother-in-law would grill fish over vine stalks, and would hang baby lambs from a tree for butchering. I had never butchered meat as a girl in Busoler—that was grown-ups' work—but I got into it at my mother-in-law's."

Lidia had spent the preceding seven years—roughly half as much of her life as she could remember with any continuity—in the United States. As she describes the experience, revisiting her birthplace at eighteen was much like arriving in New York at twelve. Just as she had been excited by the discovery of a whole new world of food, she was now even more excited by the rediscovery of what she had left behind. "It was tremendously thrilling to work again with ingredients I remembered from my childhood," she recalls, "to reexperience flavors and aromas that couldn't quite be duplicated with American ingredients, even when they were cooked exactly as they would have been in Istria."

— 37 —

ORIGINS: A COURTYARD IN BUSOLER

Two months of eating and cooking in Europe put an end to Lidia's infatuation with convenience foods. The honeymoon was over in more ways than one, and she returned to Astoria resolved to quit fooling around with commercial mixes, frozen dishes, and all the other novelties she had found so seductively American as a teenager attempting to adapt to a brash new world. It was time to reestablish her ties to her culinary and gastronomic heritage.

Felice, too, returned with new resolve. After having noodled the idea around since he and Lidia began thinking of marriage, he was now determined to implement it: He would open a restaurant of his own. "As soon as we got home," Lidia recalls, "he was on the phone, talking all night to a prospective partner, another waiter, about the new place we were going to open."

While Felice's dream was taking shape, both he and Lidia worked in Manhattan—Felice as a waiter at Mario's Front Page and Orsini's, and Lidia as a waitress, part-time cook, and bartender at Café Roma. Eventually, the couple bought out a small French restaurant, Chez François, in Forest Hills, renamed it Buonavia after an establishment they had enjoyed in Fiume, and installed an Istrian chef of Felice's acquaintance. "We bought it for thirty-two thousand dollars we didn't have," Lidia confided at lunch one afternoon, "and we opened in August of 1971, with me behind a three-stool bar.

"We were insecure, and at first the menu was very unadventurous—parmigiana, manicotti, veal pizzaiola, things like that—but the food was abundant and the prices were right. We opened to torrential rains, but the place filled up every night because of a prominent announcement in the window and fliers that we had distributed in every apartment house in the neighborhood. After a couple of months, we started cooking things for ourselves, dishes we had grown up on, and we said, 'Why wouldn't our customers like this?' "

Among the things the couple cooked for themselves and decided to try out on their clientele was surplus venison and other game donated by the Istrian community's hunters. It was (and remains) illegal to sell shot game in this country, and at that time the market for farm-raised "game" was a minuscule fraction of what it is today. The very few New Yorkers who hankered for an occasional venison stew or chop from a beast taken in the wild could satisfy their cravings, somewhat stealthily, by cozying up to the owner of one of a handful of butcher shops obscurely located in Italian neighborhoods around town. My own bootleg source was a hole-in-the-wall establishment on East Eleventh Street, where, along with tripe, beef hearts, and other generally despised offal, I could sometimes pick up a little deer meat or a wild rabbit in season, usually on a Monday morning, after clandestine delivery of some weekend hunter's bag.

Lidia and Felice kept their operation licit by serving shot game to favored customers without charge. As Lidia puts it, "We had an understanding with special customers, people with adventurous palates, and we'd let them try our off-menu dishes on the house. The idea was to acquaint them not only with Istrian cooking, but with more authentic Italian cooking in general than most Americans were familiar with. Also, we were trying to stimulate main-course ordering, to correct the mistaken belief that pasta is the principal dish in an Italian meal.

"Felice would go down to the Fulton market at two o'clock in the morning for our fish," Lidia continued, "and then drive up to the Hunts Point market in the Bronx for our meat and vegetables. He'd always stop at Zolotto's, which specialized in innards—hearts, sweetbreads, tripe, tongue, beef testicles, and so on—which we served to special customers. We had to keep the conventional dishes on the menu; otherwise we'd have gone broke. But we always had a special cuisine for special customers, and word of it got around. People like Arthur Schwartz and Giuliano Bugialli [respectively, the *Daily News* restaurant critic and the noted cookbook author] would come out from Manhattan, and they'd pass the word along to other food professionals. Then we started doing pasta and game demonstrations, which were very popular and got us a lot of news coverage. Eventually we were serving seven hundred people a night between the two Queens restaurants [Buonavia and Villa Secondo], and we knew that if we could do that well in Queens with authentic cooking, we'd have no problem in Manhattan, where people's tastes are a lot more sophisticated."

Lidia had been the restaurant's nominal bartender and cashier when Buonavia opened. From the outset, however, she had gravitated to the kitchen, where, working under the guidance of the chef, she gradually took over a good many of his responsibilities. "I had no qualms about my ability to cook," she recalls today, "but I didn't have commercial experience. Working alongside an experienced professional chef, I learned to translate small-scale skills into large-scale production."

Fisherman negotiating price, Trieste.

As first Buonavia and, later, the couple's spinoff venture, Villa Secondo, prospered and expanded in turn, Lidia and Felice began to plow part of their increasing profits into research and development—or, as Lidia terms it, "an investigative process that sustained our growth": "We'd go back to Europe every year, and we'd travel in this country and Canada between European trips. The primary object wherever we went was to experience and familiarize ourselves with foods and techniques we might later make use of, but we found we were also developing a network of restaurateurs on two continents—people who were eager to exchange information and useful references with other restaurateurs, producers, suppliers, and winemakers.

"We had progressed beyond the point, for example, where we could still serve wild game without charge, and we had to adapt to farm-raised game, which can be cooked pink or, at the other extreme, cooked until it falls off the bone and served with a *sguazet* sauce [see page 210]. The network of restaurateurs we developed in our travels opened up a whole new network of avenues for us. You have to see what's out there and form your own cuisine from observed and acquired influences grafted onto a solid inherited foundation." In the course of their travels during the 1970s, the couple toured France, Germany, England, Hungary, Greece, Spain, Finland, Luxembourg, Switzerland, and Austria, with varying responses to what they ate. (Austria, Hungary, and Germany provided insights into certain aspects of their native Istrian cookery, as did Switzerland, to a lesser extent. They could appreciate the cooking of Spain and Greece, which derived from their own Mediterranean heritage. But neither England nor Finland excited them much, and Felice describes an interlude in the Soviet Union as a "disaster" gastronomically, "except for the caviar, which hardly any of the Russians ever even tasted," although he concedes that the museums might have made the trip worthwhile.)

Lidia's ongoing culinary education went somewhat beyond exploratory travel and informal exchanges with her peers. Although by then a highly successful restaurateur, she continued during the 1970s to take college-level and advanced-education courses in the science, history, and anthropology of food, the physiology of taste, practical cookery, recipe tasting and composition, and the like, mostly at Queens College and, in Manhattan, at Hunter College and the New School—all while raising two young children and largely supervising the operation of two phenomenally successful restaurants. And during her periodic sojourns in Italy, she served various internships in the kitchens of her network of mutually supportive restaurateurs. (Today, she often returns the compliment by allowing visiting Italian chefs free rein in the kitchen of Felidia.)

Early one afternoon about a year ago, as Lidia, her daughter Tanya, a visiting Istrian cousin of hers, and I lunched on *osso buco* classically accompanied by saffron-tinctured *risotto alla milanese,* we sampled an exceptional Grignolino from a producer Lidia had met in Italy the previous summer. I remarked that the rural and small-town Europeans of my acquaintance seldom were knowledgeable about any wines but their own regional specialties or, in most cases, the locally produced table wine.

"I agree that many people in Europe are not great wine connoisseurs, although they are great wine drinkers," Lidia said, "but I was exposed to some very fine wines, even as a child in Pula and Busoler. My family wasn't rich, but we were better off than a lot of people. As a teacher, my mother was compensated from time to time for special tutoring with fresh eggs or a goose or a few bottles of some special wine. My father often was paid for the use of his trucks in olive oil or wine or little regional specialties like *speck,* prosciutto, marinated cabbage, and locally celebrated liqueurs.

Joseph, Lidia, Tanya, and
Felice Bastianich.

"Because I shuttled back and forth between my parent's middle-class home and my grandmother's peasant home, I was exposed to the best of both of those worlds. I had good wines that often went far beyond regional specialties at my parents', and the best of the regional country wines when I stayed with my grandmother, who bartered her produce for them. Later, at my aunt's in Trieste, I was exposed to a different wine with each course, and that made a lasting impression on me."

Needless to say, in southern Europe, where moderate indulgence in wine is approved from midchildhood on, anyone with access to a relatively diversified cellar has a long head start toward oenological connoisseurship. For an uncommonly exploratory young girl with a precocious palate, the advantages of being born into a family of discerning wine bibbers are incalculable vis-à-vis the average American's belated introduction to the subject. Consequently, the American wine buff often talks a much better game than he drinks, whereas the reverse usually holds true for the native European to the manner born. As Lidia inhaled her Grignolino on the afternoon in question, she employed conventional terminology ("a fine nose"), but the look of near-rapture on her face and in her eyes was more expressive by far than anything she, or any of the owlishly solemn pedants who usually turn up at professional wine-tastings, could have put into words.

Shopping for the day's food,
Pula.

Russell Baker once drew an elegant distinction between the seriousness of poker players and the solemnity of joggers. Aided and abetted by the late Nino Laurenti, a veteran maître d' and the restaurant's resident sommelier, Lidia took her wines with the utmost seriousness, but no undue solemnity. I've traveled around Italy with her when in her dual capacities as an independent restaurateur and a member of the Ordine Ristoratori Professionisti Italiani (O.R.P.I.) she made it her business (mixing business with pleasure) to visit and sample the produce of large and small vintners in every region we passed through. (Lidia since has become the vice president of O.R.P.I. International. The organization is devoted to the furtherance, promotion, and codification of authentic Italian cookery, which, despite its enormous current popularity in the United States, remains improperly understood, at least in the view of the O.R.P.I membership.) Making generous allowances for the tendency of commercial winemakers to suffer even fools gladly if the fools happen to represent potentially lucrative retail outlets, I was impressed by Lidia's easy rapport with both legendary and obscure winemakers, and by their invariable treatment of her as a respected peer. During the course of meal after meal, I was equally impressed by the wine jargon I *didn't* hear when the real experts sat down to enjoy themselves. Although a good deal of technical information necessarily was exchanged, conversation always was restricted to plain factual data devoid of the judgmental effusions and lyric imagery usually to be heard when amateurs flaunt their putative expertise.

"Come with me to the kitchen," Felice said one early-autumn evening, before the arrival of the dinner crowd. "I want you to see something." He was all but quivering with excitement, a symptom betokening the acquisition of some edible wonderment or another. For some time, Felice had been promising to select the most active pair of scampi from the live shipments the restaurant was receiving and race them down the bar. With the bar not yet populated for the evening, I assumed that the great event was at hand. I was led into the walk-in box, where, if any scampi were in residence, they were crowded out of sight by a dozen or more outsized produce cartons. The chamber had been turned into a mycological Fort Knox; it was crammed with more wild mushrooms than I'd ever seen in one place, wholesale and retail markets included, "Lidia and I picked them this morning in less than an hour—one hundred pounds," Felice crowed. "I knew we'd find plenty because it rained so much the past few days, but, my God—*one hundred pounds!*" Sad to say, not one of the hundred pounds would be consumed at the restaurant; the entire haul was destined for home use over the course of a year or so.

During the restaurant's first few years, various wild mushrooms gathered on Long Island by Lidia, Felice, Dante, and Nino Laurenti (who was *born* a mushroom expert in a small town outside Parma, just as his brother Dante was born a prosciutto maker) were served regularly in their various seasons. Some varieties were to be found nowhere else in the city, but the display of, say, an unwashed fifty-pound clump of hen-of-the-woods *(Polypilus frondosis)* or a basketful of honey mushrooms *(Armillaria mellea)*, with fallen leaves, twigs, soil, and other detritus, gave way to prudence, when, at the urging of legal counsel, Lidia and Felice reluctantly concluded that any unrelated bellyache could lead to a ruinous lawsuit. The restaurant hasn't been quite the same since, although Lidia does what she can with wild mushrooms gathered by professional foragers on two continents and with those species that lend themselves to domestication by small growers.

Lidia and I were chatting in the kitchen one morning when the day's porcini—named for their supposed resemblance to plump piglets—arrived. The mushrooms were subjected to a rigorous inspection while the delivery man waited. When I remarked that the porcini, many of whose stems were as thick as the business end of a baseball bat, looked flawless to my unpracticed eye, Lidia replied, "Yes, but let's see what's underneath the top layer." She flipped a case over, unceremoniously dumping its contents onto a counter. Satisfied that there wasn't a blemished specimen in the lot, she signed the receipt and let the man go.

Later, as I basked happily in the warmth of a steaming bowl of *minestra di funghi selvatici* [recipe page 75] that exuded a compelling earthy redolence, Lidia reminisced about the Big Move to Manhattan. "When Felice and I finally made the decision, we sold the two Queens restaurants," she said. "We came out with two hundred and fifty thousand dollars in cash, but the architect estimated that we'd need three hundred and fifty thousand, *minimum.* He gave us a choice of three quality grades for every proposed installation, every detail, and we chose the best in every case."

The previous occupant of the chosen site on East Fifty-eighth Street had been a minuscule installation whose narrow dining room comprised little more than what is now Felidia's bar and ended where the present ground-floor dining room begins. The restaurant Lidia and Felice envisioned was to be a duplex layout some four times larger than the former establishment, with a much larger kitchen in the rear and additional kitchens in the basement. The plan called for extension of the existing brownstone building into a backyard, and entailed major construction that ultimately resulted in a cost overrun of a hundred and fifty thousand dollars. In aggregate, the couple spent three-quarters of a million dollars on the restaurant before opening its doors. "We had to go a long way backward before we could go forward," Lidia said, as I mopped up the last of the soup with a bit of bread. "We had come to this country as immigrants, with nothing, and now we were immigrants again, and had nothing again. We had put everything we had into the new place, mortgaged our house to raise more, and tapped my parents' resources. My mother was feeding us—we were back to eating chicken wings—and even my son Joseph chipped in what he earned on a paper route. We'd cook big pots of mussels for the construction crew, to stimulate them to work faster, and we did a lot of the detail work ourselves. We stripped all the wood paneling [salvaged from a Connecticut estate] at home in our garage, with the kids, and we finished and upholstered all the chairs ourselves. Still the work seemed to drag on endlessly, with the city building department hassling us on every move and with money running out constantly."

It occurred to me that the tactic of serving mussels to the construction crew might have been counterproductive: A guy feeding for free on *cozze in salsa verde* [recipe page 51] might be in no rush to move on to another job with no such epicurean perks. Despite, or thanks to those big pots of mussels, as the case may have been, and with the indulgence of their bankers, Lidia and Felice finally saw their dream come to fruition. As Lidia now puts it, "It took us nine months to a year after we opened to polish our act." If so, a good many Manhattanites were quick to recognize a diamond in the rough. The restaurant prospered phenomenally, virtually from Day One, thereby ensuring Felidia's continuance in a landlord-dominated era that has witnessed the demise of innumerable highly regarded ventures as leases ran out and renewal demands approached stratospheric altitudes. Lidia and Felice had purchased the property two years before opening the restaurant.

By the mid-1980s, Lidia and Felice not only had installed private party facilities on the restaurant's second floor, but had acquired another piece of property: a home atop a rise overlooking Little Neck Bay, in the Douglaston section of Queens. As might be expected, its centerpiece is an enormous state-of-the-art kitchen, complete with an open rotisserie on which a whole lamb and a suckling pig simultaneously can be done to a turn.

Along with two hundred-odd other friends of the family, I turned up for the first Christmas party at the Douglaston house. The quantity and variety of foods was stupefying, as was the volume consumed by Istrian émigrés who, like their hosts, had known the hard times in the Old Country. It was as joyous an event as I've ever attended. In the midst of those she loved, Lidia beamed with an unworldly radiance, celebrating life through the sharing of food.

Lidia's brother, Franco, and his wife, Margaret, watch as Lidia checks the oven for Thanksgiving dinner.

Lidia and Felice in the restaurant.

ORIGINS: A COURTYARD IN BUSOLER

PART TWO

Recipes: Memories of the Feast

1

Antipasti e Minestre
Appetizers and Soups

COLD ANTIPASTI

◆

Cozze in Salsa Verde

Insalata di Gamberetti e Fagioli Misti

ABOUT LUMACHE

Insalata di Lumache e Finocchio

Insalata di Branzino

Insalata di Polipo e Patate

ABOUT BACCALÀ AND STOCCAFISSO

Baccalà Mantecato

Cervella Fredda al Limone

Insalata di Trippa

HOT ANTIPASTI

◆

ABOUT WHITE TRUFFLES

Uovo Tartufato

Asparagi e Uova per Merenda

Crostata di Funghi

Frico Croccante

Formaggio in Crosta

Polenta con Fonduta e Funghi Porcini

SOUPS

◆

ABOUT SOUPS AND STOCKS

Brodo di Carne

Brodo di Manzo

Brodo di Vitello

Brodo di Pollo

Brodo di Pesce

Riso e Patate

Zuppa di Pesce con Riso

Brodo Brostula

Minestra di Verdure Miste con Finocchio

Minestra di Funghi Selvatici

Yota

COLD ANTIPASTI

Cozze in Salsa Verde
Mussels in Parsley Vinaigrette

SERVES 6

Mussels were an integral part of my childhood. They were always available for the taking when other seafoods were scarce. We kids would pack a sandwich of home-made bread and maybe a slice of prosciutto, and walk to the beach at Stoia. When we began to get hungry, we'd gather mussels from the rocks and steam them over driftwood fires in an old tomato can. With the mussels and our sandwiches, we'd have a fine meal. When we were more ambitious, we'd gather *datteri* (sea dates), which were similar to mussels, but required more work, because they bore into soft rocks, and you'd have to break the rocks apart to get at them. They were worth it.

3 pounds medium-large mussels (see Note)
4 bay leaves
6 tablespoons minced Bermuda onion
6 tablespoons minced roasted peppers
3 tablespoons minced seeded peperoncini (see Note)

3 tablespoons minced Italian parsley
3 tablespoons virgin olive oil
3 tablespoons red wine vinegar
Salt and freshly ground pepper
Lemon wedges and parsley sprigs

In a nonreactive pot large enough to accommodate the mussels with room to spare, bring 2 cups of water to a boil, add the mussels, and cook, covered, about 5 minutes, shaking the pot occasionally, until all the mussels have opened. Drain the mussels in a colander, discarding any that have remained closed, and, if desired, reserve the liquor for another use. Remove and discard the upper shells of the mussels, leaving the meats attached to the lower shells. On a serving tray, arrange the mussels in a concentric, radiating pattern, like flower petals, and allow them to cool in the refrigerator.

In a bowl, blend all other ingredients except the lemon wedges and parsley sprigs. When the mussels have cooled sufficiently (they should not be over-chilled), spoon about 1 teaspoon sauce over each and decorate with lemon wedges and parsley sprigs.

Note: Mussels may be scrubbed and rinsed in advance of use, but should not be debearded until just before they are cooked. Peperoncini, hot pickled green peppers, can be found in Italian groceries and most supermarkets.

Insalata di Gamberetti e Fagioli Misti
Shrimp and Mixed Bean Salad

SERVES 4

It's the Tuscans who are known as *mangia fagioli,* or bean eaters, but the Istrians eat their share as well. Perhaps both regions inherited a taste for legumes from the Etruscans, who civilized Tuscany and whose archaeological remains prove that they traveled in Istria. I like this salad for its harmony of textures, colors, and, of course, flavors.

1 pound fresh fava beans, shelled

1 pound fresh cranberry beans, shelled

½ small onion

2 bay leaves

1 small carrot, sliced

1 rib celery, cubed

1 pound large (about 14–20) shrimp, shelled except for the fantails, and deveined

3 tablespoons olive oil

3 tablespoons wine vinegar

¼ teaspoon salt

Freshly ground pepper to taste

In two separate pans of boiling water, cook the beans until tender, about 4 and 8 minutes for the favas and cranberry beans, respectively. Drain and refresh the beans under cold running water, and remove the outer skins from the favas.

In a medium saucepan, boil the onion, bay leaves, carrot, and celery in 6 cups of water for 20 minutes. Add the shrimp and cook just until opaque throughout, about 1 minute. Remove and drain the shrimp and allow them to cool.

In a serving bowl, whisk together the olive oil, vinegar, and salt and pepper. Add the beans and shrimp, and toss to coat the solids thoroughly. Serve warm as an appetizer.

Recommended wine—I'd serve a Ribolla Gialla with this dish. The grape has been cultivated in Friuli and Istria since around the turn of the thirteenth century and has undergone a resurgence of popularity during the last ten years or so. It's a dry white with balanced acidity, soft yellow color, elegant nose, and a pleasant complexity that complements antipasti and light main dishes.

Lumache (snails) have been eaten in various European regions since prehistoric times and were highly regarded by the cultures of classical antiquity. They also have been eaten in the Orient since time immemorial. Despite their popularity in both Italy and China, however, they seldom, if ever, turn up on Italian or Chinese restaurant menus in this country, possibly because Americans associate them more or less exclusively with French gastronomy.

As a child in Istria, I gathered land snails as naturally as I did any of the other wild foods in which the region abounded. They were good, they cost nothing, and the time and work their initial preparation entailed was its own reward for a small girl permitted to perform adult tasks.

Tinned escargots can be substituted for live snails for the recipe that follows, but they will be inferior in texture and flavor to fresh snails, which can be found at some fancy fishmongers' establishments and in some ethnic (particularly Chinese) markets. They are not only preferable to, but significantly less expensive than the commercial product. If the use of canned snails is unavoidable, look for the medium-size variety: 18–24 pieces per 7-ounce can.

To prepare live snails for use, figure on 2 pounds in the shell for ¾ pound usable meat.

Sprinkle bread crumbs over the bottom of a cardboard box or a tightly woven basket (either of which should be tightly covered; snails are prone to wanderlust and cover more ground more quickly than it's generally supposed they can). Place the snails in the box and let them rest for 24 hours, during which time they will begin to cleanse their digestive tracts of undesirable substances. Next, wash them well in cold running water and drain them thoroughly. Clean out the box or basket, sprinkle the bottom again with bread crumbs, and allow the snails to purge themselves over an additional 5-day period, cleaning and sprinkling the container with fresh bread crumbs daily. (It's advisable, incidentally, not to form any sentimental attachments with the critters, and to refrain from naming or otherwise individualizing them; you're raising food, not pets.)

Rinse the snails well and soak them in a large pot for 2 hours in a mixture of 4 quarts water and 2 cups vinegar. Then boil them for 20 minutes in 3 quarts of fresh water, salted to taste, with 3 bay leaves. Drain well, discard the bay leaves, and allow the snails to cool. With a wooden pick or small shellfish fork, extract the snails from their shells, discarding the shells. With your fingers, remove and discard the cloaca, or food sac (a tightly curled spiral at the end of the edible portion) from each snail.

Insalata di Lumache e Finocchio
Snail and Fennel Salad

SERVES 4

In Istria and many other European regions where edible land snails are found, these terrestrial mollusks feed extensively on wild fennel, which perfumes and adds a hint of its flavor to their flesh. This sprightly salad reunites the little gastropods with a staple of their natural diet.

1 young fennel bulb, trimmed

1 pound cooked snail meats (page 53)
(about 2¼ pounds, 2 7-ounce cans,
raw in the shell)

3 tablespoons olive oil

Juice of 1 lemon

Salt and freshly ground pepper to taste

2 tablespoons chopped Italian parsley

Halve and thinly slice the trimmed fennel bulb. In a serving bowl, combine the snails and fennel, tossing well. Add the remaining ingredients, again toss well, and serve at room temperature.

Insalata di Branzino
Striped Bass Salad

S E R V E S 4

The translation is somewhat arbitrary. *Branzino,* an Old World rockfish, isn't found in American waters, but striped bass makes a reasonably close substitute. For that matter, any firm-textured, non-oily fish, such as sea bass, or if you prefer real elegance, salmon, adapts comfortably to this dish, which was a warm-weather favorite when I was growing up. Essentially, salads of this sort make frugal use of leftovers, and I hope that's the way you'll prepare them.

2 pounds skinless striped bass fillets

2 bay leaves

1 small onion, sliced

1 medium carrot, sliced

2 tablespoons white wine vinegar

Salt

¼ cup olive oil

3 tablespoons red wine vinegar

Freshly ground pepper

2 tablespoons chopped Italian parsley

2 medium cucumbers, peeled, seeded and thinly sliced

1 medium red onion, halved vertically and thinly sliced

Tie the fish in cheesecloth, keeping it flat. In a nonreactive pot large enough to hold the fish with water to cover generously, boil together sufficient water, the bay leaves, small onion, carrot, white wine vinegar, and 1 teaspoon salt for 15 minutes. Lower the heat, add the fish to the pot, and simmer 20 minutes.

Remove and drain the fish and allow it to cool thoroughly in the refrigerator. With the fingers, roughly break the fish into 1″ morsels.

Whisk together oil and red wine vinegar. Add salt and pepper to taste and the parsley. Stir in the cucumbers and red onion. Add the fish and toss gently.

Recommended wine—The acidity of this dish calls for a Pinot Grigio, although the grape isn't indigenous to Friuli, the home of the best of the Pinot Grigios, but was introduced there fairly recently. It's a wine with a tight nose, solidly structured, and goes well with appetizers, soups, pastas, and light main courses.

Insalata di Polipo e Patate
Octopus and Potato Salad

SERVES 4

This is a dish with a "secret" ingredient: If you put a wine cork in the pot while the *polipo* cooks, the enzymes in the cork will tenderize the octopus. I know of no scientific documentation for this, but I know it works.

Although the dish may seem simple, there are subtleties involved in its preparation. First, only Idaho potatoes should be used; they throw off a starchy residue that gives a distinctive body to the finished product. Originally included for volume—to bulk out a scarce and relatively costly principal ingredient—potatoes have a neutral character that absorbs and tones down the richness of the octopus. One of my uncles, Emilio, was a fisherman in Istria. He fished at night and kept a light burning at the stern of his boat. He would drag white cloths behind the boat to attract octopuses, then hook them with a *parangal,* a local-dialect term for a grapnel-like cluster of barbs.

1½–2-pound octopus, cleaned	*6 tablespoons olive oil*
1 wine cork	*3 tablespoons red wine vinegar*
2 bay leaves	*1 Bermuda onion, thinly sliced*
Salt and pepper to taste	*2 tablespoons chopped Italian parsley*
2 medium Idaho potatoes, whole	*Lemon wedges for garnish*

Place the octopus, wine cork, bay leaves, and salt and pepper in a large pot with water to cover generously, and bring to a boil. Reduce the heat and cook the octopus at a vigorous simmer until tender but slightly al dente, about 25 minutes. (*Polipetti*, or baby octopuses, are wonderful in this preparation also.)

Meanwhile, in a second pot, cover the potatoes with cold water and bring to a boil. Cook about 25 minutes, until just tender, then cool, peel, and cut them into 1" cubes.

Drain the octopus, discarding the bay leaves and cork. Cut the tentacles away where they join the head and, if desired, strip away the skin and suction cups by drawing the tentacles through the bunched fingers of one hand. (This is a purely cosmetic procedure which may, and I think should, be omitted.) Clean the octopus head by squeezing out the core with your fingers, and slice the meat thin. Cut the tentacles into 1" lengths and toss all the meat with the warm potatoes and remaining ingredients, except lemon. Garnish with lemon wedges and serve.

Recommended wine—This is another dish with which I'd serve a Pinot Grigio.

ABOUT BACCALÀ AND STOCCAFISSO
Salt-cured and Air-dried Cod

The various methods of preserving foods—curing, smoking, pickling, and the like—originated as expedients for extending shelf life beyond seasonal availability or normal rates of spoilage. Centuries before the advent of refrigeration, when European sailing ships spent months harvesting cod in the northwestern Atlantic, the catch had to be preserved in one manner or another for its long journey home. The two most efficient means of preservation produced what we Italians term *baccalà* and *stoccafisso:* respectively salt-cured and air-dried cod.

Today, factory ships equipped with enormous freezers return to their home ports after months at sea, carrying thousands of tons of fish in approximately the same condition they were in when netted, and the difference between fresh and frozen cod is relatively negligible. Like most foods subjected to older methods of preservation, however, *baccalà* and *stoccafisso* have distinctive characteristics altogether unlike those of fresh or frozen fish. Like prosciutto di Parma vis-à-vis fresh ham, dill pickles vis-à-vis fresh cucumbers, or smoked vis-à-vis fresh salmon, *baccalà* and *stoccafisso* are no longer considered mere substitutes for fresh cod, but are esteemed as delicacies in their own right, preferable for some uses to freshly caught fish.

Both products are highly regarded and extensively eaten throughout southern Europe, significantly in regions with ready access to an abundance of fresh fish. In this country, where fresh cod is plentiful, there traditionally has been little demand for cured and dried cod, except in various ethnic communities. A taste for both is well worth acquiring, however, and the products can be found wherever ethnic Italians, Spaniards, Portuguese, Greeks, and some West Indians shop for their food.

Baccalà, the less costly of the two, is boneless and relatively moist but too salty for immediate use, and must be soaked overnight or longer in several changes of water. It can be poached, fried, baked, or used in pâtés, mousses, and sauces. *Stoccafisso* (from the English "stockfish") is much drier, with a woody texture and appearance, and usually is given a light pounding, to break down its fibrous texture, before being soaked in the same manner as *baccalà.* It is then boiled, cleaned from the bone, and, typically, beaten to a mousselike consistency with oil or cream.

In Istria, we used both products more or less interchangeably, and the dish we ate as *baccalà mantecato* actually was made with stockfish. Well, we grew up with both and always knew which was which, whatever we chose to call it.

My family's recipe for *baccalà mantecato,* made with *stoccafisso,* follows. For a true salted cod recipe, see *baccalà con patate al forno* (page 155).

Baccalà Mantecato
Whipped Stockfish

SERVES 6 – 8

In many parts of Italy, La Vigilia, the meal eaten on Christmas Eve, consists entirely of seafood in various forms. *Baccalà mantecato* was always a part of my family's Christmas Eve dinner, and our stockfish would be soaked for two or three days in advance, until the whole house smelled of it. The dish was considered a real delicacy, and it was my late father's specialty, although he wasn't a great cook otherwise. We still honor the tradition every year, and I always feel that my father is with us at Christmas when we make *baccalà mantecato*.

1 whole dried cod (stockfish), about 1½ pounds	2 cups olive oil
3 cloves garlic, chopped fine	¼ cup fish stock (recipe page 70)
	Salt and pepper to taste

Lightly beat the surface of the stockfish with a wooden mallet. Soak it overnight in several changes of cold water. Cut the fish into four parts and poach it in 6 quarts of water until the fish begins to fall from the bones, about 1½ hours. Drain and cool, then remove and discard the bones, but not the skin and cartilage.

Place the fish and garlic in a food processor and, with the motor running, gradually add the oil and stock in thin streams and alternating batches. With the motor turned off, taste the mixture and add salt and pepper to taste. Restart the processor and let it run until the mixture is light in color and texture, like a mousse.

Serve as a spread for toast, crackers, or plain Italian bread.

Recommended wine—A Spumante would set off the richness of this dish well. Look for one vinified in the *méthode champenois* by Ca' del Bosco, Berlucchi, or Ferrari.

Cervella Fredda al Limone
Calf's Brain Salad with Lemon

———

SERVES 4

During my childhood, the animals we raised for food were loved and respected. We killed them to subsist ourselves, but to waste any part of them would have been unthinkable, sinful. When calves, lambs, or goats had to be slaughtered, we ate their delicate brains, most often in a *frittata,* or omelet, at *merenda,* the light midmorning meal. Cooked that way, the texture and weight of the organ tended to get lost: brain and eggs were hardly distinguishable from each other. In this salad, however, the mild flavor and elusive texture of the main ingredient can be appreciated. The lemon juice sharpens the relative blandness of the *cervella* without overwhelming its subtlety.

1 pound calf's brain	*Salt and freshly ground pepper to taste*
½ cup white wine vinegar	*1 tablespoon chopped Italian parsley*
6 tablespoons olive oil	*2 tablespoons small pickled capers*
3 tablespoons lemon juice	

Pick over and trim the brain of all membranes and surface blood vessels. In a bowl, combine the vinegar with 1 quart water, add the brain, and refrigerate 2 hours, to blanch.

Rinse the brain well under cold running water, then cook 15 minutes in lightly salted boiling water to cover. Drain well and rinse under cold running water. Cool to room temperature, then refrigerate until cold. Trim off any remaining bits of membrane, cut the brain into 4″ slices and arrange on serving plates.

In a bowl, whisk together the olive oil, lemon juice, and salt and pepper. Dress the sliced brain with this lemon sauce. Garnish with parsley and capers.

Recommended wine—Tocai has a nutty, almost almondy dry finish well suited to the butternut flavor of *cervella.* Try one produced by Livio Felluga, Schioppetto, or Vigne del Leon.

Insalata di Trippa
Tripe Salad

SERVES 4

Meat was scarce in Istria during my childhood, so none of a slaughtered animal went to waste. In this country, many people think they don't like tripe, but it usually turns out that they've never tried it. At Felidia, we offer this dish every day. Once our customers try it, they order it again and again. I can understand an initial reluctance to taste it. As a child, I had a love-hate feeling about tripe. First of all, it was my unwelcome chore to have to wash it ten times and boil it innumerable times. Also, I loved the flavor but wasn't crazy about the texture. Today, tripe is sold cleaned and bleached, and what I like most about it is its silky gelatinous texture. This dish is best when served just a bit below room temperature.

2 pounds honeycomb tripe	3 tablespoons white wine vinegar
2 bay leaves	2 tablespoons chopped Italian parsley
1 small onion	1 clove garlic, minced fine
6 black peppercorns	Lemon slices for garnish
5 tablespoons olive oil	Parsley sprigs for garnish

In a large nonreactive pot, cover the tripe with plenty of boiling water and add the bay leaves, onion, and peppercorns. Boil the tripe 1–1½ hours, testing after the first hour by inserting a fork into the thickest part. When the fork penetrates without resistance and slides out easily, the tripe is done.

Drain and allow the tripe to cool, discarding the remaining contents of the pot. Trim the tripe and cut it into large rectangles. Turn the tripe honeycomb side down and scrape off all fat and membranes. Cut tripe into julienne strips, toss with the oil, vinegar, parsley, and garlic, and serve garnished with lemon slices and parsley sprigs.

Recommended wine—With tripe, which has lots of character and resistance, I'd serve a relatively intense wine such as Cabreo by Ruffino or Cervaro della Sala by Antinori.

ABOUT WHITE TRUFFLES

The *tartufo bianco (Tuber magnatum)*, the white truffle dug from the ground in its most sensuous manifestation around Alba, is regarded as the finest, most aromatic truffle among some three hundred known edible varieties, although the French, who prefer the black truffle *(Tuber melanosporum)* disagree. Perhaps it's a matter of temperament or cultural outlook; we Italians prefer our foodstuffs with their essential characteristics undisguised, whereas the French tend to impose their culinary will on what they eat. The big difference between "white" (actually tan) and black (sometimes dark brown) truffles is that the white almost always are added raw to dishes, whereas the black usually are a cooked ingredient.

The white truffle grows underground, as all truffles do, only in symbiotic relationships with oak, hazelnut, and linden trees (although just what benefits the trees may derive from the association is uncertain). Most commonly, in its marketable form, it grows from the size of a walnut, to as large as a potato, and larger. Jay reports once having been given one "the size of Einstein's brain." Either Jay has extraordinarily generous friends or Einstein wasn't the intellectual he was cracked up to be.

To harvest truffles, dogs or pigs are used—canines more commonly in Italy, swine in France. In Italy, the dog is trained by withholding its food for several days, after which time it is fed a fractional bit of truffle. The dog records the unique olfactory sensation in its memory bank and infallibly recognizes its faintest subterranean traces thereafter. The beast is restrained from devouring its quarry (which its master pockets) by the substitution of a different edible treat.

Generally, *i tartufai,* the truffle hunters, set out at dusk and operate under the cover of darkness, when their activities are least likely to be observed by rivals who know that truffles grow in the same spots year after year. Aside from saffron but including the very finest caviar, which Felice appreciates more than I do, white truffles are the costliest foodstuff known and hence should be shopped for with the utmost prudence. When buying a white truffle, its size is of some importance, but the crucial factors are its freshness and pungency; its aroma should combine the muskiness of old earth and leaf mold with the sharpness of garlic. A fresh truffle should be as hard and crisp as a fresh turnip and, ideally, as near to egg-shaped as possible, with no erratic protrusions or indentations.

Fresh truffles are sold retail by the ounce and average about forty dollars an ounce when plentiful. As a rule of thumb, an ounce is sufficient for four portions of a given dish—pricey enough, but within reason for grand occasions and well worth the investment.

Truffles of ultimate freshness can be kept up to ten days if buried in rice in an airtight container and refrigerated. (They will add an indescribable perfumed dimension to the rice, which should be used to make risotto.) Their color varies from pale ivory to pale brown, and their seasonal availability lasts from early October until late December. They can be found in specialty food shops, or, in Jay's phrase, belly boutiques.

Uovo Tartufato
Truffled Egg

SERVES 6

White truffles are found in Istria, near Montona, although their quality is a bit shy compared to their Alba cousins. I had this dish for the first time when Guiseppina Fassi, chef and owner of Gender Neuf Restaurant in Piedmont, prepared it for lunch here in New York to celebrate the release of Ceretto's Brico Rocche Barolo.

3 ounces white truffles
3 tablespoons butter plus extra for greasing the ramekins
6 tablespoons heavy cream

6 tablespoons milk
6 large eggs
Salt and freshly ground pepper
Toasted Italian bread

Clean the truffles of all loose soil with a vegetable brush and use a paring knife to remove only dirt that is embedded. Preheat the oven to 325°F. Butter six 3″ ramekins and place 1 tablespoon cream, 1 tablespoon milk, and ½ tablespoon butter in each. Break a whole egg into each ramekin, add salt and pepper to taste, and shave rough edges of truffle over the eggs.

Set the ramekins in a baking pan and pour in enough hot water to reach halfway up the outside of the ramekins. Bake 8–15 minutes, depending on whether you prefer your eggs soft, medium, or firm. Remove the ramekins from the oven and water bath, shave the remaining truffle over the eggs, and serve with toasted Italian bread cut into ½″ × ½″ × 4″ batons and freshly ground pepper.

Recommended wine—Uovo Tartufato is a wonderfully smooth dish with intense flavor. Ceretto's Bricco Rocche is a superbly balanced Barolo that captures the soul of the Piedmont, where the finest white truffles are found.

Asparagi e Uova per Merenda
Asparagus and Eggs for Brunch

SERVES 4

Merenda (which goes by the same name in Spanish) is a late-morning meal eaten mostly by the *contadini* (farmers) who have been working the land since early morning. In springtime in Istria, we'd often make this dish with the slenderest wild asparagus spears, and if any grow near where you live, I think you'll find them a little tastier than the earliest cultivated spears.

1 pound pencil-thin asparagus
2 tablespoons olive oil

Salt and freshly ground pepper to taste
8 eggs

Remove and discard the tough lower ends of the asparagus. Wash and cut the spears into 1½″–2″ lengths. In a heavy skillet, sauté the asparagus spears in olive oil, sprinkling them lightly with salt. Cover the pan and cook over medium heat, stirring occasionally, until asparagus is tender but still firm, about 5 minutes.

Beat the eggs lightly in a bowl, with salt and pepper. Add the eggs to the asparagus, scrambling the mixture lightly with a fork. Cook 2 minutes or less, depending on the texture desired, and serve immediately.

Recommended wine—Contrary to widespread belief, asparagus and wine can be paired successfully if some precautions are taken. The mild astringency of both asparagus and artichokes derives from cynarin and tends to distort our perceptions of other flavors, imparting an exaggerated sweetness to wines served with either vegetable. When I eat asparagus or artichokes, I take a small sip of the accompanying wine, pass it around in my mouth, and rest for 30 seconds or so while my threshold of taste readjusts. Then I can taste the wine's true character. A good fresh Merlot, preferably from Livio Felluga, would be my choice with this dish.

Crostata di Funghi
Mushroom Pie

SERVES 4 – 6

Traditionally, professional chefs and restaurateurs knew the particular culinary repertory they had been trained to prepare and serve, but were too busy minding the store to dine out very often themselves. Typically, their customers were far better informed about restaurants in general than they themselves were. Once established, the menus of most restaurants became something like Holy Writ and remained virtually unchanged year after year. Today, however, an increasingly savvy, well-traveled general public demands more variety and adaptability than it did in the past. To accommodate that demand, progressive restaurateurs literally have made it their business to eat out regularly and to expose their chefs to the innovations and regional specialties of their colleagues.

Felice and I dine out as often as we can, separately or together, in order to keep abreast of significant or interesting developments, both in this country and abroad. In New York, we visit our colleagues' places as often as we can, just as they drop in at Felidia, on evenings they've devoted to research, to check on what we're up to. And in our travels abroad, we constantly look for worthwhile regional specialties that may be incorporated into our own menu at Felidia. We found this savory mushroom pie at a Piedmontese restaurant and loved it.

½ pound puff pastry dough
(recipe page 235)
½ cup milk
3 tablespoons unsalted butter
1 tablespoon flour
½ pound porcini mushrooms,
sliced (see Note)

2 ounces prosciutto, diced
1 tablespoon finely minced shallots
Salt and pepper to taste
1 egg, beaten
2 ounces Montasio or Fontina
cheese, shaved

Keep the puff pastry dough refrigerated until needed. In a small saucepan, scald the milk. In a second small saucepan, melt 1 tablespoon of the butter, add the flour, and cook over medium heat, stirring constantly, until the mixture foams, about 2 minutes. Whisk the boiling milk into the butter and flour mixture and cook until the white sauce is boiling and thickened, 2–3 minutes.

Meanwhile, heat the remaining butter in a sauté pan, add the mushrooms, prosciutto, and shallots, and sauté until the mushrooms are tender. Add the mushroom mixture to the white sauce, season to taste, and cool.

Preheat the oven to 375°F.

On a wooden or marble surface, roll out the pastry dough into a sheet ¼″ thick and cut two circles from it, 7″ in diameter. Butter a 7″ pie pan and line with one pastry circle. Spread the mushroom mixture evenly over the pastry base, leaving a ¾″ border all around the edge, and brush the border with beaten egg. Top the filling with shaved cheese, cover with the remaining pastry circle, and press down tightly all around the border to seal the edges. Brush the pastry with the remaining beaten egg and bake until nicely browned, about 30 minutes. Serve warm.

Note: Morels, chanterelles, or other wild mushrooms can be substituted.

Recommended wine—Mushrooms are wonderful to work with—earthy, sensuous, comforting, and stimulating. You can accentuate their qualities by serving big wines such as Brunello or Barolo, or keep things on the lighter side with Chianti, Merlot, or Cabernet.

Frico Croccante
Cheese Chips

———

YIELDS 14–16 PIECES

These simple, tasty chips are popular in the mountains of Friuli. I pass them around to party guests, along with glasses of Tocai Friulano.

½ teaspoon unsalted butter

¾ pound Montasio cheese (rind removed), shredded

In a 7″ nonstick skillet, melt the butter. Sprinkle a 3½″ area to each side of the pan with 2 tablespoons of the cheese. Spread the cheese evenly and cook over moderately low heat, turning once with a spatula, until golden, about 4 minutes on each side. Transfer to paper towels to drain, and repeat the process until the cheese is used up. (To save time, use two or more skillets simultaneously.)

Formaggio in Crosta

Cheese in a Crust

SERVES 4

I was given this recipe, which owes something to French cooking, at a restaurant called La Contea, near Alba, in Piedmont. Either Gorgonzola or ripe Taleggio can be used as filling, and either will provide a delightful textural contrast with the pastry.

6 ounces Gorgonzola or
½ pound ripe Taleggio (or mixed)

12 ounces puff pastry, chilled
(recipe page 235)
1 egg yolk, beaten

Preheat the oven to 475°F. Crumble the Gorgonzola, or remove the rind and shred the Taleggio. Divide the cheese in four parts and lightly shape into balls (they should just hold together, not be compacted).

On a lightly floured surface, roll out the pastry ⅛″ thick and, using a 5″ bowl as your guide, cut out four rounds. Place the pastry rounds on a heavy baking sheet and center a cheese ball on each. Brush the edges of the pastry with beaten egg and fold the pastry over to form half-moon shapes. Press lightly around the curved edges to seal, and brush the tops lightly with beaten egg. Bake until browned, risen, and crisp, 10–15 minutes.

Serve warm.

Recommended wine—If you make this dish with Gorgonzola, Barbaresco would be a fine choice. A softer Dolcetto would be better if you use the Taleggio.

Polenta con Fonduta e Funghi Porcini
Polenta with Fontina and Porcini Mushrooms

SERVES 6

This dish derives from a Piedmontese specialty. Polenta and cheese are quite complementary, and porcini work well with both.

½ pound Italian Fontina cheese
1 cup milk
2 tablespoons soft unsalted butter
2 egg yolks
Salt to taste

1 walnut-size white truffle from Alba, brushed clean (optional)
Polenta (recipe page 129)
½ pound porcini
Olive oil to sauté

Preheat the broiler. Cut the Fontina in ½" cubes and soak in the milk for 1 hour. Transfer to a double boiler and cook gently until cheese is melted. Add the soft butter and the egg yolks, one at a time, and mix well. Add salt to taste. If used, shave the rough corners of the truffle into the *fonduta,* and mix.

Grill or pan-brown the polenta slices for a few minutes on each side. Place in a large gratin dish in a single layer and top with very hot *fonduta*. Set under the broiler until golden, about 1 minute. In the meantime, sauté the porcini and serve with the polenta, shaving truffle over the dish if desired.

Recommended wine—On a chilly fall evening, my choice would be either a Gattinara or a Spanna. Reliable producers include Antoniolo, Nervi, Trovaglini, and Vallana.

Bella, an expert truffle hound, on the job near Motovun. The German short-haired pointer and the Labrador retriever are the breeds of choice in Istria, and bitches generally are preferred to males, which have greater endurance but tend to be less diligent workers. Because prospective truffle hounds don't respond to training until they are six months old, those born in January are the most highly prized, for their education—a ten-day process— commences in June, when the subterranean truffles grow closest to the surface and are most easily detectable.

SOUPS

ABOUT SOUPS AND STOCKS

In my family, soup always was taken for granted as a prelude to a serious dinner. My father expected soup at the start of the meal, except on the hottest summer days. When a multicourse dinner was prepared, the soup usually was made with fresh-killed chickens and garnished with a little rice or fidelini—very thin egg pasta.

I suppose every culture hails the medicinal properties of its chicken soup, and ours is no different. When someone was ill or recovering from childbirth, the aroma of chicken soup filled the house, in keeping with accepted folk wisdom. As a child and young woman, I knew that I felt better when I ate soup, but it wasn't until later that I deduced why; that the chemical and psychological effects of hot soup on the system stimulate some organic processes and relax others, making the digestive tract more receptive to subsequent courses. The warmth of the ingested soup, for example, activates the flow of the gastric juices in the digestive tract and increases the capillary blood supply, thereby allowing the stomach to work more efficiently. Also, the warm soup combines with the gastric juices and forms a digestive solution to break down solid food more easily.

With a supply of stock on hand, a good soup can be put together in minutes. For this reason—and because many of the recipes in this book call for a cup or two of stock—I suggest that you cook up a batch of stock periodically and keep it in reserve. It freezes well and, in concentrated form, takes up little storage space. Very concentrated stock, produced by boiling away most of the water content, can be poured into an ice cube tray and used by the cube as needed. (Once frozen, it can be stored in plastic bags.) The addition of hot water will reconstitute the stock for use in soups and sauces or as a flavorful braising liquid. The quantity of water will depend on the concentration of the stock.

Wine note—With soups, I usually continue with whichever wine accompanied the antipasto. Exceptions would be emphatically flavorful soups, such as wild mushroom (recipe page 75) or *yota* (recipe page 77). For them, I'd choose a bigger wine that also can be served with the main course. Too many wines complicate a meal unnecessarily and detract from the enjoyment of the food.

Brodo di Carne
Basic Stock

YIELDS 8–10 CUPS

---

1 pound chicken backs and wings

1 pound veal shin bones

1 pound short ribs of beef

Salt to taste

2 ribs celery

1 small bunch Italian parsley

¼ celery root (celeriac), peeled (optional)

2 large carrots, halved

4 whole cloves garlic

1 medium-large onion (see Note)

4 whole peppercorns

Trim the meats of excess fat, rinse, and place in a stockpot. Cover generously with cold water, salt very lightly, and slowly bring to a boil. Add all the other ingredients, lower the heat, and simmer 3–4 hours, depending on the desired concentration of flavor. (I'd suggest more rather than less; for a lighter soup, a concentrated stock always can be quickly diluted with water.) Skim the surface of froth and fat as they accumulate.

Remove from the stove, strain through a very fine sieve, and refrigerate overnight. The next day, skim off the solid surface fat. The stock then can be kept under refrigeration up to 3 days or frozen for several months.

Note: Peel and cut the onion in half and brown it over an open flame or under the broiler. For a more deeply colored stock, the meats and vegetables can be browned in a roasting pan with a little olive oil.

VARIATIONS: With the same quantities of vegetables and seasoning, beef, veal, or chicken stock can be prepared using the following amounts of meat and bones.

Brodo di Manzo
Beef Stock

1 pound each beef bones (preferably marrow bones), beef shin, and short ribs or oxtails

Brodo di Vitello
Veal Stock

1½ pounds each veal shin bones and muscles or neck and breast of veal, bone in and fat removed

Brodo di Pollo
Chicken Stock

3 pounds chicken backs and wings

Brodo di Pesce
Fish Stock

YIELDS ABOUT 5 CUPS

1 pound fish heads and trimmings, preferably red snapper or sea bass

2 quarts water

2 medium carrots, quartered

1 small onion, halved

3 sprigs parsley

1 rib celery, quartered

6 whole black peppercorns

1 teaspoon olive oil

Salt and pepper to taste

Rinse the fish heads and trimmings well under cold running water. In a large pot, combine all ingredients and bring to a boil. Reduce the heat and simmer very gently for 45 minutes, skimming off the surface foam.

Strain the stock through a sieve lined with a double thickness of moistened cheesecloth. The stock can be used at once, refrigerated up to 2 days, or frozen for several weeks in ½-cup or 1-cup containers.

Note: A vegetable stock can be substituted in most fish recipes. To make one, proceed as above, without the fish heads and trimmings, and with the water reduced by half.

Riso e Patate
Rice and Potato Soup

SERVES 6

This is a quick soup and very economical.

2 potatoes, peeled and diced small
3 tablespoons olive oil
2 carrots, shredded
2 ribs celery, halved crosswise
2 teaspoons tomato paste
10 cups hot chicken stock
(recipe page 69)

2 bay leaves
Salt and freshly ground pepper to taste
1 cup long-grain rice
Grated Parmigiano

In a deep pot or large saucepan, cook the potatoes in the olive oil, turning occasionally, until browned, about 5 minutes. Add the carrots and celery, and cook 2–3 minutes over medium heat, stirring with a wooden spoon. (The potatoes may stick slightly to the bottom of the pan. No harm done—in fact they'll take on added flavor—so long as you don't let them burn.)

Add the tomato paste, hot chicken stock, bay leaves, and salt and pepper. Cover the pot and simmer 40 minutes over medium-low heat. Add the rice and cook 12 minutes longer, until the rice is tender. Remove and discard the celery and bay leaves, adjust the seasoning, and serve sprinkled with grated cheese.

Zuppa di Pesce con Riso
Red Snapper Soup with Rice

SERVES 6

In Istria, this would be called *zuppa di triglie con riso* and would be made with a species of small red mullet common to the Adriatic and the Mediterranean. Although Felice sometimes finds a few in the markets of Astoria, fresh *triglie* are seldom available in this country. At the restaurant, we substitute filleted red snapper for the red mullet, both for that reason and because few of our customers will eat whole fish on the bone. If you prefer a more authentic—and more flavorful—soup, cook your fish bones and all.

Note: For this recipe, use a medium-size pot for each of the two lists of ingredients.

FOR THE SOUP

⅓ cup olive oil	2 cups boiling water
1 medium onion, chopped	1 stalk celery
Head, tail, bones from red snapper (see below)	2 sprigs fresh thyme
½ teaspoon salt (or to taste)	2 leeks (green part only)
1 tablespoon tomato paste	

For the soup, heat the oil in a medium-size pot and sauté the onion until translucent, 2 minutes. Add the fish head, tail, and bones, and sauté until golden, 3–5 minutes. Add the salt and tomato paste, mixing well, then add the 2 cups boiling water. Bring to a boil again, add the celery, thyme, and leeks. Reduce the heat and simmer 25 minutes. Strain the liquid into a clean receptacle and set it aside. Discard the solids.

FOR THE RICE

4 teaspoons olive oil	2 pounds red snapper fillet
1 medium potato, peeled and cubed	⅔ cup long-grain or Arborio rice
1 cup shredded carrot	6 flakes dried Italian hot pepper
¾ teaspoon salt	2 tablespoons chopped Italian parsley
2 cups boiling water	Freshly ground black pepper to taste
1 teaspoon white vinegar	

Begin the rice while the soup is simmering. Heat the oil in a second medium-size pot, add the cubed potato, and brown on all sides, tossing occasionally, about 4–5 minutes. Add the shredded carrot and salt, and sauté, stirring constantly, 2 minutes.

Add 2 cups of boiling water and the vinegar, cook 10 minutes, and add the reserved liquid from the first pot. Cook at low boil 15 minutes longer, meanwhile cutting the fish fillet into ½″ cubes. Stir the rice into the pot, cook 10 minutes, and add the cubed fish and pepper flakes. Continue to cook 5 minutes longer, until the rice is done. Season with additional salt to taste. Add the parsley and serve with freshly ground pepper.

Brodo Brostula
Toasted Soup

————

SERVES 6

At home, during my early childhood, *brodo brostula,* an extremely simple "poor man's" dish, was considered a "lean" soup and usually was eaten on meatless Fridays. Still, its texture was fairly dense and almost reminded me of morning oatmeal. It was comforting and earthy, and I thought of it as a "fond" soup.

4 cloves garlic, lightly crushed
1 cup unbleached flour
3 tablespoons olive oil
8 cups chicken stock (recipe page 69)

4 eggs, beaten
1½ cups croutons
Freshly ground pepper to taste

In a heavy saucepan, brown the garlic and flour in heated oil, stirring constantly over low heat, 3–5 minutes. Add the chicken stock and mix well, scraping all the flour from the sides of the pan. Simmer 20 minutes, skimming occasionally. Pass the mixture through a sieve, discarding the garlic and any lumps of flour.

In a clean pan, bring the mixture to a boil and slowly add the beaten eggs, continuously beating with a fork during the process. Return to the boil, remove immediately from the heat, and serve with croutons and freshly ground pepper.

Minestra di Verdure Miste con Finocchio
Vegetable Soup with Fennel

SERVES 12–16

At home in Istria, this fragrant soup is eaten in the spring and early summer, when the fennel shoots are still young and tender. During my childhood, wild fennel, which I haven't seen in this country, was used, and the soup often was served as a meal in itself, sometimes with sausage added. (Sausage and fennel have a natural affinity.) Because its preparation takes some time and its character develops after a night or two in the refrigerator, when it is *riposada,* or rested, I always make this soup in big batches to be enjoyed over two or three days.

2 cups Great Northern white beans
2 fresh pork hocks (see Note)
2 large Idaho potatoes, peeled
2 large carrots
5 fresh bay leaves
4 cloves garlic, chopped fine
4 tablespoons olive oil
1 cup chopped peeled tomatoes

1 pound spinach, shredded
1 pound Swiss chard, shredded
10 ounces corn kernels, frozen if need be (see Note)
10 ounces fresh peas, or frozen (see Note)
1 pound fennel, diced fine
Salt and freshly ground pepper to taste

Pick over and rinse the beans, and soak them overnight in plenty of water.

In a large pot, bring 5 quarts water to a boil. Add the drained beans, pork hocks, potatoes, carrots, and bay leaves.

In a skillet, lightly sauté the garlic in the olive oil until golden, add the tomatoes and sauté 10 minutes longer. Add the contents of the pan to the boiling pot, lower the heat, and simmer gently, covered, 1 hour.

Meanwhile, in a large saucepan, bring 3 quarts water to a boil. Add the spinach, Swiss chard, corn, peas, and fennel, and parboil 10 minutes. Drain, and set aside.

At the end of the first hour, remove the carrots and potatoes from the pot, mash them together with a fork, and return them to the soup. Add the reserved vegetables, season to taste, and simmer another 30 minutes, uncovered, skimming and stirring occasionally. Remove the pork hocks (which may be eaten separately) and the bay leaves. Adjust the seasoning and serve with crusty Italian bread or focaccia (recipe page 229).

Note: One fresh and one smoked pork hock may be used to invest the soup with a somewhat more intriguing flavor. If frozen corn kernels and peas are used, they should not be parboiled and their final cooking time should be halved.

Minestra di Funghi Selvatici
Wild Mushroom Soup

SERVES 6

Every cook in our part of Istria had her own version of wild mushroom soup. This one was devised by my Great Aunt Santola, a widow, who cooked the soup for the whole courtyard at Busoler. She would come home and pick over the mushrooms she had gathered, separating those to be sautéed from those earmarked for other uses. Mostly trimmings and stems were reserved for her soup. When I was old enough to begin gathering my own mushrooms, I was allowed to pick only the unmistakably safe varieties, like champignons and porcini, and forbidden to eat any before my aunt approved them. The traditional belief was that the poisonous mushrooms could be detected by cooking them in water with a piece of brass; if the brass turned green, the mushrooms were unsafe. As a further precaution, the oldest woman in a household had the dubious honor of tasting the mushrooms before they were served to other members of the family.

Note: The soup is best when made with several varieties of fresh wild mushrooms (porcini, shiitake, chanterelle, hen-of-the-woods, etc.), but even a single variety will produce an excellent soup. Other types of dried mushrooms may be substituted for the dried porcini specified, but porcini are preferable.

Mountain forager weighing mushrooms, Udine.

8 pieces (²/₃ ounce) dried porcini mushrooms

5 tablespoons olive oil

2 slices bacon, chopped fine

1 medium onion, chopped

2 medium potatoes, peeled

2 medium carrots, whole

1 large shallot, chopped

2½ quarts chicken stock (recipe page 69)

½ teaspoon salt, or to taste

In 1½ cups of warm water, presoak the dried porcini about 20 minutes, until softened. Drain, reserving all but the last 2 teaspoons of the steeping liquid (to avoid unwanted sediments), remove and rinse the softened porcini.

In the 5-quart pot, heat 5 tablespoons olive oil, add the bacon and onion, and sauté until translucent. Add the potatoes, carrots, and shallot, and cook 2 minutes over medium heat, stirring constantly. Add the stock, drained porcini, reserved soaking liquid, and salt, and bring to a boil. Reduce the heat and keep on low boil about 10 minutes, until the vegetables are tender.

FOR THE FRESH MUSHROOMS

5 tablespoons olive oil

2 pounds wild mushrooms, cleaned and sliced

Freshly ground pepper to taste

¼ cup chopped Italian parsley

To prepare the fresh wild mushrooms, heat the olive oil in the large skillet and sauté them in batches, over medium-high heat, until all water has evaporated, about 7 minutes per batch. Transfer the mushrooms to the soup pot and simmer 30 minutes, skimming occasionally. Add the pepper and parsley, and serve piping hot.

Yota

Sauerkraut and Bean Soup

SERVES 12–16

In Trieste and throughout Istria, *yota* (alternatively *jota* or *iota)* plays much the same role that onion soup plays for Parisians at the end of a bibulous night on the town. This is a winter dish: lusty stick-to-the-ribs fare with a pronounced Slavic accent. It's best made in big batches, and improves after a day or two in the refrigerator.

1½ cups dried red kidney beans

1 lb. pork butt

4 cloves garlic

¼ pound bacon

2 bay leaves

2 pounds sauerkraut, washed twice

3 medium starchy potatoes, peeled and quartered

Salt and freshly ground black pepper to taste

Pick over and rinse the beans, and soak them overnight in 4 cups cold water.

Rinse the pork butt and cut into small cubes. With a sharp knife or in a processor, mince garlic and bacon together, to form a paste.

Drain the beans and put them in a large pot with the pork butt, bay leaves, and 4 quarts water, and bring to a boil. Reduce the heat, add the bacon mixture, and simmer gently 1 hour.

Add the sauerkraut and potatoes, and cook until the potatoes are tender, about 30 minutes. With a slotted spoon or skimmer, remove the potatoes from the soup, mash them roughly, and return them to the pot. Add salt and pepper and cook 15 minutes longer, adding a little water if the soup seems overly thick.

Discard the bay leaves and serve the soup piping hot.

2

Insalate e Verdure

Salads and Vegetables

Olive oil is the staple cooking fat and culinary lubricant of the cuisines indigenous to southern Europe, where its use was propagated during the spread of the Roman Empire. I grew up on olive oil and use it as a basic ingredient in most of my cooking. During my childhood, it was used for cosmetic and medicinal purposes as well: as a pomade and massage oil, for example, and in the treatment of earaches. I've often wondered why olive oil is such an effective remedy for a mild infection of the ear, and my guess is that either the heat of the warm oil brings additional blood to the infected area or the oil's sealing properties cut off the oxygen supply to the bacteria. So much for my medical theories.

Most of my salads are dressed with olive oil, and I often use raw olive oil to amalgamate sauces. To tighten a sauce, I just dribble some olive oil into it toward the finish and shake the pan back and forth. The oil molecules expand as they are heated, and the agitation of the pan incorporates air into them, making the sauce fluffier.

Olive oil from the first and second pressing of the fruit is labeled "Pure Olive Oil." Oil exclusively from the first pressing is graded as follows, according to its oleic acid content:

4 percent = Virgin
3 percent = Fine
1.5 percent = Superfine
1 percent = Extra Virgin

The percentage of oleic acid indicates the degree to which fat molecules have been broken down into their fatty acid components and is a determining factor in establishing the smoking point of a given grade of oil. When frying foods, I usually mix equal amounts of vegetable oil and olive oil for flavor and to lower the smoking point.

STORING OLIVE OIL: There is no need to store olive oil in the refrigerator, where it will solidify. Stored properly in a cool, dark place, it will keep as long as two years without spoilage. Remember, however, that olive oil will become rancid when oxidized by repeated exposure to air. Therefore, oil bought by the gallon should be transferred to smaller bottles, which are corked well and opened one at a time. The addition of such fresh herbs as sage, rosemary, and garlic will not only inhibit oxidation but impart their flavors to the oil.

ABOUT BALSAMIC VINEGAR

The finest balsamic vinegar—so called because it is considered a balm—is made in the area of Modena, from the juice of the Trebbiano grape. The late-harvest grapes are crushed, whereupon the must is filtered and boiled, with no fermentation taking place during the process. The must is reduced from 30 to 70 percent during its boiling, depending on the sugar content, left to age for a year, then transferred successively at one-year intervals to casks of chestnut, cherry, ash, and mulberry. The initial cask contains sixty liters, of which about 10 percent will be lost to evaporation each year. Hence, at the end of the fifth year there will be about ten liters of vinegar left in the last cask. The same casks are used, without cleaning, for decades; therefore, the "mother," a bacterial mass that generates natural fermentation, remains in the casks as they are refilled year after year. Balsamic vinegar continues to age after it has been bottled—in some cases for a century or longer—and with the passage of time, it's transformed from a condiment to a *digestif* and finally to a medicinal remedy.

When shopping for balsamic vinegar, look for the legend "aceto balsamico tradizionale," which indicates that the product is the result of the traditional method involving five years in the wood. The vinegar so labeled is far superior to other, nontraditional balsamic vinegars and is accordingly quite expensive. Its characteristics are a molasseslike consistency, lively brown color, a mildly acidic "nose," and a smooth, subtle interplay of sweet and sour flavors.

Insalata di Fagiolini e Patate
String Bean and Potato Salad

SERVES 6

There isn't much to be said about this dish, except that we ate a lot of potatoes during my Istrian years and worked out many ways of dressing them up. This was one of my favorites when my grandmother's earliest string beans were harvested. Try it as picnic fare.

2 medium-to-large Idaho potatoes
1 pound fresh string beans, trimmed
3 tablespoons olive oil
3 tablespoons white wine vinegar
¼ teaspoon salt
Freshly ground pepper to taste
1 small red onion, thinly sliced

Boil the potatoes in 2 quarts salted water for 20 minutes. Add the beans and boil 7 minutes longer, until the beans and potatoes arc just tender. Strain into a colander, remove and set aside the potatoes. Refresh the beans under cold running water and drain well.

When the potatoes are cool enough to handle, peel and slice them ⅓" thick.

If the beans are long, halve them crosswise.

In a large bowl, whisk together the oil, vinegar, salt and pepper. Add the onion, potatoes, and beans, and toss very gently to dress all ingredients without breaking the potatoes.

Recommended wine—In the ordinary format of a meal, a wine chosen specifically for the salad course is unnecessary. If you opt to serve wine with the salad (a practice frowned upon by many wine buffs), just stay with whatever you've poured previously. If salad is the main course, however, go for a high-acidity white, such as Pinot Grigio, or a big white with wood, such as Chardonnay.

Insalata di Asparagi

Asparagus Salad

SERVES 4

All the elements of this simple salad can be prepared in advance, but the dish should not be assembled until just before it's served. When they're available, the first pencil-thin asparagus spears of the season make this a special treat.

2 pounds asparagus, trimmed and peeled

½ teaspoon salt (or to taste)

2 hard-cooked eggs

3 tablespoons white wine vinegar

4 tablespoons olive oil

Freshly ground pepper to taste

In a large nonreactive pot, steam or boil the asparagus with lightly salted water just until tender, about 6 minutes. Drain immediately in a colander and refresh under cold running water. Pat the asparagus dry and cut into ½" pieces. Separate the egg whites and yolks, and coarsely chop each.

In a bowl, blend the vinegar, oil, salt and pepper. Add the asparagus and toss well. Add the egg whites and yolks, and combine thoroughly.

Scarola Affogata
Smothered Escarole

SERVES 4

This is the treatment of choice for leafy vegetables throughout Italy and the Italian-speaking regions of Istria, and any other leafy vegetable—spinach, *broccoli di rape*, or the like—can be prepared the same way. During my childhood, we often added bacon or sausage to *scarola affogata* and had it as a main course for *merenda*. I'd be sent off to play with a big sandwich of *scarola affogata* for my lunch. By the time I was tired and hungry enough to eat it, the thick bread had absorbed some of the vegetable juices and the cooking oil. I loved those sandwiches. As a side dish, this marries best with drier foods like roasts and fried chicken. It's not as appropriate with stews, braised dishes, or boiled meats served with their cooking broth.

1 pound (approximately 2 medium heads) escarole

6 cloves garlic, crushed

3 tablespoons olive oil

½ teaspoon salt

¼ teaspoon hot red pepper flakes

Fresh black pepper, 4 twists of the mill

Remove the outer leaves of escarole if damaged or discolored. Cut off the bases, wash the leaves twice in abundant cold water, and drain. In a large pot, sauté the garlic in oil until golden but not brown. Add the remaining ingredients, cover, and cook over moderate heat 3–4 minutes, stirring occasionally. Remove and discard the garlic; serve immediately.

Broccoli di Rape e Salsicce

Leaf Broccoli and Sausage

SERVES 4

This is a variation on the preceding escarole recipe. *Broccoli di rape* is especially good with sausage because the bitter-almond flavor of the vegetable sets off the sweetness of the meat.

1 pound broccoli di rape	½ teaspoon salt
10 ounces sweet Italian sausage	¼ teaspoon hot pepper flakes
6 cloves garlic, crushed	Fresh black pepper, 4 twists of the mill
3 tablespoons olive oil	1 tablespoon water

Preheat oven to 500°F.

The choice parts of *broccoli di rape* are the slender green florets; therefore, clip off the large stems, remove the tough upper leaves, and, if the main stem is tough, peel it with a standard potato peeler. Wash in plenty of cold water and drain.

Prick the sausage with a fork, set it on a metal plate or skillet, and bake in oven 15 minutes, turning occasionally.

Remove to another plate and cool.

In a 4–5-quart pot, sauté the garlic gently in oil until golden but not brown. Add the *broccoli di rape* and, successively, the salt, pepper flakes, fresh black pepper, and water. Mix well, cover, and cook 5–7 minutes. Meanwhile, slice the sausage. Mix lightly with the *broccoli di rape*. Remove and discard the garlic; serve at once.

Verze e Patate
Savoy Cabbage with Potatoes

SERVES 6

Simple but satisfying, this was a family favorite during my childhood.

3 medium starchy potatoes

1 large Savoy cabbage (about 2½ pounds)

4 cloves garlic, lightly crushed

¼ cup olive oil

2 teaspoons unsalted butter

Salt and freshly ground pepper

Peel and quarter the potatoes. Core the cabbage and cut the remainder into 1″ cubes. Bring 4 quarts water to a boil, add the potatoes, and cook until half-done, about 10 minutes. Add the cabbage and cook until both vegetables are tender, 10–15 minutes longer. Drain the vegetables thoroughly.

In a large skillet, brown the garlic lightly in the olive oil. Add the cabbage, potatoes, butter, salt and pepper. Mash the vegetables coarsely, leaving plenty of lumps. If the mixture is too moist, continue to sauté it a little longer, taking care not to scorch it. Adjust seasoning, discard the garlic cloves, and serve.

Lenticchie

Lentils

SERVES 4 – 6 AS A SIDE DISH

Among the most versatile and nutritious of the legumes, lentils (Esau's mess of pottage) originated in central Asia in ancient times and have been popular in Italy at least since the days of the Roman Empire, when they were imported by the shipload. In Mediterranean Europe, they're often served together with pork, especially with cotechino (recipe page 196) in Italy.

1½ cups lentils

2 tablespoons olive oil

1 small onion, chopped

1 large shallot, chopped

3 small carrots, finely chopped

2 small ribs celery, finely chopped

2 bay leaves

½ cup crushed peeled tomatoes

1½–2 cups chicken stock (recipe page 69)

Salt and freshly ground pepper

Rinse and pick over the lentils. In a medium saucepan, boil the lentils 10 minutes in water to cover and drain them well. Meanwhile, heat the oil in a medium casserole. Add the onion and shallot and sauté over moderately high heat until golden. Add the carrots, celery, and bay leaves, and sauté 2 min-utes longer. Add the tomatoes, lentils, and 1 cup of the chicken stock, and season to taste. Simmer over moderately low heat, adding stock as needed, until the lentils are tender, 25–30 minutes. The finished product should not be soupy.

Frico con Patate

Cheese and Potato Cake

SERVES 4

Except for the inclusion of cheese, *frico con patate* would be essentially the same dish as the French *pommes Anna*. With a simple salad and a piece of fruit for dessert, it can be served as the main course of a light meal.

2 medium-large baking potatoes
¼ pound Montasio cheese

2 tablespoons unsalted butter
Salt and pepper to taste

In water to cover, boil the potatoes in their jackets 25–30 minutes, keeping them on the firm side. While the potatoes cook, remove rind from the Montasio and cut the cheese in small dice.

When the potatoes are cool enough to handle but still warm, peel and slice them ¼″ thick. Melt the butter in a 10″ nonstick skillet. Off the heat, arrange the potatoes, slightly overlapping the slices, in concentric circles, working from the center outward and covering the bottom of the pan. Season with salt and pepper, sprinkle evenly with cheese, and cook, covered, over moderate heat until browned on the bottom, about 8 minutes.

Invert a large plate over the uncovered pan and then invert the potato cake onto the plate. Slide potato cake back into pan and cook uncovered until the cheese browns, about 8 minutes longer.

Once again invert the potato cake onto the plate and pat it with paper towels to remove any excess grease. Cut into 4 wedges and serve.

For a more appealing presentation, the ingredients can be divided into four parts, cooked separately in 5″ pans, and served as individual cakes.

Chifeletti di Patate
Fried Potato Crescents

When we made gnocchi at Busoler, we'd often put aside some potatoes and flour for *chifeletti,* which were served with roasts as a sop for the sauce. Sometimes we kids would snitch a few from the kitchen and sprinkle them with sugar for an impromptu dessert.

½ pound Idaho potatoes	1 tablespoon unsalted butter, melted
1 egg	½ cup flour
¼ teaspoon salt	2 cups vegetable oil

In a medium saucepan, boil the potatoes in salted water to cover until tender, about 25 minutes, and drain well. When cool enough to handle, peel the potatoes and rice them into a bowl. Allow the potatoes to cool thoroughly. Beat the egg with the salt and add with the butter to the potato mixture. Add the flour and blend well. Working with about 1 tablespoon of dough at a time, roll it into a cylinder about 3" long and ½" thick. Bend cylinders into U shapes.

In a medium skillet, heat the oil just short of the smoking point. Add potato crescents in batches and fry until golden brown.

Finocchio alla Griglia
Broiled Fennel

SERVES 4

The distinctive characteristic of young bulb fennel is its clean sweet flavor. I use it often to refresh the palate between more complex, deeply flavorful courses.

2 bulbs fennel, about 2 pounds

4 tablespoons unsalted butter, cut into dots

½ cup grated Parmigiano

Preheat the broiler. Trim the fennel, discarding the tough outside parts and reserving the greens for soup. Cut the fennel bulbs in half vertically and slice each half vertically through the core, into slices about ¼" thick. In a medium saucepan, bring 3 cups water to a boil.

Add the fennel and cook until tender, about 12 minutes. Drain the fennel and reserve 1 cup of the cooking liquid.

Transfer the fennel to a baking dish. Dot with butter and sprinkle evenly with cheese. Add the reserved liquid and broil 2–4 minutes, until golden brown.

Radicchio Trevisano al Tegame
Braised Treviso Radicchio

SERVES 4

Trevisans refer to their best-known specialty, radicchio, as *il fiore che si mangia,* "the flower which is eaten," and insist that theirs is the only true radicchio. A second, quite different variety is grown around Castelfranco Veneto, about twenty miles away, but is scorned by the Trevisans, who refuse to dignify it with the name radicchio, and refer to it, disparagingly, as *rose.* Both varieties now are sold in this country and are widely considered to be interchangeable. They really aren't. The superior Treviso type can be distinguished by its more elongated shape, deeper color, and sharper flavor. Although milder and not as striking, Belgian endive makes an acceptable substitute for this treatment.

2 tablespoons olive oil

8 cloves garlic, crushed

4 heads (about 1½ pounds total) radicchio trevisano, *trimmed at bases*

¼ cup hot water

4 anchovy fillets, coarsely chopped

¼ cup dry white wine

In a medium nonreactive skillet, heat the oil, add the garlic, and sauté until golden. Add the radicchio carefully (it splatters) and the water, cover immediately, and cook over moderately high heat, stirring occasionally, until tender, about 6 minutes (7 minutes if Belgian endive is substituted). Add the anchovies, lower the heat to medium, and cook 3 minutes longer.

Transfer the radicchio to a serving plate. Add the wine to the skillet and cook over moderate heat, stirring occasionally and scraping the bottom to incorporate the pan drippings with the wine. Discard the garlic and pour the lightly thickened sauce over the radicchio.

Zucchine al Tegame
Sautéed Zucchini

SERVES 4

This way of treating zucchini originated in Trieste, the penultimate station on the old spice route from Asia to Venice. I'm not sure that every early Triestine experiment with spices succeeded, but cinnamon complements zucchini surprisingly well.

2 tablespoons olive oil
1 pound small zucchini, cut in ¼" rounds
2 cloves garlic, crushed

Salt and freshly ground pepper
1 tablespoon chopped Italian parsley
Cinnamon to taste

In a large heavy skillet, heat the oil, add the zucchini and garlic, and season with salt and pepper. Sauté over moderately high heat, stirring often, until the zucchini is tender and lightly browned, about 7 minutes. (The garlic should not be permitted to burn and become bitter.) Discard the garlic, add the parsley, mix well, and serve piping hot, dusted with cinnamon.

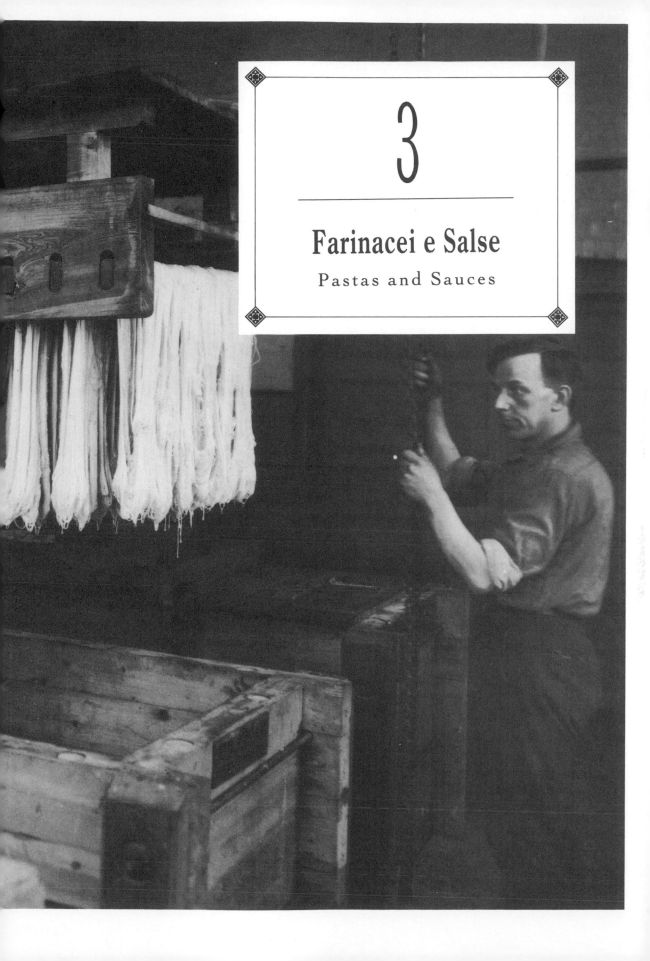

3

Farinacei e Salse

Pastas and Sauces

GNOCCHI

◆

Gnocchi

Salsa alla Salvia

Parenci

Gnocchi di Zucca

Gnocchi di Susine

Gnocchi di Melanzane

Salsa di Pomodoro

Gnocchi di Ricotta

Contessa Sauce

Roulade di Ricotta e Spinaci

POLENTA

◆

ABOUT POLENTA

Basic Polenta

Fried Polenta

Grilled Polenta

Polenta con Fonduta di Funghi Porcini e Tartufi

Lumache con Polenta

ABOUT WINES AND PASTA

When choosing wines to serve with pasta dishes, the primary consideration should be the fat content of the sauce. If the sauce contains a high quantity of olive oil, cream, or butter, serve a wine high in acidity, such as Gavi, Soave, Pinot Grigio, or Spumante.

Attention also should be paid to the intensity of the sauce's flavor. With sauces of moderate intensity, fresh, up-front wines like Merlot or Refosco would be good choices. Tignanello, Taurasi, or Cabernet would be more appropriate to meat sauces or *sguazet*, while sauces of game call for Barbaresco, Barolo, Cabreo, or Sassicaia.

Lidia and Felice with Dante and Nino, and some of Felidia's carefully selected wines.

DRY PASTA

◆

ABOUT DRY PASTA

When buying dry pasta, avoid any that breaks easily or looks chipped, blotchy, or dull. The product should have a lively, even, almost translucent tone.

1 pound pasta | *2 tablespoons coarse salt*
4 quarts water

Add the pasta to rapidly boiling salted water in a tall pot. Cook half-covered, stirring occasionally, until al dente. (Cooking time will vary according to the type and brand of pasta.) Drain and proceed with sauce. Do not add oil while cooking and do not rinse under cold water unless you are preparing a cold pasta dish.

The water is a very important element. The softer the water (the fewer the minerals), the better the pasta cooks. Hard water has a high salt, calcium, and magnesium content, and therefore leaves unwanted deposits in any cooking vessel, negatively affecting the color of the principal ingredient. Most major cities filter their water with lime to eliminate excess calcium and magnesium.

Ziti con Broccoli di Rape e Salsicce

Ziti with Broccoli di Rape and Sausage

SERVES 4

*B*roccoli di rape is one of several tart, acidic, leafy greens that many Italians find particularly appealing. In this dish, the vegetable acts as a near-perfect foil for the rich sweetness of the sausage, while the neutral pasta mediates between the two.

This dish requires fairly precise timing, but with a little advance preparation, the sauce can be made while the ziti is cooking, and both should be ready at about the same time. The cooking time of dried pasta varies from 8 to 14 minutes, depending on its shape and quality, after the water returns to a boil. The ziti should be drained as soon as it's al dente, even if the sauce isn't quite finished by then. It will reheat sufficiently when combined with the sauce.

½ pound sweet Italian sausage	*¼ teaspoon salt*
2 pounds broccoli di rape	*¼ teaspoon hot pepper flakes*
3 tablespoons coarse salt	*2 teaspoons unsalted butter*
1 pound ziti	*1 cup chicken stock (recipe page 69)*
¼ cup olive oil	*½ cup grated Parmigiano*
3 large cloves garlic, crushed	

*G*rill or broil the sausage in advance. When cooled, slice it thin and set aside. Wash and drain the *broccoli di rape* and set it aside.

In a large pot, put 10 quarts water on to boil, with 3 tablespoons coarse salt added, and immediately start preparing the sauce. Add the ziti to the pot when the water boils and cook until al dente.

In a large, deep, heavy skillet with a fitted lid, heat the olive oil, add the garlic, and sauté, uncovered, until golden, about 2 minutes. Add the *broc-coli di rape,* ¼ teaspoon salt, and pepper flakes, cover, and steam 5 minutes, stirring occasionally. Stir in the sausage. Add the butter and chicken stock, and cook over high heat, uncovered, about 3 minutes, until the liquids are slightly reduced.

Add the drained pasta to the sauce and toss gently. Sprinkle on ½ of the cheese, toss again, serve immediately, and distribute the remaining cheese over the pasta.

Recommended wine—A Fiano di Avellino by Mastroberardino would be my first choice for this dish. The wine's volcanic element sets off the spicy earthiness of the *broccoli di rape* to perfection.

Spaghetti con Salsa di Gamberi e Basilico
Spaghetti with Shrimp and Basil Sauce

SERVES 4 – 6

We didn't use much basil in our cooking at home in Istria, and I didn't really discover its possibilities until I traveled to Liguria, where it's the dominant herb. *Basilico,* I've since learned, goes well with almost anything, particularly tomatoes and seafood. I like this dish for its simplicity, fragrance, and freshness.

1 pound medium shrimp
1 pound spaghetti
6 tablespoons olive oil
4 cloves garlic, crushed
1 tablespoon minced shallots
1 cherry pepper, seeded and chopped
Salt and freshly ground pepper

1 cup white wine
18 fresh basil leaves, quartered
2 tablespoons minced Italian parsley
4 mint leaves, minced
½ cup boiling water from the spaghetti pot

While bringing 6 quarts salted water to a boil, peel, devein, and halve the shrimp crosswise. Add spaghetti to the boiling water and start sauce, stirring the spaghetti occasionally. The spaghetti will be done in 10–12 minutes, by which time the sauce should be ready.

In a large pan, heat 4 tablespoons of the olive oil, stir in the garlic and shallots, and sauté until the shallots are translucent. Add the cherry pepper and shrimp, taking care not to crowd the shrimp lest they steam in their own juices. Sauté 2 minutes, add the wine, salt and pepper to taste, and boil 1 minute. Remove the shrimp with a slotted spoon and set aside.

Add the remaining 2 tablespoons olive oil, basil, parsley, mint, and boiling water. Bring to a vigorous boil for 2 minutes, reduce the heat, and return the shrimp to the pan for a few seconds. Off heat, pour ¾ of the sauce into a second pan, drain and stir the spaghetti into the second pan, and add the remaining sauce. Mix the sauce and pasta well, and serve immediately.

Recommended wine—The wines and dominant flavors of a given region seldom fail to harmonize. For this dish, a nice Pigato di Albenga, grown in Liguria, would be a natural.

Capellini Capricciosi
Spicy Capellini

SERVES 4 – 6

The first time I tasted this dish was at the Sabatini restaurant in Florence. I asked for the recipe but was turned down. Back in New York, I reconstructed it to the best of my ability and liked the results. The next time I visited Sabatini, the owners conceded that my interpretation was very close to their original version. They still refused, however, to part with the precise recipe.

8 slices bacon, chopped	3 cups peeled Italian tomatoes, crushed
1/3 cup olive oil	1/4 teaspoon salt, or to taste
2 medium onions, thinly sliced	1 pound capellini
8 Tuscan peperoncini, seeded and chopped (see Note)	3/4 cup grated Parmigiano

In a nonreactive skillet, sauté the bacon in 3 tablespoons of the olive oil until lightly browned. Add the onions and cook, stirring, over medium heat until golden. Add the peperoncini, tomatoes, salt, and simmer 10 minutes.

While the sauce is simmering, cook the capellini in 4 quarts salted boiling water until al dente (tender but still firm), about 3 minutes. Drain the pasta and toss with the remaining olive oil. Stir in the sauce, add the cheese, toss well, and serve immediately.

(This is the only exception in tossing pasta with olive oil before adding the sauce. The capellini are so thin that the coating of oil limits their absorption of the hot sauce and helps to keep them al dente for a longer period while eating them.)

Note: Peperoncini (pickled hot Italian peppers) are available at specialty shops and most supermarkets.

Recommended wine—A dear friend, Teresa Lungarotti, and her father, Dr. Giorgio Lungarotti, produce wonderful wines in Torgiano, Umbria. A Rubesco Lungarotti or Montepulciano d'Abruzzo would match this dish well.

◆

Tagliatelle ai Porri
Tagliatelle with Leek Sauce

SERVES 4

Although Italians consume vegetables in greater variety and quantity per capita than any other Western Europeans, certain veggies seem to flare up in the public consciousness from time to time, just as they do in America. Leeks, for example, have been very much in vogue all over Italy since the mid-1980s. This is a dish from the Piacenza area, where the locals claim leeks always have been in style.

2 sweet Italian sausages

2 tablespoons coarse salt, or to taste

2 large leeks

2 tablespoons olive oil

1 teaspoon minced shallot

4 tablespoons unsalted butter

1 cup chicken stock (recipe page 69)

Salt and freshly ground pepper to taste

1 pound fresh tagliatelle

½ cup grated Parmigiano, and more for table

Grill the sausages, slice them thin, and set aside.

Bring 6 quarts water to the boil with the 2 tablespoons coarse salt, or to taste, and start the sauce as soon as the water is on the stove.

Trim the leeks and discard the top ⅓ of tough green portion. Slice the remainder in ½″-thick rounds, and rinse in several changes of cold water to remove all soil and grit. Drain well.

In a large skillet, heat the olive oil, add the leeks, and sauté over moderately high heat, stirring, until softened, about 5 minutes. Add the reserved sausages and the shallot, and cook, stirring, 1 minute. Add half the butter and the stock, and simmer gently 5 minutes. Season to taste.

Add the tagliatelle to the boiling water, stirring with a wooden spoon. The pasta will be done as soon as the water returns to the boil, ½–1 minute. Drain the pasta well, add the leek sauce, and toss well to coat the pasta with sauce. Add the remaining butter and sprinkle with cheese. Toss well and serve with additional cheese on the side.

Recommended wine—A Pomino or Galestro from Tuscany or an Orvieto from Umbria would be good with this dish. All three are clean, crisp, light wines with a nice fruity body that stands up well to the sweetness of the leeks.

Pappardelle in Salsa di Porcini Freschi
Pappardelle with Fresh Porcini Sauce

SERVES 4

A little butter is included in this recipe because our customers seem to like the richness it provides, but I omit it when cooking the dish at home, and recommend that you do too. Simple clarity—the pristine, unmuddled flavor of olive oil and mushrooms with a background of garlic—is what I want here, and butter clouds the issue.

¼ cup olive oil

1 pound fresh porcini, trimmed and sliced (morels, shiitake, or frozen porcini can be substituted)

4 cloves garlic, lightly crushed

Salt and freshly ground pepper to taste

2 tablespoons unsalted butter (optional)

3 tablespoons chopped Italian parsley

¾ cup chicken stock (recipe page 69)

1 pound fresh pappardelle (see Note) (recipe page 108)

½ cup grated Parmigiano

While bringing 6 quarts salted water to the boil for the pasta, begin the sauce. In a large skillet, heat 2 tablespoons of the oil. Add half the mushrooms and garlic, season to taste, and sauté until the mushrooms are lightly browned on both sides. Do not stir the porcini, or they will break; rather, turn them gently with a spatula. Transfer the porcini to a plate, and proceed as before with the remaining oil, garlic, and porcini.

Discard the excess oil from, and return all the porcini to, the pan and add the butter, if desired, and the parsley. Adjust the seasoning, add the stock, and simmer over medium heat about 1 minute, meanwhile adding the pappardelle to the boiling water. As soon as the pappardelle is done (1–1½ minutes), drain it well, add to the sauce over low heat, and toss gently, adding 4 tablespoons of the cheese. Serve immediately, with the remaining cheese at the table, to be added according to individual taste.

Note: Fresh pappardelle cooks so quickly that it should be added to the boiling water just before the sauce is finished.

Recommended wine—With porcini, as already noted, I like an earthy, complex wine. Try a fine Barbaresco with this dish.

Tortelloni
Stuffed Ring Dumplings

SERVES 8

Tortelloni require less time and work than the more familiar tortellini, simply because they're larger and only about half as many have to be cut out, filled, and shaped for each portion. This is Dante Laurenti's recipe for a specialty of Parma, where extensive use is made of cream, butter, and cheese.

FOR THE DOUGH

4 cups flour	*½ teaspoon salt*
6 eggs, beaten	*½ teaspoon olive oil*

Make a well in the flour and add the eggs, salt, and olive oil. Work with your hands, or use a mixer, to form a ball of very smooth consistency, neither sticky nor hard, adding more flour if needed.

Divide the dough into two parts and roll each to the thickness of a linen napkin. With a round cookie cutter or an inverted tumbler, cut out circles of dough approximately 3″ in diameter.

FOR THE STUFFING

1 pound ricotta cheese	*½ cup cooked and finely minced Swiss chard or spinach*
½ pound salted ricotta	*1 teaspoon salt*
½ cup grated Parmigiano	*1 teaspoon freshly ground pepper*
1 egg	

Blend all the stuffing ingredients well and place 1 teaspoon of the mixture in the center of each dough circle. Fold the dough over the filling to form semicircles, and press around the edges to seal them. Roll each piece around your index finger, with the stuffing facing the fingernail. Turn the thin edge of dough up against the stuffed portion and press the ends of dough together, forming a ring. Slide the dumpling off your finger and repeat the procedure until all the components are used up. Boil the tortelloni in salted water 2 minutes, or until they rise to the surface. Drain well and serve with sauce (below).

1 cup unsalted butter
1½ cups heavy cream

½ cup grated Parmigiano
Freshly ground pepper to taste

In a large saucepan, melt the butter, stir in the cream, and bring to a gentle boil. Add the cooked tortelloni, stir gently, and add grated cheese and pepper. Stir gently until the sauce has a honeylike consistency, and coats the tortelloni. Serve immediately.

Recommended wine—The outstanding winemaker Giacomo Bologna is the personification of Piedmontese gastronomy and oenology. His rendition of Barbera is wonderful. For this dish, I'd cross regional boundaries and pour Barbera Monella by Giacomo Bologna. It adds new meaning to the term Barbera.

Krafi
Wedding Pasta

———

SERVES 8

In Istria these ravioli-like dumplings are served on particularly festive occasions, especially weddings, because their sweetness is supposed to augur well for a happy marriage, and their richness symbolizes future prosperity. Neither citrus fruits nor rum was indigenous to Istria. Traditionally considered foreign trade ingredients, they were included in krafi as tokens of esteem for the occasion, the principals, and the assembled guests. As Jay reminds me, pineapples played a similar role in American social life during the post-Revolutionary era, when the few that survived the journey from the West Indies were offered to honored guests.

FOR THE DOUGH

3 whole eggs plus 1 yolk
¼ teaspoon salt

2½ cups flour

Beat the eggs, yolk, and salt well. Sift the flour, forming a mound, and make a well in the center. Add the eggs and mix with your fingers until the dough comes together. Knead until soft and pliable, adding flour, 1 tablespoon at a time, if dough feels sticky, or water, 1 teaspoon at a time, if dry and crumbly. Knead the dough until smooth and elastic, about 10 minutes, or use an electric mixer. (If you use a mixer, beat the eggs and salt together and alternately add small amounts of flour and water until the proper consistency is reached.) Cover with plastic wrap and let the dough rest while preparing stuffing.

½ cup golden raisins	¼ pound freshly grated Parmigiano
2 tablespoons dark rum	¼ cup fresh bread crumbs
2 eggs, beaten with a pinch of salt	½ teaspoon grated lemon zest
1½ teaspoons sugar	½ teaspoon grated orange zest
¾ pound Fontina cheese, shredded	

Soak the raisins in the rum. In a large bowl, beat together the eggs and sugar. Add the Fontina, parmigiano, and bread crumbs, mixing well. Add the remaining ingredients and combine well, using your hands. Cover and set aside.

Lidia's mother, Erminia, on her wedding day.

Divide the dough into three parts and roll out each part to form a rectangle about 1/16″ thick. If using a pasta machine, pass the dough through successively narrower openings, ending with the next-to-thinnest setting. (Keep the remaining dough covered while working each portion.) Set the rolled dough on a work surface with the long side facing you and spoon the filling onto the upper (farthest) half, by the tablespoonful, at 3″ intervals. Lightly moisten the dough with water along the edges and around the mounds of filling. Fold the unfilled bottom half of dough over the top, aligning the borders, and press around the mounds and along the edges to seal.

Using a 2¾″ round cookie cutter, stamp out the krafi. Press each filled portion lightly to fill the air pockets with stuffing, check the edges to be sure they are completely sealed, and set the krafi on a floured cloth. Repeat the procedure until the filling is used up.

Boil the krafi in a large pot of salted water until al dente but cooked through, 6–8 minutes. Drain and serve with veal or beef *sguazet* (recipe page 181) or toss well with ⅔ cup melted unsalted butter, sprinkle liberally with grated Parmigiano, and serve with freshly ground pepper and additional Parmigiano.

Recommended wine—The wines of Friuli are crisp, fruity, and vivacious. With krafi, I'd serve a Schioppettino by Ronchi di Cialla, one of the great Friulian producers.

Pasutice, Fuzi, Pappardelle

SERVES 6

*P*asutice and *fuzi* are unique to Istria and are always made fresh at home. As legend goes, a young man courting a woman would go to her house, and after having had *fuzi* for the Sunday dinner, would reach for the wooden board the dough had been rolled on. If he found traces of old dough on the board, that was the end of the courtship. As stated earlier in Jay's text, the Istrian pastas known as *pasutice* and *fuzi* represent two stages of a single process. *Fuzi*, served mostly with game and meat sauce, is simply *pasutice* (best with seafood sauces) carried one step further.

4 cups unbleached flour

2 eggs, beaten

½ teaspoon salt

1 teaspoon olive oil

½ cup warm water

On a marble or wooden surface, make a mound of 3½ cups of the flour, reserving ½ cup, and form a well at the mound's center. Place the eggs, salt, and olive oil in the well and, while beating with a fork to incorporate all ingredients, add the water slowly, in a thin stream.

Sprinkle your hands liberally with the reserved flour, rubbing them together to remove any scraps of dough from your skin. With a knife, loosen any dough attached to the work surface and knead the mass for 20 minutes, or use a mixer to process it, until smooth and satiny. Allow the dough to rest 2 hours in a covered bowl, refrigerated, before rolling it out.

Cut the rested dough into four parts and roll them out one at a time on a lightly floured surface until very thin, or feed the dough through the rollers of a pasta machine at successively narrower settings, stopping short of the narrowest opening. With a knife, cut the dough into 1½″ strips. Flour them lightly and lay them atop one another, forming three stacks, then cut the strips crosswise at a slight angle at 2″ intervals, forming lozenges. At this point you have *pasutice.*

To convert *pasutice* to *fuzi,* roll the pasta lozenges around the tip of the left index finger (assuming righthandedness) or the tip of a wooden dowel; pressing ends lightly as they meet and overlap, to form quill shapes. Line them up on a floured clean kitchen towel or a cornmeal-dusted baking sheet until they are to be cooked.

To make pappardelle use the same recipe and procedures as for *pasutice* and *fuzi.* When you have cut the dough into 1½″ strips and have formed the stacks, cut the stacks at 5″ intervals. At this point you will have ribbonlike pasta, pappardelle. Set them on a clean kitchen towel dusted with flour.

To cook *pasutice, fuzi,* or pappardelle, bring 6 quarts of water to the boil with 1 tablespoon of coarse salt. Drop in the pasta a handful at a time, stirring it as it drops in the boiling water. Mix well and cook until the water reaches a full boil and pasta rises to the top, approximately 3–5 minutes. Drain well and coat with the sauce of your choice.

Bigoli
Egg, Milk, and Butter Pasta

SERVES 4

Bigoli might be termed the spaghetti of Venice. Typical of most things Venetian, it's rich, lively, and resilient. As noted in the introduction to the recipe for *Piccione con Bigoli o Polenta* (page 216), it isn't taken lightly in its region of origin.

4½ cups unbleached flour plus 1 cup to work with

4 whole eggs

½ cup warm milk

1 tablespoon unsalted butter, melted in the milk

½ teaspoon salt

On a marble or wooden work surface, mound 4½ cups of the flour. Make a well in the center, add the remaining ingredients, and knead until the dough is smooth and silky, using remaining flour as needed to work with. Set dough aside to rest for 20 minutes. (If using an electric pasta machine, combine all ingredients and mix until the proper consistency is attained.)

Cut the dough into quarters and pass it through the smallest opening of a meat grinder. As the dough is extruded, cut it off at 8″ intervals. Sprinkle the strands of dough with flour, separate them, and lay them one by one on a floured baking sheet, taking care not to let them overlap. Continue until the dough is used up.

Boil the bigoli in salted water for 10–12 minutes, drain, and toss with 8 tablespoons of the sauce of your choice. Top with grated Parmigiano and serve.

RISOTTO

♦

ABOUT RISOTTO

Until the relatively recent popularity in this country of the cuisines of northern Italy, risotto seldom was listed on restaurant menus. Even today it isn't likely to be served in small, family-operated places without plenty of kitchen help, simply because its preparation requires more hands-on work than such establishments can afford to devote to a dish that must be cooked to order from a standing start: a consideration that doesn't apply to home cooks, who more conveniently can give sixteen to eighteen minutes of undivided attention to the preparation of a rewarding family meal.

The word translates literally as "rice," one of the great Italian triumvirate of starchy staples, ranking between pasta and polenta in general popularity and favored over both in some regions. In less literal usage, though, risotto is not only the generic grain itself, but Italian-grown short-grain rice cooked in a certain manner.

The distinctive characteristic of properly cooked risotto is the creaminess of its finish, an effect obtained without the use of actual cream, but by the gradual release of amylopectin, or soluble starch, of which some varieties of short-grain rice have a much higher content than the long-grain varieties and thereby can absorb far greater amounts of liquid. In effect, amylopectin is a starch that is released by each grain of rice and combines with the cook-ing liquids and fats. (For this reason, risotto, unlike long-grain rice, never is cooked in plain water, but always with gradual increments of broth or stock.)

When buying rice for risotto dishes, look for shiny kernels of uniform pearly color, with no blotchiness, and a smooth surface that doesn't feel floury to the touch. Carnaroli, Arborio, Padano, and Vialone Nano are the short-grain varietals best suited to your purposes, and none should be washed before cooking, as contact with water will initiate premature release of starches.

The best cooking vessel for risotto is a wide, heavy, nonreactive skillet that evenly disperses heat and allows evaporation to occur uniformly. The proper ratio of rice liquid is one to three-and-a-half parts, and the yield of cooked risotto will be double the bulk of the raw rice.

What produces the distinguishing texture of a well-made risotto (a slight resistance to the tooth beneath the characteristic creaminess) is the result of several procedures: first, the even, gradual release of the starch, which initially is controlled by toasting the unwashed rice in olive oil or butter, a process that simultaneously tempers each kernel's outer layer of starch and coats the grain with a liquid-resistant substance, thus inhibiting overly rapid absorption of the cooking liquid. Release of starch is further controlled by the gradual addition of boiling broth; boiling because the cooking temperature of the rice must be kept constant to prevent coagulation and loss of creaminess. Finally, the rice must be stirred constantly, to prevent the released starch from scorching and to amalgamate fat and starch.

It's imperative that risotto be served and eaten immediately. Otherwise, the rice will continue to absorb moisture, release too much starch, and become *pappa,* or soft and gummy—baby food.

Once the basic technique is understood, risotto can be flavored any way you wish; it's just a matter of orchestrating the cooking times of the rice and its accompaniments—seafood, meats, vegetables, mushrooms, truffles— everything's good with risotto.

Risotto all'Ammiraglia
Risotto Admiral's Style

SERVES 4

Seafood risotti of one sort or another are cooked in most regions of Italy. One of the best I've had was made with *vongole*— clams—at a place called Da Nico, in Grado, near Trieste. I tried to reproduce it when I returned to New York, but found that littleneck clams just didn't duplicate the flavor on their own. In combination with other seafoods, though, they make a marvelous risotto.

1 dozen littleneck clams

1 pound (about 20) shrimp

½ pound bay or sea scallops

½ cup minced onion

½ cup minced shallots

½ cup olive oil

1½ cups Arborio or Carnaroli rice

½ cup dry white wine (preferably Pinot Grigio)

5–6 cups boiling water, lightly salted

¼ teaspoon saffron threads

2 cloves garlic, crushed

2 tablespoons Cognac or other dry brandy

Salt to taste (see Note)

Freshly ground pepper to taste

2 tablespoons minced Italian parsley

Shuck and quarter the clams, reserving their liquor. Shell, devein, and cut the shrimp in thirds. If using sea scallops, slice them in half.

In a wide, heavy saucepan, sauté the onion and shallots in 3 tablespoons of the olive oil until lightly golden. Add the rice and stir to coat completely with oil. Toast the rice lightly, stirring constantly, 1–2 minutes. Add the wine and cook, stirring constantly, until it evaporates. Add 1 cup of the boiling water and simmer, stirring constantly. Add the saffron and gradually add more boiling water as previous additions are absorbed, always stirring.

When the rice is almost done (about 10 minutes), heat 3 tablespoons of the remaining oil in a deep skillet, add the garlic and sauté until lightly browned. Remove and discard the garlic, add the shellfish to the skillet, and sauté 2 minutes.

Stir in the reserved clam liquor and quickly add the contents of the skillet to the rice. Mix well, add the brandy, beat in the remaining oil, and cook 3–4 minutes longer, adding boiling water as needed.

Off the heat, season risotto to taste, stir in the parsley, and serve immediately.

Note: Use salt sparingly, allowing for the salinity of the clam liquor.

Recommended wine—Definitely Greco di Tufo by Mastroberardino. In Campania, "Mastro's" native region, Aglianico is the indigenous varietal, and he does wonders with the fruits of this volcanic terrain.

Risotto con Porcini

Creamy Rice with "Piglet" Mushrooms

SERVES 4

This is one of my daughter, Tanya's, favorite dishes and was one of mine when I was even younger than she is now. In those days, it was prepared when everyone in the family was at home at the same time, because risotto must be served the moment it's ready and can't be held for latecomers. Any meaty mushrooms may be substituted for porcini.

5 tablespoons olive oil

1 cup minced onion

2 tablespoons minced shallots

12 ounces fresh porcini mushrooms, sliced

2 cups Arborio rice

½ cup dry white wine

6½ cups hot chicken or veal stock (recipe page 69)

½ teaspoon salt

2 tablespoons butter, cut into bits

½ cup freshly grated Parmigiano

Freshly ground pepper to taste

In a medium casserole, heat the olive oil and sauté the onion and shallots until golden. Add the mushrooms and sauté until tender, about 5 minutes. Add the rice and stir to coat it with oil. Add the wine, stir well, and add ½ cup of the hot chicken stock and the salt. Cook, stirring constantly, until all the liquid has been absorbed. Continue to add hot stock in small batches (just enough to completely moisten the rice) and cook until each successive batch has been absorbed, stirring constantly, until the rice mixture is creamy and al dente.

Remove from the heat, beat in the butter and cheese, season with pepper to taste, and serve immediately.

Recommended wine—One of the nonvarietal Sangiovese wines would be my choice here. The first producer to blend these grapes was Antinori. Try his Tignanello or Solaia.

Risotto con Fiori di Zucca e Zucchine
Risotto with Squash Blossoms and Zucchini

SERVES 4

At home in Busoler, we had risotto very similar to this regularly during the summer. Years later, I was served a wonderful version at Antica Trattoria Boschetti in Tricesimo near Udine. This is the recipe, slightly adapted. Baby zucchini with their blossoms still attached can be found in farmers' markets and at roadside produce stands during the summer. They'll be that much better, of course, if you grow them yourself and pick them minutes before they're to be cooked. For this risotto, Arborio or Carnaroli rice is the best, and Pinot Grigio would be the ideal cooking wine. The chicken or veal stock (recipe page 69) should be very light. If what you have on hand is strongly concentrated, dilute it with water.

1 pound baby zucchini, blossoms attached

2 tablespoons olive oil

½ cup minced onion

1 tablespoon minced shallot

1½ cups Arborio or Carnaroli rice

½ cup dry white wine

¼ teaspoon salt, or to taste

4½–5 cups boiling chicken or veal stock

¼ teaspoon saffron threads

6 tablespoons unsalted butter, in 6 pieces

1 cup grated Parmigiano

Freshly ground pepper to taste

Separate and wash the zucchini and blossoms. Slice the zucchini in ¼" rounds and the blossoms crosswise into thirds.

In a wide, heavy skillet, heat the olive oil and sauté the onion and shallot until translucent. Add the zucchini and blossoms and sauté until wilted. Add the rice and toast it lightly, turning constantly, until well coated with oil. Add the wine and cook until it evaporates. Add salt, 1 cup of the boiling stock, and the saffron, and cook 18–20 minutes, stirring constantly and adding stock repeatedly as previous batches are absorbed. (The finished risotto should be creamy, not milky.)

Remove from the stove and stir in the butter, incorporating it thoroughly. Then stir in the cheese and freshly ground pepper, and serve immediately.

Recommended wine—With this dish, I'd pour an Arnais, and the one that comes to mind is produced by Bruno Giacosa, who also makes a to-die-for Barbaresco Santo Stefano.

Risotto Nero con Seppie
Black Risotto with Cuttlefish

Although it also turns up in a slightly different version in Tuscany, this is a signature dish of Venetian cookery.

1½ pounds cuttlefish	4¾ cups fish stock (recipe page 70)
3 tablespoons olive oil	1½ cups Arborio rice
1 medium onion, finely chopped	2 tablespoons unsalted butter
1 clove garlic, minced	1 teaspoon Cognac
Salt and freshly ground pepper	
1 cup dry white wine (preferably Pinot Grigio)	

Clean the cuttlefish by removing the blade-shaped interior "bone" (if you keep cage birds, save it for them), skin, and innards, reserving the ink sacs (two will be sufficient for the dish; any surplus can be frozen for other uses). With a mortar and pestle, work the contents of the ink sacs to a smooth consistency, discarding the sacs themselves. Cut the tentacles from the cuttlefish just below the eyes, squeeze any hard matter from the centers of the clusters and discard. Cut the body sacs lengthwise in ⅓" × 2½" strips, and quarter the tentacle clusters lengthwise. Wash all fleshy material and pat dry.

In a medium casserole or Dutch oven, heat the olive oil. Add the onion and sauté over moderate heat until glossy, about 2 minutes. Add the garlic and sauté until fragrant but not browned. Add the cuttlefish, season with salt and pepper, and simmer 5 minutes. (The cuttlefish will exude a good deal of liquid.) Add the wine and ¾ cup of the fish stock, and simmer until the cuttlefish is tender, about 1 hour, adding fish stock as needed, to keep the cuttlefish nearly covered.

Add the rice, first toasted as in recipe on p. 113, and stir well over moderately high heat until the rice absorbs the liquids. Stir in the cuttlefish ink and the butter. Add fish stock gradually in small batches as rice absorbs previous liquid additions, and simmer, stirring frequently, until the rice is tender and creamy but still al dente, 18–20 minutes. Add the Cognac during the last minute of cooking and serve at once.

GNOCCHI

◆

Gnocchi

Potato Dumplings

———

S E R V E S 6

I've made gnocchi ever since I can remember. In Istria, we kids loved to make them, because we could express ourselves by creating different shapes and textures. At home, we usually had gnocchi on Sunday, when there was time to make enough for a large family gathering. This is my recipe for basic gnocchi, which is compatible with a great many sauces. Serve with Sage Sauce (recipe follows), or with another of your choice.

Note: I've specified Idaho or russet potatoes because they're the only kinds suitable for the proper weight and texture of gnocchi, which should be as light and fluffy as possible. Please don't blame the recipe for the results obtained from any substitutes.

6 large Idaho or russet potatoes	*4 cups unbleached flour*
2 tablespoons plus 1 teaspoon salt	*Grated Parmigiano for serving*
Dash of freshly ground white pepper	
2 eggs, beaten	

Boil the potatoes in their skins about 40 minutes, until easily pierced with a skewer. When cool enough to handle, peel and rice the potatoes, and set them aside to cool *completely,* spreading them loosely to expose as much surface as possible to air. (The reason for this is to allow as much evaporation of moisture as possible to avoid the need of additional flour, therefore keeping the gnocchi light.)

Before proceeding further, bring 6 quarts water and 2 tablespoons of the salt to the boil.

On a cool, preferably marble work surface, gather the cold riced potatoes into a mound, forming a well in the center. Stir the remaining 1 teaspoon salt and the white pepper into the beaten eggs and pour the mixture into the well. Work the potatoes and eggs together with both hands, gradually adding 3 cups of the flour and scraping the dough up from the work surface with a knife as often as necessary. (Incorporation of the ingredients should take no longer than 10 minutes. The longer the dough is worked, the more flour it will require and the heavier it will become.)

Dust the dough, your hands, and the work surface lightly with flour and cut the dough into six equal parts. Continue to dust dough, hands, and surface as long as the dough feels sticky.

Using both hands, roll each piece of dough into a rope ½″ thick, then slice the ropes at ½″ intervals. Indent each dumpling with a thumb, or use the tines of a fork to produce a ribbed effect. (This facilitates adhesion of the sauce. As a child, I'd sometimes lightly press the dough against a cheese grater, to produce a different pattern.)

Drop the gnocchi into boiling water a few at a time, stirring gently and continuously with a wooden spoon, and cook 2–3 minutes, until they rise to the surface. Remove the gnocchi from the water with a slotted spoon or skimmer, transfer them to a warm platter, adding a little sauce of choice, and boil the remaining pieces in batches until all are done. Sauce as desired, add freshly ground white pepper to taste and, if appropriate, grated cheese, and serve immediately.

Salsa alla Salvia
Sage Sauce

SERVES 4

1 cup (½ pound) butter	½ cup grated Parmigiano
12 leaves fresh sage	Freshly ground pepper to taste
1 cup heavy cream	8 ounces dry ricotta, preferably smoked
Cooked gnocchi (see previous recipe)	

Cut the butter into pieces to facilitate melting. In a skillet, distribute the butter and sage, and stir over low heat until the butter has melted. Add the cream and cooked gnocchi, and cook over moderate heat, turning gently with a wooden spoon until the gnocchi are coated with sauce and heated through, about 1–2 minutes. Transfer the sauced gnocchi to serving plates, sprinkle with Parmigiano and pepper, top with shaved dry ricotta, and serve immediately. If dry ricotta is not available, do without—it's just as good.

Parenci
Spoon Gnocchi

SERVES 4 – 6

When time was short, my mother used to make these simple, rather rustic gnocchi in our cast-iron polenta kettle. Often, she'd flavor them with a little rendered pancetta and some stock, and sauté them for a quick lunch. They're not as refined as the lighter, fluffier potato gnocchi, but they're tasty and, for me, poignantly nostalgic.

1 envelope active dry yeast
¼ cup warm water
2 cups unbleached flour
½ pound freshly grated Parmigiano
½ teaspoon salt
½ teaspoon freshly ground white pepper
3 eggs, at room temperature

½ cup warm milk
1 tablespoon olive oil
2 tablespoons chopped Italian parsley
6 tablespoons unsalted butter
8 leaves fresh sage
Freshly ground pepper to taste
½ cup grated for serving (optional)

In a small bowl, dissolve the yeast in warm water, stirring with a fork if clumps form. ("Warm water," incidentally, is the operative term; hot water will abort the development of the yeast, a living organism.)

In a medium bowl, thoroughly blend the flour, ½ cup of the cheese, the salt and white pepper. In a large bowl, beat the eggs, then whisk in the milk. Add the yeast and the flour mixture to the egg mixture, along with the oil and parsley, and blend well by hand or with an electric mixer, about 5 minutes.

In a wide pot, bring salted water to a boil. Fill a large pastry bag, fitted with a ½" or ¾" round nozzle, with the dough mixture. Working over the pot and taking care not to splash yourself with hot water, pipe out the dough, snipping the gnocchi off with scissors at ½" intervals and letting them slip into the water.

(Alternatively and more traditionally, the pastry bag can be dispensed with and the dough shaped with two teaspoons. For true "spoon" gnocchi, dip both spoons into the boiling water and fill ¾ of one spoon with dough, working against the side of the bowl, to facilitate cutting off the excess. Using the second spoon, roll the dough into the water from the first.)

Cook the gnocchi 2–2½ minutes in batches of about twenty. With a slotted spoon or skimmer, transfer them to a large plate and keep them warm while cooking succeeding batches. In a large skillet, melt the butter and add the sage. Add the cooked gnocchi and reserved Parmigiano, tossing gently with a wooden spoon until the dumplings are well coated. If the sauce seems too dry, add a little of the cooking water and toss once more. Serve with freshly ground black pepper to taste and, if desired, grated cheese.

Note: These gnocchi also are excellent with Fresh Tomato Sauce (recipe page 123). If you choose to serve them this way, eliminate the sage, add 6 tablespoons tomato sauce to the butter, and bring to a simmer before adding and tossing the gnocchi.

Gnocchi di Zucca
Butternut Squash Gnocchi

SERVES 4

According to Jay, whose culinary heritage I don't share, the only civilized use for butternut squash is to fill the cavity with bourbon whiskey, add a lump of butter, oil the exterior, and roast the squash in the embers of a campfire, preferably on a riverbank. Little, if any, bourbon can be found in Friuli, but gnocchi made with butternut squash is a specialty of the region. This recipe is from Trattoria Da Toni.

1 butternut squash (about 1½ pounds)	*1¼ teaspoons salt*
2 eggs, beaten	*1½ cups flour*

Starting the night before, preheat the oven to 350°F. Halve the squash, wrap it loosely in foil, place on a baking sheet, and bake until tender when pierced, about 35 minutes.

Scoop out and discard the seeds. With a large spoon, scoop the pulp from the skin directly into a fine sieve. Set the sieve over a bowl to catch the liquids, cover, and allow the squash to drain overnight in the refrigerator.

Next day, puree the squash in a food processor, transfer the puree to a large bowl, and add the eggs and salt. Mix well, add the flour, and blend thoroughly. The dough should be soft and quite sticky.

Bring a large pot of water to the boil. Using a teaspoon, scoop up some of the dough (about a walnut-size piece) and use a finger to slide it into the water. Cook the gnocchi in batches of ten to fifteen, poaching them for 2 minutes after they rise to the surface. Remove them with a slotted spoon. Set them aside to drain, and repeat the process until the remaining dough is used up.

Serving suggestions—These gnocchi lend themselves to various sauces, including Fresh Tomato Sauce (recipe page 123), Sage Sauce (recipe page 118), or a simple dressing of melted butter and grated cheese.

Recommended wine—A good Tocai from Friuli.

Gnocchi di Susine

Plum Gnocchi

YIELDS 16 PIECES

This is a Trieste-Istrian specialty of Austro-Hungarian derivation, and a particular favorite of my brother Franco's. When our plums were fully ripened, we had these gnocchi as a main dish—not as dessert. If any were left over, we'd eat them at room temperature the next day.

Preferably, these dumplings should be made with Italian-type prune plums, which make a tidier, more symmetrical little package, but half their number of round red or purple plums (easier to find in this country) may be substituted. In either case, the fruits should be fully ripened but still firm.

---

16 Italian-type prune plums or 8 round red or purple plums

⅓ cup sugar

½ recipe potato gnocchi dough (page 117), made without pepper

6 tablespoons unsalted butter

1¾ cups unseasoned bread crumbs

2 teaspoons cinnamon

If using Italian-type plums, halve them lengthwise, remove the pits, fill each cavity with ½ teaspoon of the sugar, and re-form the plums by pressing the halves together.

If using larger round plums, halve them crosswise, separate the halves, neatly remove the pits with a small melon baller, and fill the cavities with sugar as above. Do not press halves together.

Hand-roll the dough to form a cylinder 2″ in diameter, and slice it evenly into 16 rounds. Flatten each round in the palm of one hand, place a plum (or half plum) in the center of each, and carefully gather the dough up around the fruit, enclosing it completely with no breaks or tears in the dough. Pat the covered plums between your hands to seal and even the dough.

To a wide pot of boiling water, add the gnocchi 8 at a time, stirring gently to prevent sticking, and cook 5 minutes after they surface. Remove the gnocchi with a slotted spoon, set them aside, and keep them warm while proceeding with the second batch.

Meanwhile, melt the butter in a heavy skillet. Add the bread crumbs and toast over medium heat, stirring almost constantly, until golden brown, about 7 minutes. Add the remaining sugar and the cinnamon, and blend thoroughly.

Roll the cooked and drained gnocchi in the bread crumb mixture until all are well coated. Arrange on a serving plate and sprinkle with any bread crumbs remaining in the skillet.

Gnocchi di Melanzane
Eggplant Gnocchi

SERVES 4–6

Gnocchi are very accommodating little dumplings that can be varied by adding cheese, vegetables, herbs, and even fruit to the basic dough. At home, we'd often make gnocchi with peas, basil, or parsley—or this way when eggplant was in season.

2 pounds firm eggplant	1¼ teaspoons salt
Coarse salt	¼ teaspoon freshly ground pepper
Olive oil	12 leaves basil, minced
1 pound Idaho potatoes	2 cups flour
⅓ cup freshly grated Parmigiano	Fresh Tomato Sauce (recipe follows)
2 eggs, beaten	Grated Parmigiano to taste

Halve the eggplant lengthwise, sprinkle the cut sides generously with coarse salt, and set aside for 30 minutes. Preheat the oven to 375°F. Rinse the eggplant well, pat dry, and brush the exposed pulp with olive oil. Place the eggplant cut sides down on a baking sheet, and bake until very tender, about 40 minutes (or less if using smaller eggplants of equivalent aggregate weight). When cool enough to handle, scoop the flesh from the eggplant, and puree in a processor until smooth. Allow to cool completely.

While the eggplant bakes, boil the potatoes in water to cover until tender, 25–30 minutes. When cool enough to handle, peel the potatoes and rice them into a large bowl. Cool completely.

Add the eggplant puree and cheese to the potatoes and mix well. Add the eggs, salt, pepper, and basil, and mix to blend. Add the flour and mix to incorporate the ingredients thoroughly but not densely.

In a large pot, bring 6–8 quarts salted water to the boil. Meanwhile, fill a pastry bag with eggplant-potato mixture. When the water boils, squeeze the mixture out, holding the pastry bag over the pot, and, with scissors, cut the dough into ½″ pieces as it is extruded, allowing the gnocchi to drop into the water. Continue rapidly until the dough is used up, stirring the pot occasionally. With a slotted spoon, remove the gnocchi from the water as they rise to the surface, drain, butter lightly, and keep them warm.

In a sauté pan heat 5–6 tablespoons Fresh Tomato Sauce (see below) and mix in grated Parmigiano to taste. Arrange the gnocchi in a serving bowl, sprinkle with additional grated cheese, and top with sauce.

Salsa di Pomodoro
Fresh Tomato Sauce

YIELDS ABOUT 2 ½ CUPS

During my early girlhood, the tomato sauce we made was for immediate consumption at the height of the season. For winter use, we made tomato paste, but preferred our sauce fresh and did without when the season was over. Because this is a quick sauce, its flavor won't be affected by the inclusion of tomato seeds, which impart some bitterness to slowly cooked sauces. If you prefer to eliminate the seeds for aesthetic reasons, lightly squeeze the tomatoes over a sieve, set over a bowl to catch the juice, after peeling them. Reserve juice. If you like your sauce very smooth (I don't), puree the tomatoes in a food processor.

2½ pounds ripe plum tomatoes	Salt to taste
1 cup minced onion	Freshly ground pepper to taste
3 tablespoons olive oil	8 fresh basil leaves, minced

With the point of a paring knife cut out and discard the stem bases of the tomatoes, removing small cones about ¼″ deep, then lightly cut X-shapes on the tomatoes' opposite ends.

Bring water to boil in a large saucepan, drop in the tomatoes, and cook 5 minutes. With a slotted spoon, transfer the tomatoes to a colander, run cold water over them, and slip their skins off with your fingers.

In a nonreactive saucepan, lightly sauté the onion in the olive oil. Add the tomatoes, crushing each directly over the pan as it is added. Add the reserved juice if the tomatoes have been seeded. Season to taste and simmer 20 minutes, stirring occasionally. Add the basil before serving.

Recommended wine—A Cabernet or Merlot from Friuli.

Gnocchi di Ricotta

Ricotta Dumplings

YIELDS 1 ⅔ POUNDS

I often serve these light dumplings with Contessa Sauce (recipe follows), which blends the complementary flavors of ham and cheese, while the pine nuts add textural contrast.

1 pound ricotta cheese

2 cups flour, plus more as needed

2 eggs, beaten

1¾ teaspoons salt

½ teaspoon pepper

¼ teaspoon ground nutmeg

1 teaspoon chopped Italian parsley

Drain the ricotta overnight in a sieve.

Make a well in the 2 cups flour and add the ricotta, eggs, salt, spices, and parsley. Gradually incorporate the elements until a soft dough forms, adding more flour if the mixture is sticky.

Cut the dough into 6 pieces, roll each into a rope ½″ thick, and cut the ropes at ½″ intervals. Roll each piece over the floured tines of a dinner fork, identing the gnocchi slightly with your thumb as you do so. Cook in 4 quarts lightly salted boiling water until the gnocchi rise to the surface, about 7 minutes. Drain and keep them warm.

Contessa Sauce

1 stick (¼ pound) unsalted butter

4 thin slices prosciutto, cut into julienne strips

10 fresh basil leaves, quartered

¼ cup pine nuts (pignoli)

1½ cups heavy cream

½ cup chicken stock (recipe page 69)

½ cup freshly grated Parmigiano

In a large nonreactive skillet, melt the butter. Add the prosciutto, basil, and pine nuts, and brown lightly. Add the cream and chicken stock, increase the heat, and boil until thickened, about 8 minutes.

Add the drained gnocchi to the sauce over moderate heart. Slowly stir in the grated cheese and simmer, stirring and shaking the pan, until the sauce is creamy and coats the gnocchi. Serve at once.

Roulade di Ricotta e Spinaci
Ricotta and Spinach Roll

SERVES 8–10

I don't remember the name or exact location of the place, but it was a small family trattoria somewhere between Trieste and Venice, and we were served this dish in a courtyard. It was interesting to find potato dough used this way, and I realized that this would be a great substitute for more time-consuming gnocchi when large groups were invited for meals. Before starting the dish, note that the ricotta for the filling must be drained overnight.

FOR THE DOUGH

1½ pounds Idaho potatoes	*¼ cup freshly grated Parmigiano*
2 egg yolks	*¼ teaspoon salt*
¼ teaspoon freshly grated nutmeg	*1½ cups flour*

Boil the potatoes in their jackets until tender, about 30–40 minutes; peel, rice, and spread over a generous area to cool thoroughly. When completely cooled, scrape the potato together to form a mound, make a well in its center, and add the egg yolks, nutmeg, cheese, salt, and 1 cup of the flour. Blend the ingredients to form a dough, adding flour as needed to reduce the stickiness, but taking care not to overwork the mixture, thus keeping it light.

FOR THE FILLING

1 lb. fresh spinach or ½ cup frozen	*1 lb. ricotta cheese (see Note)*
4 tablespoons softened unsalted butter	*Salt and freshly ground pepper*
1 clove garlic, finely minced	

Clean and steam the spinach, squeeze to express as much liquid as possible, and mince fine. In a skillet, melt the butter and sauté the garlic until fragrant. Add the spinach and drained ricotta, stir until well blended, and season to taste.

Note: In a cheesecloth-lined sieve, drain the ricotta overnight.

On a floured work surface, roll the dough to form a 12″ × 15″ rectangle and evenly spread the entire surface with filling.

Starting from one of the rectangle's longer sides, tightly roll the filling-spread dough as you would a jelly roll. Wrap the roulade tight in a triple thickness of cheesecloth, tie the ends with string, and lower into boiling salted water to cover generously. Reduce the heat and simmer 30 minutes. Remove the roulade from the water, drain, and allow to stand about 15 minutes. Meanwhile, make the sauce.

Unwrap roulade, cut into ½″ slices, top with sauce, and serve with additional grated Parmigiano for those who wish it.

FOR THE SAUCE

1 cup butter	*1 cup grated Parmigiano*
10 leaves fresh sage	

Melt the butter over moderate heat until creamy but not oily, taking care not to clarify it. Add the sage and simmer 1 minute. Spoon over the slices of roulade and sprinkle with cheese.

Recommended wine—A good Chardonnay. Chardonnays now are produced extensively in Italy and include superb wines by Maurizio Zanella of Ca' del Bosco, in Lombardia, and Angelo Gaja in Piemonte.

POLENTA

◆

ABOUT POLENTA

Pasta, risotto, polenta, and, of course, bread are the essential grain-based foods of Italian cookery, which is more dependent on cereal grains than any other Western European cuisine. Of these four categories of foods, polenta is the oldest, going back in one form or another to the rudimentary grain pastes of prehistory, to a time millennia before the discovery of bread or pasta, or the introduction of rice into Europe, and continuing down through the *pulmentum,* or *puls,* on which the Roman legions subsisted, to the corn- (maize-) based dishes enjoyed in many parts of Italy today, particularly in the northeast and along the western Istrian coast (technically now part of Bosnia).

Although, outside Italy, it's the least familiar of the starchy Italian staples, polenta plays a major role in Italian gastronomy, just as it does under other names, such as grits and spoon bread, in the American South. Until the discovery of the New World and the cultivation of Indian corn in Europe, polenta more closely resembled farina than the more flavorful and versatile food that goes by that name today, and the term more accurately reflected a cooking technique for grains in general than a specific foodstuff.

Polenta can be of varied consistency, from hard to loose to soft. As a rule, in northern mountain regions, where polenta is served with game and meat dishes, it is dense and hearty; if we move toward the coast, where seafood is dominant, polenta takes on a looser consistency.

You can be very free with the flavoring of polenta: milk might be substituted for up to ½ the required quantity of water; butter or oil can be added, and herbs, such as bay leaves, garlic, and rosemary, also may be added, then removed before serving.

Grated, shredded, or cubed cheese can be added during the last 10 minutes of cooking, grilled sausages, and parboiled vegetables, such as peas, broc-

Luigi Tuzzi grinds polenta in a century-old mill in Gorizia.

coli, zucchini, or any other combination of ingredients can be added to cooked polenta.

Polenta almost never is eaten straight out of the pot, but is allowed to rest for a few minutes. Traditionally, it's poured onto a wooden board *(tagliere)* and cut with a taut string when it has begun to set, but while the interior is still warm. Polenta also can be served with a spoon dipped in water, or it can be chilled overnight, then sliced and grilled or fried and served as a main course garnish or accompaniment, a base for various toppings and sauces, or a breakfast food to be dipped in milk. It will keep for three days, covered, in the refrigerator, and is even eaten as dessert in Istria, with a sprinkling of sugar and cinnamon.

As a general rule, the proportion of grain to water is one to two, allowing for absorption and evaporation of the water. A successful batch of polenta requires about forty minutes of close attention, which may account for its scarcity on Italian menus in the United States. The cooking time can be reduced appreciably by using "instant" (partially precooked) polenta, which yields an acceptable result but lacks the roughness and resistant texture I prefer. When you shop for the makings of polenta, I'd recommend a medium- or coarse-grind meal, but a trip to an ethnic grocery for coarser unlabeled meal is worth the time it takes. Polenta, incidentally, can be made from white or yellow meal. Istrians prefer yellow, which makes a more attractive presentation on the plate.

Although more flavorful than pasta or rice, polenta is neutral enough to serve as a vehicle for a wide variety of sauced foods.

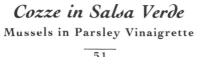

Cozze in Salsa Verde
Mussels in Parsley Vinaigrette

51

Clockwise from Top:

Insalata di Asparagi

Asparagus Salad

84

Calamari Fritti

Fried Squid

158

Insalata di Fagiolini e Patate

String Bean and Potato Salad

83

Insalata di Gamberetti e Fagioli Misti

Shrimp and Mixed Bean Salad

52

Top to Bottom:

Scarola Affogata

Smothered Escarole

85

Finocchio alla Griglia

Broiled Fennel

91

Radicchio Trevisano al Tegame

Braised Treviso Radicchio

92

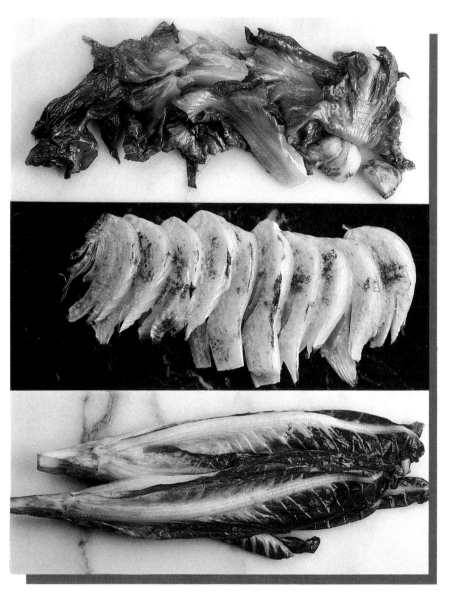

Basic Polenta

SERVES 4

4 cups water (½ milk, ½ water could be used for a richer taste)
1 tablespoon unsalted butter

1 bay leaf
2 tablespoons coarse salt
1½ cups coarse yellow cornmeal

In a medium cast-iron saucepan or other heavy pot, bring all ingredients except the cornmeal to simmer over medium heat.

Very slowly, begin to sift the cornmeal into the pan through the fingers of one hand, stirring constantly with a wooden spoon or whisk. (This operation will be greatly facilitated if the meal is scooped by the handful from a wide bowl.)

Gradually sift all the meal into the pan, continue to stir, and reduce the heat to medium low. Continue to stir constantly until the polenta is smooth and thick and pulls away from the sides of the pan as it is stirred, about 30 minutes.

Discard the bay leaf, pour the polenta into a serving bowl or onto a wooden board, and allow it to rest 10 minutes. To serve from the bowl, dip a large spoon into hot water and scoop the polenta onto individual dishes, dipping the spoon into the water between scoops. To serve from the board, cut the polenta into segments with a thin, taut string or a knife and transfer to plates with a spatula or cake server.

Fried Polenta

Spread the desired amount of hot cooked polenta in a lightly greased pan, in a layer about ¼" thick, and smooth with a rubber spatula dipped in cold water. Refrigerate the polenta until firmly set, then turn it out of the pan and cut it into squares, rectangles, triangles, etc.

In a large skillet, over low heat, melt enough unsalted butter to lightly grease the surface of the pan. Arrange the polenta pieces in the skillet, leaving space between them, increase the heat to medium, and fry about 10 minutes, turning the polenta once, until lightly browned on both sides.

Grilled Polenta

Lightly brush the polenta slices with olive oil and set them on a hot grill. Grill 4–5 minutes on each side.

Polenta con Fonduta di Funghi Porcini e Tartufi

Polenta with Fontina Cheese, Porcini Mushrooms, and Truffles

SERVES 6

This dish derives from a Piedmontese specialty. The three principal elements make, I think, an excellent dish, but the addition of fresh white truffle shavings makes it a glorious dish. Fresh truffles from Alba are available in fancy food shops in this country from early October through December. Their cost is inhibiting, but so is the cost of an extraordinary wine, and there are occasions that call for a grand splurge. If you decide to make the investment, bury the truffle in rice in a sealed jar and refrigerate for up to ten days. This will not only slow deterioration of the truffle, but will imbue the rice with its distinctive flavor and aroma, for a future risotto.

½ pound Fontina cheese
1 cup milk
2 tablespoons unsalted butter, softened
2 egg yolks
1 walnut-size white truffle (optional)
Salt and freshly ground pepper

Fried polenta (see Note)
½ cup olive oil
4 cloves garlic, crushed
20 ounces porcini mushrooms (see Note)
¼ cup chopped Italian parsley

Cut the Fontina into ½″ cubes and soak in the milk for 1 hour. Transfer the milk and cheese to a double boiler and cook over medium-low heat, stirring, until the cheese melts and blends smoothly with the milk. Add the softened butter and, off the heat, the egg yolks, one at a time, stirring until all ingredients are well incorporated. If the optional truffle is to be included, shave any irregular protrusions into the cheese mixture and blend. Season with salt and pepper to taste. Keep the mixture warm.

Preheat the broiler. Place the fried polenta in a single layer in a large gratin dish. Top the polenta with cheese *fonduta,* and set it under the broiler until *fonduta* is golden. Meantime, in a large nonreactive pan, heat the olive oil, add the garlic and mushrooms, and sauté until browned on all sides. Transfer the mushrooms to paper towels and pat dry, discarding the garlic. Sprinkle mushrooms with parsley and serve with the *fonduta*-topped polenta. If you've opted for the truffle, shave it over the *fonduta* at the table, where the release of its aroma can be appreciated.

Note: Start with the basic polenta recipe on page 129 and continue with the fried polenta recipe on page 129. If the truffle is included, it should be cleaned with a soft brush. The porcini should be scraped free of dirt with a knife, then brushed under cold running water, toweled dry, and cut in ½″ slices. Shiitake and/or other varieties of mushrooms can be substituted, although there will be some compromise of authenticity.

Lumache con Polenta
Snails with Polenta

SERVES 4

I'm particularly partial to this hearty dish, a specialty of Pazin, because it demonstrates the versatility of both its salient ingredients, snails and polenta.

1 recipe basic polenta (page 129), kept warm

2 slices bacon, coarsely chopped

½ rib celery, coarsely chopped

2 cloves garlic

3 tablespoons olive oil

1 medium onion, chopped

1½ pounds cooked snail meats (recipe page 53)

2 bay leaves

2 teaspoons tomato paste

½ cup dry white wine (preferably Tocai)

1 cup crushed tomatoes

1 cup chicken stock (recipe page 69)

Salt and freshly ground pepper

2 tablespoons chopped Italian parsley

In a food processor, combine the bacon, celery, and garlic, and process until a smooth paste forms. In a medium casserole, heat the olive oil, add the onion, and sauté until golden, about 3 minutes. Stir in the snails, bacon mixture, and bay leaves, and cook 5 minutes over moderate heat. Stir in the tomato paste and wine, bring to a simmer, and cook 5 minutes. Add the tomatoes and half the chicken stock, and season to taste. Add the remaining chicken stock as needed for desired consistency. Simmer 30 minutes.

Remove the bay leaves, stir in the parsley, and adjust seasonings. Serve the snails and sauce over the polenta.

4

Pesce

Fish

Brodetto di Frutti di Mare in Bianco

Red Snapper alla Griglia

Fillet of Red Snapper with Fresh Thyme

Tocio di Seppia e Razza con Polenta

Merlano in Bianco

Medaglioni di Rospo in Savor

Molecche al Timo Fresco

Sgombro alla Griglia

Sarde Ripiene

Trota Arrosto alla Salvia

Gamberoni alla Griglia

Gamberoni alla Buzara

Aragosta in Brodetto

Brodetto all'Istriana

Baccalà con Patate al Forno

Salmone alla Senape

Pesce Spada in Agrodolce

Calamari Fritti

Calamari al Forno

Brodetto di Frutti di Mare in Bianco
Shellfish Stew with White Wine

———

SERVES 4 – 6

Except for a narrow corridor in northwestern Valle d'Aosta, no part of Italy lies farther than a hundred miles from salt water, and over most of the peninsula's length even the innermost cities and towns are little more than half that distance from the sea. But in times past, in a prerefrigeration age of slow horse-drawn transport, "inland" regions, relatively close as they were to the coasts, had no great seafood tradition, and it was mostly the fishing ports that were celebrated for their local variations on the shellfish stew theme. Today, with easy access throughout Italy to fresh marine foods, many of the coastal specialties have migrated inland and are enjoyed everywhere. All of Istria, on the other hand (only some thirty miles across at its widest point, which is to say, no more than fifteen miles from the Adriatic at any point), has cooked and eaten its own shellfish stews since ancient times. This is one of them.

3 tablespoons olive oil	1 cup dry white wine
1 small onion, finely chopped	1 teaspoon fresh lemon juice
5 small shallots, finely chopped	2 dozen littleneck clams, scrubbed
3 cloves garlic, crushed	3 dozen mussels, washed and debearded
1 pound sea scallops	1/4 cup chopped Italian parsley
1 pound medium shrimp, shelled and deveined	1/4 cup bread crumbs
	Salt and freshly ground pepper to taste

In a large casserole, heat the olive oil. Add the onion, shallots, and garlic, and cook over moderate heat until golden, about 3–5 minutes. Add the scallops and shrimp, and cook until almost opaque, about 2 minutes. Remove the scallops and shrimp and set aside.

Increase the heat to high, add the wine and lemon juice, and bring to the boil. Add the clams and mussels, cover, and steam until the shells open, about 5 minutes. (Discard any that do not open.)

Push the shellfish to the sides of the casserole, clearing the center, to which add 3 tablespoons of the parsley and the bread crumbs. Stir to blend the parsley and crumbs into the pan sauce. Return to the boil, add the scallops and shrimp, season to taste, and toss all elements briefly, heating them through.

Arrange the shellfish on a serving dish, spoon the sauce over them, and sprinkle with the remaining parsley.

Red Snapper alla Griglia
Grilled Red Snapper

SERVES 4

Grilled fish is very popular on the Istrian seacoast, where every family has a set of iron *gradele* made by the local *fabbro ferraio*. The grills are set on bricks, and the cooking is done over the hot embers of grapevine cuttings, which impart sweetness to the fish. During my childhood, when nothing was wasted, the feathers were collected whenever a goose or duck was killed and all but one were tied together and used as small hand brooms or dusters. The exception was used to brush the fish with olive oil.

FOR THE SAUCE

½ cup olive oil
5 cloves garlic, sliced
¼ teaspoon salt

½ teaspoon freshly ground pepper
3 tablespoons minced Italian parsley
3 tablespoons fresh lemon juice

In a small bowl, blend all the ingredients except the parsley and lemon juice, and allow the sauce to steep while the fish cooks.

FOR THE FISH

4 cloves garlic, crushed
¼ cup olive oil
¼ teaspoon salt
Freshly ground pepper to taste

4 whole red snappers, about 1¼ pounds each, eviscerated and scaled
Lemon wedges for garnish

In a small bowl, combine the garlic, olive oil, salt and pepper. Ignite charcoal or other appropriate grilling fuel, or pre-heat oven to 475° F.

Brush fish on both sides with the olive oil mixture and enclose the tails in aluminum foil. When the embers are uniformly gray, place the fish on a lightly oiled grill and brush them once more with the oil mixture. Grill the fish 25–35 minutes, turning them twice with a spatula and brushing with the remaining oil. Since fish is so sensitive and might break in turning, I strongly recommend the wire-mesh grill. (When using a wire-mesh grill, heat it over the embers, insert the fish, close the grill, and proceed as above. If using an oven, set the fish in an oiled roasting pan and bake at 475° F. 30 minutes, drizzling occasionally with the oil mixture.)

If the grilled fish lack color, set them under the broiler for a minute or two, until browned and crisp. When the fish are ready for serving, discard the garlic from the sauce, add the lemon juice and parsley, and whisk the sauce lightly with a fork. Serve the fish with lemon wedges, and spoon 1 tablespoon of sauce over each, taking the remainder to the table for discretionary use.

Recommended wine—Malvasia is one of very few Istrian wines presently to be found in this country, although I understand others will be imported in the not-too-distant future. With this dish, try a bottle of Cuvena Istarska Malvazija, produced by Pic in Umag and imported under the Moiré label.

Sardine fisherman, Trieste.

Fillet of Red Snapper with Fresh Thyme

SERVES 4

There's no point in straining for an Italian rendering of the name of this dish; my first language has no word for red snapper, which doesn't swim in Italian waters, and everybody knows that fillet and *filetto* denote a boned piece of fish. This dish is an excellent example of an old culinary truism: One simple primary flavor paired with one distinctive complementary ingredient makes a good dish. In this recipe, the intensity of the thyme and simplicity of the red snapper are all you should be conscious of, with the remaining ingredients playing subsidiary roles. I don't like too many herbs and spices in a dish. They create confusion.

Salt to taste

Flour for dredging

2 pounds (4 pieces) red snapper fillets

4 tablespoons vegetable oil

4 cloves garlic, crushed

½ cup white wine

6 tablespoons unsalted butter

2 tablespoons olive oil

3 tablespoons fresh lemon juice

1 tablespoon fresh thyme leaves

1 cup fish stock (recipe page 70)

Freshly ground pepper to taste

Salt and lightly flour the snapper fillets, shaking off excess flour. In a large non-reactive skillet, heat the vegetable oil over moderately high heat. Add the garlic. In two batches, lightly brown the fish fillets on both sides, about 1 minute for each side, remove and pat dry with paper towels, and reserve.

Clean any excess oil and any burned particles from the skillet, add all the remaining ingredients except the reserved fillets, bring to a boil, and cook until thickened, about 7 minutes.

Return the fillets to the sauce and cook just long enough to allow the sauce to flavor the fish, about 1–2 minutes. Remove the garlic and serve fish immediately.

Recommended wine—Luna dei Feldi by Santa Margherita, or a good Pinot Grigio.

Tocio di Seppia e Razza con Polenta
Cuttlefish and Skate Sauce with Polenta

SERVES 4 – 6

Physically, cuttlefish (of the family Sepiidae) and squid (family Loligindae) are similarly constructed members of the order Decapoda, which also includes the nautiluses and octopuses. They're also similar from a culinary and gastronomic standpoint, and one often is substituted for the other. Squid can be used for this recipe if cuttlefish are unavailable, but I prefer the subtle difference that *seppia* imparts to the dish.

¼ cup olive oil

1 large onion, chopped

2 pounds cuttlefish or squid, cleaned (see page 158) and cut in ½" rings

Salt

½ teaspoon freshly ground pepper

1 tablespoon tomato paste

½ cup dry white wine

½ cup hot water

2 lbs. skinless skate wings (see Note)

Flour for dredging

½ cup vegetable oil

1 recipe basic polenta (page 129)

In a large nonreactive casserole, heat the olive oil. Add the onion and cook over moderate heat until glossy, about 2 minutes. Add the cuttlefish, ½ teaspoon salt, and the pepper, increase the heat to moderately high, and cook, stirring occasionally, until some of the liquid from the cuttlefish has evaporated, about 5 minutes.

Successively stir in the tomato paste and wine, and simmer 5 minutes. Add the hot water, reduce the heat to low, and simmer gently until the cuttlefish is tender, 45 minutes to 1 hour, adding more hot water if the liquid thickens substantially.

Meanwhile, dredge the skate strips in flour, shaking off the excess. In a skillet, heat the vegetable oil. Add the skate in batches and fry on both sides until golden, turning once. Transfer to paper towels to drain, salt to taste (lightly), add to the casserole, and cook about 5 minutes. Adjust seasonings and serve as soon as the sauce reduces to a gravylike consistency.

Serve with polenta flanking the fish and with sauce spooned over the dish.

Note: Free the skinned skate flesh from the cartilaginous ribs with a sharp flexible fish knife. Beginning at the top of the wing (away from the edges), cut down through the flesh until you reach the cartilage. Using the ribs of the cartilage as your guide, cut down toward the tip of the wing at a 45° angle to release the meat. Turn the wing over and repeat the process on the other side. Cut the flesh into 1" × 3" strips, following the grain. Alternatively (my preference), the cartilage need not be extracted. I think it imparts more flavor and texture to the dish.

Merlano in Bianco
Cold Poached Whiting

SERVES 4

Although we ate more whiting than almost any other fish during my childhood, it was always a special treat, particularly during the summer. Because of its delicacy and digestibility, it was always fed to women recovering from childbirth, which may be one reason why small girls relished it so. What I find particularly appealing about *merlano in bianco* is its simplicity: Nothing in either the cooking process or the uncooked sauce obscures the taste of the prime ingredient. The amounts given here are for a main course, but can be halved for an appetizer course.

8 whiting, 3½–4 pounds total	*4 bay leaves*
6 cups cold water	*3 tablespoons white vinegar*
1 cup coarsely sliced carrots	*1 teaspoon salt*
½ small onion, sliced	*8 peppercorns*

Clean the whiting, remove the heads, and wrap the fish in cheesecloth.

In a deep 12″ skillet, bring all ingredients except the whiting to a boil. After 15 minutes, remove the solids from the broth, reserving the vegetables for other uses, if desired.

Gently lower the whiting into the boiling broth and cook 3 minutes. With a lid that fits inside the skillet, hold the whiting lightly in place while draining off the broth, which should be reserved for other uses. Allow the fish to cool in the skillet. Unwrap the cooled fish and, with a large spatula, transfer them to serving plates. (Whiting are fragile and must be handled with care.) With a sharp knife, remove the skin, tails, and dorsal ridges from the fish. Carefully open the fish, belly to back, and remove the bones. Serve at, or slightly below, room temperature, with sauce.

¾ cup olive oil

1 tablespoon Bermuda onion, chopped fine

1 tablespoon roasted red bell pepper, chopped fine

1 tablespoon fennel leaves, chopped fine

2 tablespoons fresh lemon juice

¼ teaspoon salt

Fresh pepper, 5 turns of the mill

In a bowl, whisk all ingredients together and spoon over the fish.

Recommended wine—The delicacy of whiting calls for a Torre di Giano by Lungarotti or a nice Orvieto Classico.

Medaglioni di Rospo in Savor
Fried and Marinated Monkfish Medallions

SERVES 4

The term *in savor* has no satisfactory English equivalent. Its literal translation, "in flavor," just doesn't work. The preparation of fish *in savor* was devised centuries ago by Venetian sailors as a means of inhibiting spoilage at sea. For this recipe, I've chosen monkfish, but any type of fish lends itself to the same treatment. In Venice, for example, fishermen favor *sardelle* (sardines) *in saòr,* and on Venice's special holiday, the Feast of the Redeemer, everyone eats *sfogi in saòr*—fillets of sole. At home in Istria, if we found sardines in the market, we'd eat them fried the first day, and whatever wasn't eaten immediately became *sardelle in savor,* which would keep up to four days without refrigeration when packed in a covered crock. Another of my favorites is *sgombro* (mackerel) *in savor,* a very popular antipasto at Felidia.

This is an excellent, remarkably refreshing summer dish but can be eaten at any time. I often serve it with a chicory and white bean salad. The bitter chicory offsets the sweetness of the onion and the beans absorb some of the acidity of the marinade. If served as a first course, portions should be halved.

1½ pounds monkfish (or other) fillets	*1 sprig fresh rosemary or*
Salt and freshly ground pepper to taste	*1 teaspoon dried*
Flour for dredging	*4 bay leaves*
1½ cups vegetable oil	*1 teaspoon white wine vinegar*
1 large onion, thinly sliced	*½ cup dry white wine*
¼ cup olive oil	*½ cup chicken stock (page 69)*

Remove the membranes and any dark red portions from the fillets. Slice the fish in ½"-thick medallions. Salt and pepper, then dredge the medallions in flour. Shake off the excess flour. In a large nonreactive skillet, heat the vegetable oil and fry the fish in batches, turning once, until lightly browned and cooked through, about 4 minutes. Drain on paper towels.

In a second skillet, sauté the onion in the olive oil until pale golden but not browned, adding the rosemary, bay leaves, and salt and pepper as the onion cooks, about 12 minutes over moderate heat. Add the vinegar, wine, and stock, and simmer 10 minutes. Remove bay leaves and rosemary.

In a deep serving dish, arrange the medallions in two layers, distributing half the onion mixture over each layer. Allow the fish to marinate at least 2 hours and serve warm or at room temperature.

Recommended wine—Il Marzotto, a Chardonnay by Avignonesi.

Molecche al Timo Fresco
Soft-shell Crabs with Fresh Thyme

SERVES 4

This dish is a specialty of Venice and its environs. Because Adriatic crabs are much smaller than the Eastern Seaboard blue claws we serve at the restaurant, this recipe calls for small-to-medium crabs (specify "prime" at your fishmonger's). Properly sautéed soft-shell crabs provide a delightful contrast of textures—the interplay of crisped shell and pulpy meat. Dipping them in milk before dredging them in flour heightens their crispness. I prefer to serve crabs belly up. To me, the golden color of their undersides is more tempting than their darker backs. Besides, their legs fold more neatly when they're inverted.

FOR THE SAUCE

3 cloves garlic, crushed

8 tablespoons butter

1 tablespoon fresh lemon juice

½ cup white wine

½ cup fish stock (page 70)

⅛ teaspoon salt

1 tablespoon fresh thyme leaves

In an 8″ skillet, sauté the garlic in the butter over moderate heat. As the garlic begins to color lightly, add the lemon juice, wine, fish stock, and salt, and cook 4 minutes over increased heat, adding the thyme after 3 minutes. Remove the garlic and spoon the sauce over the crabs.

FOR THE CRABS

12 prime soft-shell crabs

Milk for dipping

½ cup flour

½ cup vegetable oil

Salt and freshly ground pepper to taste

To clean the crabs, turn them bottom-side up and, using scissors, remove the sexual flaps: a narrow tapered appendage on male crabs; a leaflike tab on females. Turn the crabs over, lift each pointed tip of the top shells, and pull away and discard the exposed feather-like strands. With a sharp knife or scissors positioned just behind the eyes, cut away and discard the articulated section of the head. Rinse crabs under cold running water and pat dry.

Dip the cleaned crabs in milk, and dredge lightly in flour, shaking off the excess. In a 12″ skillet, heat half the oil and sauté half the crabs, stomach side down, 2 minutes. Turn the crabs and cook 2 minutes longer, until golden brown. Remove the crabs from the skillet, drain on paper towels, and keep warm. Discard the oil, wipe the skillet clean with paper towels, and repeat the process with the remaining crabs and oil (see Note). Sprinkle the crabs with salt and pepper, set on serving plates, spoon sauce over them, and serve at once.

Note: Alternatively, and preferably, both batches can be cooked at once, in two pans.

Recommended wine—Either Libaio, a relatively light white, or Cabreo, a bit fuller, both by Ruffino.

Sgombro alla Griglia
Grilled Mackerel

SERVES 4

If you walk through the countryside of coastal Istria during the summer, you can smell mackerel grilling wherever you turn. As a child, I ate even more mackerel than whiting. Today, when people compliment me on my skin, I tell them I owe it to all the mackerel I ate as a kid. According to Istrian folklore, eating lots of mackerel produces a good complexion, and recent medical research tends to confirm the old belief. For this recipe, the mackerel may be grilled over charcoal or baked in the oven after identical preliminary treatment.

FOR THE SAUCE

¾ cup olive oil	*2 tablespoons chopped Italian parsley*
8 cloves garlic, sliced thick	*2 tablespoons fresh lemon juice*
¼ teaspoon salt	*Fresh pepper, 10 twists of the mill*

In a small bowl, whisk all ingredients together until well blended and allow to stand 1 hour. Before serving, remove and discard the garlic.

8 whole mackerel, about 3 pounds

8 cloves garlic, crushed

4 tablespoons olive oil

1 teaspoon salt

¼ teaspoon freshly ground pepper

Eviscerate the mackerel, taking care to remove all traces of dark liver, and remove and discard the heads. (The liver is harmless but imparts bitterness to the fish.) Deposit 1 crushed garlic clove in the stomach cavity of each fish. Arrange the mackerel in a 1″ × 11″ × 12″ roasting pan. In a mixing cup, blend the oil, salt, and pepper, and pour the mixture over the fish, coating them on all sides.

To grill the mackerel, remove them from the pan, place them on a well-oiled and heated metal rack, and broil 20 minutes over whitened coals, turning once after 10 minutes. Alternatively, leave the fish in the roasting pan with the marinade and bake 30 minutes in a preheated 475° F. oven.

Whether grilled or baked, allow the fish to cool for a few minutes. Remove the skin or not, as desired. With a small serving spatula, lift off one side of the fish and remove and discard the garlic and bones. Arrange pairs of halved fish inside-up on serving plates, and drizzle 2 tablespoons sauce over each serving, reserving the remaining sauce for use as desired.

Recommended wine—A Müller-Thurgau by Schioppetto or a Sauvignon Collio by Borgo Conventi, both superlative Friulian producers.

Sarde Ripiene
Stuffed Sardines

SERVES 4

On days when my grandmother brought the produce of her garden to the market in Pula, we'd usually pick up some fresh sardines before starting home, because I loved them and they made a quick lunch after a long morning. Every region has its own version of *sarde ripiene*. This is ours.

16 fresh sardines (about 2 pounds)
⅓ cup bread crumbs
¼ cup plus 1 tablespoon olive oil
¼ cup plus 2 tablespoons chopped Italian parsley
2 tablespoons fresh thyme
1 tablespoon grated lemon zest

Flour for dredging
¼ cup fresh lemon juice
Salt and freshly ground pepper to taste
2 cups vegetable oil
2 eggs, beaten and seasoned
Lemon wedges for garnish

Cut the heads and tails from the sardines, eviscerate, butterfly, and pull out the bones.

In a bowl, combine the bread crumbs, 1 tablespoon olive oil, 2 tablespoons parsley, the thyme, and lemon zest. Spoon 1 tablespoon of the mixture into the center of each sardine, then re-form the fish. Dredge with flour, shaking off the excess.

In a second bowl, whisk together the ¼ cup olive oil, the lemon juice, and salt and pepper to taste. Stir in the ¼ cup parsley and set sauce aside.

Heat the vegetable oil in a medium-large skillet. Dip the sardines in beaten egg to coat and fry them in batches of four, turning once, until golden, about 2 minutes per side. Drain on paper towels, sprinkle lightly with salt, arrange on serving plates, and drizzle the reserved sauce over the fish. Garnish with lemon wedges.

Recommended wine—A light Gavi white with a pleasant nose and some fruit will cut the oiliness of the sardines. Pio Cesare, a longtime family friend, produces a superb line of Vini Piemontesi, including Gavi, Chardonnay, Barolo, and Barbaresco, and a fine new varietal, Ornato.

Trota Arrosto alla Salvia
Baked Trout with Sage

SERVES 4

I tasted this dish for the first time at a very fine restaurant, Vecchia Lugana, on Lake Sirmione, while driving from Milan to Venice. I hope you'll like its clean, uncomplicated flavor as much as I do.

4 rainbow trout (¾ pound each)
Salt and freshly ground pepper
6 tablespoons unsalted butter, softened
2 tablespoons chopped fresh sage
2 tablespoons chopped Italian parsley
1 tablespoon olive oil
1 cup dry white wine

Preheat the oven to 450° F. Season the trout inside and out with salt and pepper. In a small bowl, combine the softened butter, sage, and parsley, and blend well. Divide the mixture into four equal parts, spread one portion inside each opened trout, and close the fish as you would a book. Rub a large baking dish with the olive oil, and arrange the trout comfortably within it. Add ½ cup of the wine and bake 10 minutes, basting occasionally and gradually adding the remaining wine to compensate for evaporation.

Drain the liquid into a small nonreactive saucepan, and cover the trout to keep them warm. Boil the cooking liquid until emulsified and reduced, about 5 minutes. With a spatula, carefully transfer the fish to a serving platter or individual dishes, strain, and spoon the reduced sauce over them.

Note: Have your fishmonger clean and bone the trout, leaving the heads and tails on and the flanks attached like the covers of a book.

Gamberoni alla Griglia
Broiled Shrimp

SERVES 4 – 6

I had never eaten shrimp until my family settled in America. Along the Adriatic, scampi *(Nephrops norvegicus),* an unrelated species, were the most abundant of the crustaceans and the ones we ate most often. These days, true scampi sometimes turn up in American markets. To my taste, they're preferable to shrimp for this dish. This recipe is an adaptation of one given to me by Nino Laurenti, our late downstairs headwaiter and wine steward. He cooked the shrimp right in the sauce, but I wanted more crispness.

2 pounds jumbo shrimp (10–12 per pound)
2 tablespoons olive oil

Salt and freshly ground pepper to taste
½ cup bread crumbs

Preheat the oven to 475° F. Shell the shrimp, leaving the tail and hindmost body plate attached. Using a sharp paring knife, slit the shrimp lengthwise along their backs, one third of the way to the tail. Rinse well under cold running water and remove the intestinal veins. Drain well and pat dry.

In a baking dish, season the oil with salt and pepper, add the shrimp and toss well. Transfer the shrimp to a dish containing the bread crumbs, coat well with crumbs, and shake off the excess.

Return the shrimp to the oiled baking dish and arrange, split sides down and open, with tails curled up from the surface, pressing lightly to spread the connected halves of the bodies. Roast 5 minutes, then broil until golden brown, about 1 minute. Prepare the sauce while the shrimp are in the oven.

FOR THE SAUCE

4 cloves garlic, minced	*1 tablespoon fresh lemon juice*
¼ cup chopped onion	*1½ tablespoons Worcestershire sauce*
4 medium shallots, minced	*⅓ cup dry white wine*
2 tablespoons olive oil	*Salt and pepper to taste*
2 tablespoons unsalted butter	*1 tablespoon chopped Italian parsley*
1 tablespoon tarragon vinegar	

In a medium nonreactive skillet, sauté the garlic, onion, and shallots in the olive oil until glossy, about 2 minutes. Add all other ingredients except the parsley, and simmer gently 3 minutes. Pass the sauce through a sieve and stir in parsley.

Spoon the sauce onto the center of individual serving dishes and arrange the shrimp around the sauce.

Recommended wine—Again, a Gavi. Dependable producers include La Scolca, Contratto, Villa Banfi, Dogliani, and Granduca, along with the aforementioned Pio Cesare.

Gamberoni alla Buzara
Shrimp Hodgepodge

SERVES 4 – 6

Although it may seem a product of mainstream Italian cookery, this is actually a Dalmatian Istrian dish that we seldom cooked at home but sometimes ate in restaurants.

2 pounds jumbo shrimp (10–12 per pound)

1 tablespoon tomato paste

1 cup hot light fish stock (recipe page 70)

¼ cup olive oil

½ cup finely chopped onion

2 cloves garlic, crushed

Salt and freshly ground pepper to taste

1 cup dry white wine

1 tablespoon bread crumbs

1 tablespoon chopped Italian parsley

Using poultry shears or a sharp paring knife, cut through the outer curve of the shrimps' shells from end to end, but don't remove the shells. Rinse the shrimp under cold running water and devein.

Dissolve the tomato paste in the hot stock. In a medium nonreactive saucepan, heat 2 tablespoons of the olive oil. Add the onion and garlic, and sauté over moderately high heat until golden. Season with salt and pepper, add the wine, and bring to a boil. Add the stock and tomato paste mixture, reduce the heat, and simmer 20 minutes.

Meantime, in a large nonreactive skillet, heat the remaining oil, add the shrimp, and sauté (in two batches) 1 minute on each side. Drain off the oil, return all the shrimp to the skillet and add the sauce. Cover and cook over high heat, stirring occasionally, until the shrimp are just cooked through, about 2–3 minutes. Sprinkle with bread crumbs and parsley, mix well, and cook 1 minute longer, uncovered. Serve immediately.

Recommended wine—Nothing's better than a good Pinot Grigio or Tocai with this dish.

Aragosta in Brodetto
Lobster Stew

SERVES 6 (OR 12 AS AN APPETIZER)

Although similar treatments turn up under the same name in various parts of Italy, the use of tomato paste and vinegar in this dish is unique to Istria. At home, we used the clawless spiny lobster, sometimes substituted large crabs, and tossed the sauce with spaghetti. If you choose to serve it that way, bring a potful of salted water to boil as you start the sauce, and add a pound of spaghetti to the boiling water when you add the tails of the lobsters to the sauce. If you do elect to serve the dish with spaghetti, try to find hen lobsters. Their coral is wonderful with the pasta.

6 small (1–1½ pound) lobsters (see Note)
Unbleached flour for dredging
⅓ cup vegetable oil
3 cups diced onion
½ cup olive oil

6 tablespoons tomato paste
½ cup red wine vinegar
5 cups hot water
½ teaspoon salt
4 cups crushed Italian plum tomatoes
Hot red pepper flakes (optional)

One-year-old son Joseph makes the acquaintance of a spiny lobster in Brovinje, Felice's home village near Labin (formerly Albona).

Cut off the lobster tails at the body junctures and dredge the exposed meat lightly in flour, shaking off the excess. In a large skillet, heat the vegetable oil just short of the smoking point, add the lobster tails meat side down, and sauté about 2 minutes, until golden brown. Set the tails aside.

In a large nonreactive saucepan or small stockpot, sauté onion in ⅓ cup of the olive oil until translucent, 3–4 minutes. Add the lobster body shells, stir, and cook 5 minutes. Stir in the tomato paste and cook over medium heat an additional 5 minutes. Blend the vinegar with the hot water, add to the pan, and bring to a full boil. Add the salt and tomatoes, bring to a boil, and cook 3 minutes.

Remove the lobster bodies with tongs, allowing all interior juices to drain back into the sauce. (The bodies should be reserved for other uses, or, if the meal is to be informal, they may be served on a communal platter in the center of the table. The most delicate meat is in those bodies and shouldn't be wasted.) Add the claws to the pot, cook 7 minutes, and add the reserved tails and remaining olive oil. (If the *brodetto* is to be served with spaghetti, the pasta should be added to the boiling water at this point.) Cook 3–5 minutes longer over high heat, skimming off all surface scum. Remove the tails and claws, and keep warm under aluminum foil. Boil the sauce briefly to effect a slight reduction and concentration of the flavors. Add the hot pepper flakes if desired.

To serve with spaghetti, toss the drained pasta with half the sauce, flank with the lobster pieces, and spoon the remaining sauce over them. Otherwise, distribute the lobster and sauce on serving plates.

Note: Select live lobsters in good condition, with hard shells, and claws held close to the bodies, not hanging limply. If the lobsters are to be cooked soon after purchase, have the fishmonger split them lengthwise, remove the sac, cut the claws from the bodies, and crack them. If purchased a day in advance, they should be kept alive until ready for use, then dismantled the same way.

Recommended wine—The richness of lobster demands a white with some body. I'd pour a Vintage Tunina by Jermann. Jermann was one of the first winemakers from Friuli to produce a nonvarietal wine. This one blends Tocai, Ribolla Gialla, and Picolit grapes and has some wood aging. It's a great wine.

Brodetto all'Istriana
Istrian Fish Stew

SERVES 6

Every coastal region of Italy has its distinctive version of *brodetto*. I must have been five months old when I tasted Istria's for the first time. This recipe differs from most in its use of vinegar, a sailor's contribution, to cut the sweetness of the fish. In Istria, we ate *brodetto* mostly with polenta (page 127), sometimes with *pasutice* (page 108). Red snapper has been substituted here for the *scorpena (scorfano)* of Istria, a relative of the American scorpion fish, an unjustly despised fish seldom found in the market.

Salt and freshly ground pepper to taste
Flour for dredging
One 4-pound red snapper (see Note)
1½ cups vegetable oil
1 onion, chopped fine
8 scallions (white parts only), chopped fine

½ cup virgin olive oil
2 tablespoons tomato paste
3½ cups hot water
½ cup red wine vinegar

Season and lightly flour each piece of fish, shaking off the excess flour. In a large skillet, heat the vegetable oil just short of the smoking point and, in batches, brown the fish lightly on both sides, leaving it raw on the inside. Remove the fish from the pan with a slotted spatula, drain on paper towels, and sprinkle with salt.

In a second large skillet, sauté the onion and scallions in the olive oil until golden but not browned. Stir in the tomato paste. Add the fish, including the head and tail, in one layer. (Use two pans if necessary, dividing the onion mixture between them.) Cook 3–5 minutes over medium heat, shaking the pan occasionally.

Gently turn the fish and increase the heat to high. Add salt and pepper. Mix the water and vinegar, and add to the pan. When the liquid begins to boil, lower the heat to medium and simmer 10 minutes, occasionally shaking the pan and gently prodding the fish with a wooden spoon to prevent sticking.

If you wish, discard the head and tail (the cheeks, at least, should be served; they're a delicacy it would be criminal to waste). Remove the fish from the pan with a slotted spatula and keep it warm. Boil the pan liquid until reduced to a rich gravy, about 12 minutes, adding any juices that drain from the reserved fish. Set the fish on individual plates beside polenta or *pasutice*. Spoon the pan sauce over the fish and the accompaniment of choice and serve immediately. The sauce may be strained to eliminate bones.

Note: The flavor and texture of your *brodetto* will be best if the fish is sliced vertically into six portions left on the bone, but fillets can be substituted if you insist. In any case, be sure to have the fishmonger include the head and tail with your purchase; you're paying for them anyway, and they're essential to the success of the dish. Other firm-fleshed, non-oily fish, such as sea bass or monkfish, can be used in lieu of red snapper, but their cooking time may take a bit longer.

Recommended wine—If I seem to be overselling Friulian wines, it's because there are close affinities between the cooking of Friuli and that of my native Istria, and because Friuli is one of the significant wine-producing regions closest to Istria. For this dish, my choice would be a good Friulian Sauvignon, Tocai, or Pinot Grigio.

Baccalà con Patate al Forno
Baked Salt Cod with Potatoes

SERVES 6

This isn't a dish I grew up on, but an adaptation of one I enjoyed later on, in Piacenza. The idea of using cream with salt cod seemed odd at first, but the combination tasted good. As I discovered later on, *brandade de morue,* a specialty of the south of France, is quite similar to, and probably derives from, Italian versions of the dish.

1 pound boneless, skinless salt cod

Olive oil for greasing the dish

4 large potatoes sliced 1/8" thick

Salt and freshly ground pepper (see Note)

1 large onion, thinly sliced

1 1/2 tablespoons unsalted butter, cut into bits

1 cup heavy cream

1/2 cup milk

1/2 cup fish stock (recipe page 70)

Soak the salt cod overnight in three changes of cold water.

In a nonreactive pot, poach the cod 45 minutes in 5 quarts water, until the fish begins to break apart. (Cooking time may vary, depending on the quality of the *baccalà.*) Drain and set aside.

Preheat the oven to 475° F., and oil the bottom of a medium baking dish. Line the bottom of the baking dish with a single layer of potatoes, season to taste, and successively add layers of onion and broken-up salt cod, repeating the procedure until the ingredients are used up. Dot the surface with the butter, and add the cream, milk, and stock. Cover with foil, pierced here and there to allow steam to escape. Bake until the potatoes are tender when pierced with a fork, about 35 minutes. Uncover and brown for an additional 10 minutes.

Note: Salt only the potatoes, and sparingly; there will be enough residual salt in the cod to season everything else.

Recommended wine—Either Le Moie or Verdicchio, both by Fazi-Battaglia, would be an appropriate choice.

Salmone alla Senape
Salmon with Mustard Sauce

SERVES 4

Because salmon isn't native to Istrian waters, I never tasted it until I came to the United States. This is a recipe that Felice picked up during his years as a New York restaurant worker. Neither he nor I remember where it originated, but I like it. So do our customers at Felidia.

1½ pounds skinless salmon fillet (4 pieces)
Flour for dredging
2 tablespoons vegetable oil
3 tablespoons unsalted butter
½ cup dry white wine

Salt and freshly ground pepper to taste
2 tablespoons Dijon mustard
½ cup fish stock (recipe page 70)
Juice of ½ lemon
¼ cup heavy cream

Lightly flour the salmon. In a large non-reactive skillet, heat the oil, add the salmon, and sauté over moderate heat until golden, turning once, about 3 minutes per side. Set the salmon aside and discard the oil from pan. Add the butter, wine, and salt and pepper to the pan, and bring to a simmer. Add the mustard, fish stock, and lemon juice. Simmer over moderately high heat 5 minutes.

Gradually add the cream, stirring constantly, and simmer until slightly thickened, about 5 minutes. Add the salmon to the sauce and simmer until the fish is well coated and the sauce is reduced to ⅓ cup, about 3 minutes longer.

With a spatula, carefully transfer the fillets to serving plates. Strain the sauce, spoon a little over each fillet, and serve the remainder in a sauceboat.

Recommended wine—This is a dish that could stand up to a light red such as Sfursat or Grumello, from the Valtellina, in Lombardia. (Nino Negri is a reliable label for either.) Otherwise, a lightly acidic white such as Pinot Grigio would be my choice.

Pesce Spada in Agrodolce
Swordfish in Sweet and Sour Sauce

SERVES 4

Swordfish was scarce when I was growing up, and seeing the actual sword of the fish was a big deal for most kids. Because its flesh is nearly as dense as beef, swordfish lends itself well to preparation with balsamic vinegar, which would overpower more delicate, white-fleshed fish.

Four ½-pound skinless swordfish steaks
Salt and freshly ground pepper
Flour for dredging
4 tablespoons vegetable oil
2 tablespoons small marinated capers

¾ cup white wine
10 tablespoons balsamic vinegar
2 teaspoons olive oil
2 teaspoons butter

Lightly salt and pepper the fish, and dredge each piece in flour, shaking off the excess. In a large nonreactive skillet, bring the vegetable oil to moderately high heat. Add the fish and sauté about 1½ minutes on each side, until browned and cooked through. Transfer the fish to a platter, cover with aluminum foil, and keep warm.

Discard the oil from the skillet, add a pinch of flour, and let it brown over moderate heat. Add the remaining ingredients and boil over high heat, shaking the pan, until thickened to a light syrup, about 4 minutes. Spoon the sauce over the swordfish steaks and serve immediately.

Note: If you like your fish well done, return it to the sauce and cook it an additional minute before serving.

Recommended wine—This is another fish preparation with which I wouldn't hesitate to serve a light red. If you prefer a white, I'd suggest a good Chardonnay.

Calamari Fritti
Fried Squid

SERVES 4

Squid were relatively abundant along the Istrian coast when I was a child. We usually had them fried in crisp golden rings, and a favorite accompaniment was *radicchio zuccherino primo taglio,* the first cut of the immature plant of the sweetest member of the chicory family, which grows around Trieste, Treviso, and Istria in late spring and early summer. The secret of frying squid to appetizing crispness is to have it as dry as possible before it gets floured, then shake the excess flour off before it goes into the pan; to give the squid enough space so that the oil can circulate freely around it; and to not cover it completely with the oil, but to give it air in which to breathe and expel its residual moisture.

3 pounds medium squid	*2 cups flour*
3 cups vegetable oil	*½ teaspoon salt*

To clean the calamari, gently pull the head from the body, drawing out the internal organs. Cut off the tentacles just below the eyes and reserve them, discarding the remainder of the head and the internal organs. Peel the skin from the body sac, remove the transparent "backbone" from inside the sac, and wash the tentacles and sac well with cold water. Detach the "wings" (fins) from the sac and cut them in half from base to tip. Cut the body sac into ¼″ rings, discarding the tip of the sac, which may contain residual sand. If the tentacle clusters are larger than bite size, cut them in two lengthwise. Drain all the pieces well in a colander, pat dry in a cloth towel, and divide into two batches.

In a 14″ skillet, heat half the oil until very hot but not smoking (see Note). While the oil heats, dredge the calamari in flour, and shake off the excess.

Test the oil by adding one calamari ring. If there is no visible frying action, the oil is not hot enough. When the heat is sufficient, add the calamari a few pieces at a time, spreading them around with a fork, and tilting the skillet so that the oil reaches all. Fry the calamari on one side until golden, 2 minutes; turn and fry 2 minutes longer. With a skimmer or slotted spoon, remove the calamari from the pan and drain on paper towels. Discard the oil and repeat the process with the remaining oil and the second batch of calamari. Sprinkle evenly with salt and serve immediately.

Note: Alternatively, two skillets can be used at once. This requires divided attention but insures that all the food will be served piping hot and perfectly crisp.

Recommended wine—You'll want a lightly acidic white here: a Friulian Pinot Grigio, for example, or a Lacryma Christi del Vesuvio by Mastroberardino.

Calamari al Forno
Oven-baked Squid

SERVES 4

As a child, I was fascinated by live squid. Like chameleons, they could change their coloration when threatened, and I used to poke them with my fingers to see the show. One of my chores was to clean the calamari whenever we found some in the market or my late uncle Emilio caught some. It was a messy job—the squid ink would spatter the walls—and it never was one of my favorite tasks, but I loved eating squid. For this recipe you can, if you like, substitute an equal amount of cuttlefish for the squid. This is a simple, tasty way of preparing tender young squid. Although the dish isn't at all heavy, its flavor is deep and rich. I'd serve it with nothing more than a simple green salad and some fresh Italian bread such as focaccia (recipe page 229).

8 squid, 6 ounces each (total 3 pounds)
4 cloves garlic, sliced
4 tablespoons olive oil

Salt and freshly ground pepper to taste
4 tablespoons fish stock (recipe page 70)
¼ cup chopped Italian parsley

Preheat the oven to 375° F. Clean and rinse the squid without removing the skin (see Note). Arrange the squid in a shallow cast-iron pan. Blend the garlic, olive oil, salt and pepper, mix well, and coat the squid. Cover with aluminum foil and bake 20 minutes. Remove from the oven, discard the foil, and turn the squid. Add the fish stock and bake, uncovered, 10–15 minutes, until squid is tender, turning it occasionally. Test with a fork or skewer, which will slide out easily when the squid are done.

Transfer the pan to the stove top and cook over high heat until the sauce becomes syrupy. Transfer the squid to a serving platter. Strain the sauce, add the parsley, and spoon over the squid.

Note: To clean squid, grasp the body sac in one hand and draw the head out with the other. Detach the tentacles by cutting laterally just below the eyes, discarding the base of the head and any attached body innards. With your fingers, draw the transparent "backbone" and any loose remaining innards from the body sac. Snip off the point at the rear end of the sac and flush running water through the sac. For this recipe, bake the detached heads together with the sacs and reposition them in the sac openings before serving.

Recommended wine—One of the new nonvarietals from Friuli, such as Terre Alte by Livio Felluga or Vinae by Jermann, would be a fine choice to cut the richness of this dish.

5

Le Carni

Meats

POLLAME (CHICKEN)

◆

Pollo Arrosto al Rosmarino e Arancia

Pollo in Sguazet con Polenta

Petto di Pollo con Piselli

Petto di Pollo Marinato con Funghi

Pollo alla Casalinga

VITELLO (VEAL)

◆

Arrosto di Vitello Rustico

Vitello Tonnato

Cima Genovese

Salsa Verde

Stinco Arrosto

Trippa con Patate

Rognoncini Trifolati alla Senape

Fegato di Vitello all'Aceto Balsamico

AGNELLO (LAMB)

◆

Crostata di Agnello

Agnello di Latte Arrosto

MANZO (BEEF)

◆

Manzo in Sguazet

Bistecche in Tecia

SUINO E SALUMERIA (PORK, HAM, AND SAUSAGES)

◆

INTERLUDE—"COMING BEAUTIFUL"

Curing Prosciutto

Cotechino

Salsiccia Mantovana

Salsiccia Trevisana

Luganega, or *Salsiccia al Metro*

Cappucci Guarniti

Sarma

POLLAME
(CHICKEN)

❖

Pollo Arrosto al Rosmarino e Arancia
Roast Chicken with Rosemary and Orange

SERVES 4

Whether in times of need or times of plenty, rosemary grows in abundance along the coast of Istria, where its fragrance perfumes the air indoors and out and adds a festive note to the many dishes in which it is used. Oranges, on the other hand, are not indigenous there, and when I was a child we had them only at Christmas and on a few other special occasions. This recipe (which borrows freely from the French classic *canard à l'orange),* the traditional Istrian roast chicken with rosemary—as festive a dish as I knew during my early girlhood—is infused with scents and flavors I still associate only with the most joyful occasions of those years.

2 whole 2-pound chickens
¼ teaspoon salt
¼ teaspoon pepper
3 tablespoons olive oil
2 tablespoons fresh rosemary leaves
6 tablespoons Grand Marnier

3 tablespoons fresh orange juice
2 tablespoons brandy
2 tablespoons butter
4 tablespoons chicken stock
(recipe page 69)

Split the chickens into halves. Cut out the backbones and remove the breastbones and ribs with your fingers and a paring knife. Blend the salt and pepper, and season the chickens inside and out.

Preheat the oven to 500° F.

Place the chickens skin-side down in a hot, dry 14″ ovenproof skillet and brown 5 minutes. Turn the chickens and brown 5 minutes longer, then add the olive oil. Transfer the skillet to the preheated oven and roast the chickens 30 minutes, turning them occasionally. Remove from the oven, drain off all fat, and add the remaining ingredients to the pan. Place over high flame and cook 2 minutes, frequently basting and occasionally turning the chickens. Transfer the birds to serving plates and spoon the pan sauce over them.

Recommended wine—Roast chicken classically calls for a medium-bodied red wine with balanced tannins and acidity and an elegant style. Any of today's excellent Chiantis would be my choice here.

Pollo in Sguazet con Polenta
Chicken *in Sguazet* with Polenta

SERVES 4

This is a somewhat abbreviated version of the dish described on page 30 of Jay's text. We usually had it on Sundays for the family, or when company came for dinner, or after a new baby was born. When women had given birth, they were fed *pollo in sguazet* to restore their strength, and the older kids would have the leftovers in soup. Consequently, kids with brand-new brothers or sisters invariably were nicknamed "Soupy." At home, Felice and I use a tough old stewing fowl for this dish, but younger, more readily available chickens require far less cooking time than the more flavorful older birds. The cooking time given in this recipe is for the younger chicken.

1 large onion, minced

2 slices bacon, minced

¼ cup chicken livers, minced

3 bay leaves

1 teaspoon fresh (or ½ teaspoon dry) rosemary

4 whole cloves

¼ cup olive oil

one 3-pound chicken, cut into 8 pieces

Salt and freshly ground black pepper

1 tablespoon plus 1 teaspoon tomato paste

1 cup dry white wine

1½ cups chicken stock (recipe page 69)

Polenta for serving (recipe page 129)

In a large nonreactive skillet, sauté the first six ingredients in the olive oil about 5 minutes, until the onion has wilted. Season the chicken with salt and pepper to taste, add it to the skillet, and sauté until lightly browned on all sides, about 5 minutes. Add the tomato paste and the wine, mixing with a wooden spoon, and coat the chicken pieces with the mixture. Add the stock to the skillet, scraping the bottom of the pan to loosen the particles of food, and simmer 20 minutes, turning the chicken occasionally.

Remove and set aside the chicken pieces, and continue to cook the sauce until thickened, about 10 minutes. Strain the sauce, return the chicken and sauce to the pan, and cook just until heated through.

To serve, spoon hot polenta onto center of each dish, flank the polenta with two pieces of chicken, and spoon sauce over chicken and polenta.

Recommended wine—A Spanna by Travaglini or Caldi.

Petto di Pollo con Piselli
Breast of Chicken with New Peas

SERVES 4

This isn't a dish we normally would have eaten at home, but a restaurant specialty that Felice picked up somewhere during his years as a waiter. It's simple, easy, and popular with our customers.

8 skinless, boneless chicken breast halves, slightly flattened

Flour for dredging

¼ cup vegetable oil

1 tablespoon olive oil

1 medium onion, chopped fine

¼ cup chopped prosciutto

4 tablespoons unsalted butter

½ cup dry white wine

1 cup chicken stock (recipe page 69)

2 cups new peas (petits pois; *see Note*)

Salt and freshly ground pepper to taste

Lightly flour the chicken breasts, shaking off the excess. In a large heavy skillet, heat the vegetable oil over moderately high flame. Add chicken breasts in two batches and sauté, turning once, until golden brown, about 5 minutes per side. Remove from the skillet and keep warm.

Wipe the skillet clean and add the olive oil. Add the onion and prosciutto, and sauté over moderate heat until the onion is translucent, about 5 minutes. Add the butter, wine, and stock, and bring to a boil. Reduce the heat and simmer sauce until well blended and thickened, about 5 minutes.

Return the chicken to the skillet, add the peas, and cook until just heated through, about 2 minutes. Season to taste, arrange two pieces of chicken on each serving plate, and spoon the sauce and peas over them.

Note: Peas should be thoroughly cooked if fresh, thawed if frozen.

Recommended wine—A good Chianti or a Friulian Merlot.

Petto di Pollo Marinato con Funghi
Seared Marinated Breast of Chicken with Shiitake Mushrooms

———

SERVES 6

Although we Americans eat an awful lot of chicken on the bone anywhere else, most of us demand boneless chicken in a white-tablecloth restaurant. This recipe was developed at Felidia as one response to that demand. The marination does wonders for the relatively dry and bland breast meat, and the shiitake mushrooms add an earthy note to a lean, quick, tasty dish, usually served with a crisp salad of arugula and Belgian endive.

2 pounds boneless and skinless chicken breasts, diagonally sliced into thirds, and lightly pounded

FOR THE MARINADE

½ cup olive oil
1 tablespoon minced fresh rosemary
1 tablespoon minced fresh sage

4 cloves garlic, crushed
Salt and freshly ground pepper to taste

In a shallow nonreactive vessel such as an ovenproof roasting pan, combine all the ingredients, add the chicken pieces, cover, and marinate overnight in the refrigerator.

¼ cup olive oil

4 cloves garlic, crushed

1 pound shiitake mushrooms, stems discarded

Salt and freshly ground pepper to taste

1 teaspoon brandy

1 tablespoon unsalted butter

2 tablespoons minced Italian parsley

In a large nonreactive skillet, heat the olive oil and lightly brown the garlic. In two batches, add the shiitake caps, salt and pepper, and sauté until golden brown on both sides, about 4 minutes per batch. Return all the mushrooms to the pan and cook about 2 minutes, until softened throughout. Stir in the brandy, butter, and parsley, and cook 1 minute longer. Coat a large skillet with oil from the marinade and set over moderately high heat. When very hot, sear the chicken on both sides, about 2–3 minutes on each side, until browned and cooked through. Arrange the chicken on individual serving plates and top with the mushrooms.

Recommended wine—Chianti S. Nicolo by Castellare or Chianti le Pergole Torte by Monte Vertine.

Pollo alla Casalinga
Home-style Chicken

SERVES 4

Just about every home cook in Italy prepares a version of chicken and potatoes roasted in the same pot, and no two are precisely the same. This is my family's. We used *galletti,* young spring chickens, which cook quickly, and we usually used two at a time because they were small. The dish was considered somewhat extravagant because the immature birds yielded smaller, less flavorsome portions, but they made up in tenderness for what they lacked in volume and character. This is my son Joseph's favorite dish. My mother always made it for him when he was home from Boston College, and he's always served the crispest of the potatoes.

3 pounds chicken parts of your choice

Salt and freshly ground pepper to taste

¼ cup olive oil

1½ pounds non-mealy potatoes, peeled and quartered

2 small onions, thinly sliced

1 sprig fresh rosemary

Season the chicken with salt and pepper to taste. In a 14″ cast-iron skillet, heat the olive oil over moderately high flame, add the chicken parts skin-side down, and cover the skillet. Brown the chicken, turning it once, 5–7 minutes, and move it to one side of the skillet.

Add the peeled and quartered potatoes to the clear side of the skillet and cook on medium heat 20 minutes, turning them often, until evenly browned. (At this point, both the chicken and potatoes should be crisp and brown.) Reduce the heat, add the onions and rosemary, and cook, covered, occasionally mixing gently, about 10 minutes, until the onions have softened and the flavors have blended.

Drain the oil from the pan before serving chicken and potatoes.

Recommended wine—With this robust chicken dish, I'd serve a Vino Nobile di Montepulciano. Look for the Avignonesi label. Avignonesi also produces one of the great dessert wines, Vin Santo.

VITELLO
(VEAL)

◆

Arrosto di Vitello Rustico
Country-style Roast Veal

───

SERVES 6

Jay tells me this is the best roast veal he's ever eaten. Because the meat is cooked on the bone, the dish has a higher gelatin content and more flavor than most roasts. I often add peeled and roughly hacked potatoes to the pan just after the foil has been removed. Jay tells me they're the most savory potatoes he's ever eaten.

3½ pounds veal shoulder with blade bones, hacked into 2" cubes

2 ribs celery, roughly chopped

2 large carrots, roughly chopped

1 onion, sliced

3 bay leaves

3 small sprigs fresh rosemary, or 1 teaspoon dried

1 cup dry white wine

½ cup virgin olive oil

¼ cup balsamic vinegar

Salt and pepper to taste

2 cups chicken stock (recipe page 69)

In a deep or large bowl, toss all ingredients except the stock, and marinate overnight in the refrigerator. Return to room temperature before roasting.

Preheat the oven to 475° F. Place all ingredients, including the stock, in a roasting pan, cover with aluminum foil, and roast 30 minutes.

Remove the foil and roast meat 1 hour longer, turning and basting it reg-ularly. Using a slotted spoon, transfer the meat to an ovenproof serving dish.

Set the roasting pan over high heat to reduce the liquid, about 15 minutes. Strain the juices over the meat and re-turn it to the oven. Roast, turning the meat frequently, until very tender and browned all over, about 30 minutes.

Recommended wine—For this, a good Refosco or Teroldego. Both these Friulian wines are characterized by what we Italians call *asputa*—a little movement against the palate—and both have plenty of character.

Vitello Tonnato
Tunnied Veal

In my travels over the years, I've tasted hundreds of the countless versions of *vitello tonnato* to be found in Italy. This is my version, but you're encouraged to play with the recipe and work out your own variations. The dish can be served as an appetizer or main course, and its tanginess and freshness make it wonderful summertime eating.

FOR THE VEAL

2 small carrots	2 bay leaves
2 ribs celery	1 cup dry white wine
2 pounds (1 piece) lean fillet of veal, trimmed	6 whole black peppercorns
1 small onion, quartered	½ teaspoon salt

Slice one each of the carrots and celery ribs into julienne strips about 1½″ long. Slice the remaining carrot and celery crosswise. Using a thin skewer, make a horizontal hole in the meat, and insert a piece of the carrot julienne. Continue the process, alternating carrot and celery pieces inserted at varying levels and turning the meat frequently until "larded" throughout with the julienne vegetables. This will flavor the meat and form a mosaic pattern when the veal is sliced.

Set the meat in a nonreactive casserole and add the sliced carrot and celery, the onion, bay leaves, wine, peppercorns, and salt. Bring to a simmer and cook, covered, 1¼ hours. Allow the meat to cool in its cooking liquid.

One 6½-ounce can oil-packed white tuna, drained

1 tablespoon each carrots, celery, and onion from the casserole

1 tablespoon capers

2 anchovy fillets

½ cup cooking liquid from the casserole

2 tablespoons olive oil

3 small cornichon pickles

3 tablespoons mayonnaise

1 teaspoon Dijon mustard

1 teaspoon white vinegar

Salt and pepper to taste

Additional capers for garnish

Place tuna, vegetables, capers, anchovies, cooking liquid, olive oil, and cornichons in a blender. Blend until smooth, about 10 minutes, or use a food processor, which will do a much faster job. Transfer the mixture to a bowl, successively fold in the mayonnaise, mustard, and vinegar. Season to taste and refrigerate the sauce and meat separately until chilled.

Thinly slice the chilled meat against the grain, arrange it on a serving platter in a petal-like pattern, and spread the sauce over it. Sprinkle with capers and serve, preferably with steamed mixed vegetables vinaigrette. For an excellent variation on the theme, substitute turkey breast for the veal.

Recommended wine—Ordinarily a Chardonnay, but a light red such as Dolcetto would be fine in cooler weather.

Cima Genovese
Stuffed Breast of Veal

SERVES 8

Genoa's two most distinctive contributions to the Italian menu are pesto and *cima genovese*, the beautiful mosaiclike cousin of the French *ballottine de veau*. Although *cima* is eaten year-round, it's ideal for summer serving. This recipe was given to me by our former chef, Nino Palmieri, who now lives in retirement in Genoa.

1 medium carrot, pared and trimmed

1 medium zucchini, trimmed

1 medium red bell pepper, halved and seeded

1/4 pound prosciutto, sliced 1/8" thick

1/2 cup olive oil

3 ounces fresh spinach, large stems removed

1/2 cup shelled fresh peas

6 raw eggs

1/2 cup milk

Salt and freshly ground pepper to taste

1 breast of veal, about 6 1/2 pounds (see Note)

4 hard-boiled eggs, shelled

1 onion, sliced

1 carrot, sliced

3 bay leaves

Salsa Verde (recipe follows)

Cut the pared and trimmed carrot, the zucchini, and red pepper in julienne strips 1/4" × 1/4" × 2". Cut the prosciutto into thin julienne strips.

In a large skillet, heat the olive oil over a medium flame, add the julienne vegetables, spinach, and peas, and cook, tossing lightly, until softened, about 5 minutes.

In a small bowl, lightly beat the raw eggs and the milk together. Add to the skillet and cook, stirring, until the eggs are scrambled loosely. Off the heat, stir in the prosciutto and season with salt and pepper to taste. Spoon the mixture into a colander set over a bowl and allow it to cool to room temperature.

Cut a piece of butcher's twine long enough to reach completely around the breast of veal three times lengthwise, keeping in mind that the meat will be thicker when it is stuffed, and thread the twine into a trussing needle. On a flat surface, open the veal as you would a book, with the longer side facing you. Season the surface with salt and pepper, then spread the drained egg mixture over one side of the veal breast, leaving a 1" border along the edges. Arrange the hard-boiled eggs end-to-end over the length of the filling. Fold the other half of the veal over the filled side, as you would close a book, and tightly stitch the open edges together, drawing the twine through the meat at 1" intervals. Wrap the veal breast tightly in a double thickness of cheesecloth and tie the package crosswise at 2" intervals with butcher's twine.

Fill halfway with cold water a deep pot, large enough to hold the veal comfortably. Add 1 tablespoon salt, the sliced onion, sliced carrot, and bay leaves, and bring to a simmer. Slip the veal roll into the water and adjust the heat to maintain a gentle simmer until the veal feels tender when pierced with a skewer, about 2¼ hours.

Transfer the drained veal to a roasting pan and set a second, smaller, roasting pan, a loaf pan, or the like, on top of it. Place about 4 pounds deadweight, such as a couple of large cans of tomatoes, in the second pan, and allow the *cima* to cool to room temperature. To serve, unwrap the cooled *cima*, remove the stitches, slice as you would a jelly roll, and spoon the salsa around the meat.

Note: Have the butcher bone and butterfly the breast of veal.

Salsa Verde

YIELDS ¾ CUP

8 shallots, minced	*½ cup minced pimento*
2 anchovy fillets	*1 hard-boiled egg, minced*
½ cup plus 3 tablespoons olive oil	*¼ cup minced Italian parsley*
¼ cup red wine vinegar	*½ small red onion, minced*
Salt and freshly ground pepper to taste	*¼ cup minced celery*

In a medium skillet, sauté the shallots and anchovy fillets in 3 tablespoons of the oil until the shallots are translucent and the anchovies have dissolved, about 5 minutes, and allow to cool. Mix the remaining oil, the vinegar, salt, pepper, and minced ingredients. Add the shallot-anchovy mixture and blend thoroughly.

Recommended wine—*Cima genovese* goes best with a crisp white such as Pinot Grigio, Arnais, or Gavi.

Stinco Arrosto
Roasted Veal Shanks

SERVES 4

Here we have a case of languages in collision. A perfectly innocent Italian term for the shank of the calf sounds suspiciously smelly where English is spoken. Felice and I debated long and hard about what to call this dish on our menu. We finally decided to play it straight, and found that our customers have no problem with the term and love the dish. I like it served with steamed, buttered Brussels sprouts. One of the best versions of *stinco* I've ever had was prepared at the Antica Trattoria Suban, in Trieste, where my good friend Mario Suban roasts meats over an open fire as his customers inhale the mouth-watering aromas.

2 veal shanks, 2–2½ pounds each
Salt and freshly ground pepper to taste
6 tablespoons olive oil
1 large carrot, chopped
1 small onion, sliced
1 large celery rib, chopped
2 cloves garlic, crushed

2 tablespoons fresh rosemary or 2 teaspoons dried
6 leaves fresh sage, or ½ teaspoon dried
1 cup dry white wine
3 cups veal or chicken stock (recipes page 69)

Preheat the oven to 475° F. Season the shanks with salt and pepper. In a large roasting pan on top of the stove, heat 4 tablespoons of the olive oil, add the shanks, and brown on all sides. Transfer the pan to the oven and roast 30 minutes, turning occasionally.

Meanwhile, in a skillet, heat the remaining oil, add all the vegetables and herbs, season with salt and pepper, and sauté until softened, about 10 minutes.

Discard all oil from the roasting pan and add the wine, vegetables, and 2 cups of the stock. Roast, turning and basting the shanks occasionally and adding stock as needed, until the meat is very tender and its surface is nicely car-amelized, about 1 hour. Remove the shanks from the pan and strain all the vegetables and the sauce through a fine sieve. Mash the carrot and retrieve as much vegetable puree as possible. Skim off the excess fat. Return the meat to the sauce and roast in the oven for another 10 minutes, or until the sauce is syrupy and forms a brown glaze on the meat.

There should be 5 tablespoons of sauce per shank. To serve, hold the *stinco* by the bone with a towel, and with a carving knife or an electric knife, cut ¼″ slices, turning the bone until all meat is off. Set on a serving plate and spoon sauce over the meat.

Recommended wine—As for Arrosto di Vitello Rustico, a Refosco or a Teroldego.

Trippa con Patate
Tripe with Potatoes

SERVES 6 – 8

Piazza Giardini was the social center of Pula, my hometown. There was a restaurant there that was celebrated for its tripe. When my mother, who taught school, didn't have time to cook, I'd be sent there with a stack of covered pots, called a *gamella,* and they'd be filled with hot *trippa,* which I'd carry home for dinner.

4½ pounds honeycomb tripe

½ cup olive oil

3 medium onions, chopped

2½ ounces pancetta or bacon

3 bay leaves

1 cup dry white wine

1 teaspoon salt, or to taste

½ teaspoon crushed red pepper

3 tablespoons tomato paste

2 cups Italian plum tomatoes, peeled and diced

1¼ pounds potatoes, in ¾" cubes

6 cups chicken stock (recipe page 69)

1 cup grated Parmigiano

Freshly ground pepper to taste

In a large nonreactive pot, simmer the tripe in 6 quarts water for 2 hours. Drain, cool, and scrape off all the fat and membrane. Cut into ½" × 2½" strips, wash, and drain. (Tripe can be treated a day in advance.)

In a large casserole, heat the olive oil, add the onions, pancetta (or bacon), and bay leaves, and sauté until the onions are golden, about 8 minutes. Add the tripe and sauté, stirring, until most of the water from the tripe has evaporated, 8–10 minutes. Add the wine and boil until evaporated, 8–10 minutes. Add the salt, crushed red pepper, and tomato paste, and mix well. Add the tomatoes, reduce the heat, and simmer, stirring frequently, about 10 minutes. Add the potatoes and enough of the chicken stock to cover, and simmer 30–45 minutes, gradually adding the remainder of the stock until the tripe is tender but slightly resistant to the tooth. At this point, there should be sauce enough to coat the tripe and potatoes.

Serve sprinkled with the cheese and fresh pepper. (Leftover tripe will keep very well for 2–3 days in the refrigerator.)

Recommended wine—Merlot.

Rognoncini Trifolati alla Senape
Veal Kidneys in Mustard Sauce

SERVES 4

I really didn't become acquainted with mustard until after I left Istria, where it isn't used much. Except for the addition of mustard, a touch borrowed from the standard French dish *rognons de veau à la moutarde,* this recipe is typically Istrian. I like mustard because it marries well with organ meats and intensifies their flavor while adding almost nothing to their caloric content.

2 pounds whole veal kidney	1/2 cup dry white wine
1 cup white vinegar	6 tablespoons butter
5 cups water	1 teaspoon fresh lemon juice
1/4 teaspoon salt	4 tablespoons Dijon mustard
1/2 teaspoon freshly ground pepper	1/2 cup heavy cream
4 tablespoons vegetable oil	1/2 cup chicken stock (recipe page 69)
2 tablespoons brandy	1 teaspoon Cognac or brandy

Remove all exterior fat from the kidney. Rinse and let soak in the vinegar and water for 2 hours, then wash in cold water and pat dry in a towel. Cut the kidney lengthwise into three sections and then crosswise into 1/4" slices, removing the interior fat as it becomes exposed. (Kidney fat retains odor and should be scrupulously removed.)

Blend the salt and pepper, and season the kidney with the mixture. In a thin 14" sauté pan, heat oil until very hot but not smoking. Add the kidney, spreading out and stirring occasionally until lightly browned, 3–5 minutes, adding 2 tablespoons brandy as it cooks. Set the cooked kidney aside to drain in a colander.

In a clean, heated 14" pan, blend the remaining ingredients and bring to boil, stirring. Continue to boil 2 minutes, and add the drained kidney. Sauté 1–2 minutes, until the reduced sauce clings to the kidney, and serve.

Recommended wine—A good Gattinara with flavor and bouquet, balanced but without an overwhelming palate. Superior producers include Antoniolo, Cadi, Travaglini, and Nervi.

Fegato di Vitello all'Aceto Balsamico
Calf's Liver with Balsamic Vinegar

SERVES 6

I've cooked calf's liver with vinegar as long as I can remember, but I didn't discover balsamic vinegar, a specialty of Modena, until about twenty-five years ago. I've experimented with this cask-mellowed, highly concentrated essence ever since, and have learned a great deal about its properties and uses from two Modenese, Gianni Salvaterra and Marta Pulini. Really fine balsamic vinegar, aged in wood for many years, can be more expensive than some of the great vintage wines, but a little goes a long way and the results are worth the splurge.

2 pounds calf's liver
1 pound white onions
1 tablespoon sugar
4 bay leaves
3 tablespoons olive oil
½ teaspoon salt

Freshly ground pepper to taste
1 teaspoon flour
½ cup balsamic vinegar
1 tablespoon white wine
5 tablespoons vegetable oil

Trim the liver of its outer covering, blood vessels, and any blemishes. Pat dry, cut in julienne strips (2″ × ½″ × ½″), and set aside.

Slice the onions thin, working with the grain. In a nonreactive skillet, melt the sugar until it caramelizes, add the onions and bay leaves, and mix well. Add 3 tablespoons of olive oil, the salt and pepper, and sauté over moderately high heat until the onions are golden brown but not limp. Stir in the flour, blending well, add the vinegar and wine, and simmer about 2 minutes, until the sauce thickens.

Meanwhile, in a skillet large enough to hold the strips of liver in a single layer (use two pans if necessary), heat the vegetable oil, add the liver, and sauté, stirring occasionally, about 2 minutes.

With a slotted spoon, drain the liver and transfer it to the sauce, tossing gently until well coated, about 1 minute. The sauce should be quite adhesive, not runny.

Serve immediately with boiled (page 129) or fried polenta (page 129).

AGNELLO
(LAMB)

◆

Crostata di Agnello
Rack of Lamb

SERVES 4

Although I devise or adapt the overwhelming majority of the recipes we use at Felidia, I can't claim any credit for this wonderful rack of lamb, one of the most popular selections on our menu. This is the creation of our chef de cuisine, Edgar Torres, whose excellent palate and reverence for his raw materials is evident in every dish he serves. Edgar and his brother David came highly recommended to Felidia. Edgar was a veteran with more than twenty years' experience in the preparation of Italian cuisine. Nonetheless when I hired him I stood beside him and observed his methods closely. It was quite evident from the very start that this man loved what he did; he literally caresses particularly fine meats and tries to determine which would be the best method to prepare them. Edgar and I have been working side by side for ten years, and I have been consistently impressed by his symphonic style. For this dish, the sauce is made in advance.

FOR THE SAUCE

1½ pounds lamb bones and scraps	*1 tablespoon fresh sage*
3 tablespoons olive oil	*1 tablespoon fresh thyme*
1 tablespoon flour	*Salt and freshly ground pepper to taste*
½ cup chopped onion	*3 cups chicken stock (recipe page 69)*
¼ cup sliced carrot	*½ cup dry white wine*
¼ cup sliced celery	*1 cup water*
1 tablespoon fresh rosemary	*1 cup young peas, parboiled if fresh*

Preheat oven to 425° F. Trim the lamb scraps of all fat, place together with the bones in a roasting pan, and toss with 1 tablespoon of the olive oil. Roast for 30 minutes, then sprinkle with the flour and roast 15 minutes longer, until nicely browned.

Meanwhile, in a large nonreactive saucepan, sauté the onion in the re-

maining oil for 5 minutes over moderate heat. Add the carrot, celery, rosemary, sage, thyme, salt and pepper, and cook 15 minutes, stirring and occasionally adding small amounts of stock to prevent the vegetables from burning.

Transfer the browned bones and meat scraps to the vegetable mixture. Drain all fat from the bottom of the roasting pan. While the roasting pan is still hot, add the wine and water, and scrape the bottom of the pan to release all coagulated drippings. Simmer, skimming frequently, 1 hour and 15 minutes, or until the liquid has reduced to about ¾ cup. Discard the bones and strain the sauce through a fine sieve, pressing down hard on the solids to express as much liquid as possible. Return the sauce to the heat and reduce to the consistency of gravy. Add the peas before serving with rack of lamb.

FOR THE RACKS

3½–4 pounds rack of lamb (see Note)
2 teaspoons olive oil

1 teaspoon each salt and freshly ground pepper

Have the butcher trim the racks, leaving protruding rib bones 2½″ long and reserving the between-bone scraps for the sauce, but leaving the blanket of fat intact. (In profile, the rack should take the configuration of the number six.)

Preheat the oven to 500° F. Wrap the exposed rib bones in aluminum foil and brush a mixture of the oil and seasonings over the exposed meat. While the sauce is reducing, place the racks, fat down, in a preheated roasting pan and roast 30 minutes.

Note: Racks are unseparated chops from the loin section. For this recipe, young lamb, yielding eight relatively thin chops per rack, is what you want. The yield per serving is four small chops.

TO FINISH THE RACKS

1 cup bread crumbs
2 tablespoons olive oil
1 tablespoon chopped Italian parsley
2 teaspoons grated Parmigiano

1 clove garlic, finely minced
¼ teaspoon dried oregano
Salt and freshly ground pepper

Blend all ingredients well.

Remove the racks from the oven and trim away all outside fat. Spread the bread crumb mixture evenly over all surfaces of the racks and tamp down well. Return the racks to the oven and bake 5 minutes, until the crumbs are crisped. (This treatment will yield a medium degree of doneness; for rare or well-done meat, adjust the timing accordingly. I recommend a rare rack.)

Let the racks rest off the heat for 5 minutes before serving. To serve, cut the chops apart and arrange four per portion on serving plates with sauce spooned over them.

Recommended wine—An older Brunello di Montalcino, smooth and silky, would be an ideal choice here.

Agnello di Latte Arrosto

Roast Baby Lamb

SERVES 6

I always had mixed emotions about this dish as a little girl. Traditionally, it was served at the first meal after Lent, a joyous occasion to which everyone looked forward, including me. Still, there was an element of personal sadness: My pet was being eaten. At Busoler I spent long hours playing in the fields with lambs and young goats, and always found sentiment struggling with appetite at Easter. When the appearance of the first peas of the season coincided with Easter, they'd be shelled and added to the dish at the last moment.

5-pound baby lamb shoulder with bone,
cut in 2" cubes
2 ribs celery, coarsely chopped
2 medium carrots, coarsely chopped
1 large onion, sliced
1 cup dry white wine

½ cup olive oil
¼ cup balsamic vinegar
3 small sprigs fresh rosemary
¼ teaspoon freshly ground pepper
½ teaspoon salt
2 cups beef stock (page 69)

In a large bowl, toss all ingredients except the beef stock until well blended. Cover and refrigerate 24 hours, tossing occasionally.

Preheat the oven to 425° F. Transfer the contents of the refrigerated bowl to a roasting pan large enough to accommodate a single layer of vegetables covered by a single layer of meat. Add the stock and roast, basting and turning the lamb frequently, until the meat is very tender, about 1 hour 45 minutes.

Reduce the oven temperature to 350° F. Remove the lamb from the pan and set it aside. Skim and discard as much fat as possible from the pan liquids. Place the pan over high heat and boil until the liquids reduce to about 1¼ cups. Transfer the meat to a smaller roasting pan and strain the reduced sauce over it. Place the meat in the oven and roast, turning the meat every 10 minutes, until extremely tender, brown, and caramelized, about 30–40 minutes.

Strain the juices from the pan and, if necessary, reduce further over moderately high heat; there should be ½ cup of finished sauce. Transfer the lamb to a serving platter and spoon the sauce over it.

Recommended wine—I like Abbazia di Rosazzo's Ronco dei Roseti with roast baby lamb.

MANZO
(BEEF)

◆

Manzo in Sguazet
Beef *in Sguazet*

SERVES 8

One of the basic Istrian sauces, *manzo in sguazet* usually is made with the tougher, cheaper, more flavorful, more gelatinous cuts of beef—muscles, chuck, flank, skin, and the like. It can be used with pasta, risotto, polenta, or in hero sandwiches, and it freezes well. During my childhood, paprika and sour cream sometimes were added to provide a Hungarian accent. See "About Sguazet," page 210.

½ ounce (about 6 pieces) dried porcini mushrooms

⅓ cup olive oil

2 large onions, minced

2 beef marrow bones

3½ pounds stewing beef, cut in 1" cubes

4 bay leaves

2 whole cloves

¼ teaspoon salt

1 cup dry red wine, Chianti or Barolo

4 teaspoons tomato paste

4 cups chicken stock (page 69)

Soften the dried porcini about 30 minutes in a cupful of warm water, trim, and reserve the strained liquid.

In a large skillet, heat the oil and sauté the onions for about 10 minutes over medium-high heat, until transparent. Add the bones, meat, bay leaves, cloves, and salt, and sauté 10 minutes longer. Add the wine, raise the heat, and cook about 10 minutes, until the wine has reduced by half. Add the tomato paste and the porcini. Stir slowly and thoroughly, and add the reserved mushroom liquid. Simmer 5 minutes.

Add half the chicken stock, bring to a boil, reduce to a simmer, and cook until the sauce thickens, about 2 hours. As the mixture cooks, add the remaining stock little by little. When the *sguazet* is finished, there should be about 6 cups of thick, chunky sauce.

Serve with *fuzi* (page 108) and grated Parmigiano to taste.

Recommended wine—A reputable Chianti or a non-DOCG Sangiovese blend such as Cabreo Rosso, Peppoli, or Vinattieri Rosso.

Bistecche in Tecia
Pan-fried Shell Steaks

SERVES 6

I seldom had this dish as a child, but when I did, it was made not with beef, but with horse meat. Because red meat of any kind was scarce at the time, it was prepared mostly for anemic children. Beef still is eaten sparingly along the Mediterranean and Adriatic, where steaks seldom conform to American notions of a proper beefsteak. In general, the meat is grass fed and much leaner, with little marbling and no introduced hormones or chemical additives. Moreover, steaks are eaten in much smaller, nutritionally sensible portions. For this recipe, I've specified 1½ pounds of beef, which works out to 4 ounces per serving—enough to satisfy a craving for the taste of red meat while remaining well within safe nutritional guidelines. I like to serve the steaks with Swiss chard and potatoes.

6 boneless shell steaks, ½" thick (1½ pounds in all)
Salt to taste
Flour for dredging
¼ cup olive oil

2 cloves garlic, chopped fine
2 teaspoons butter
Freshly ground pepper to taste
½ cup beef stock (recipe page 69)
¼ cup finely chopped Italian parsley

Trim the steaks of all fat and gristle, and pound to ¼" thickness. Salt the steaks and dredge them in flour, shaking off the excess.

In a large heavy skillet (or two, if necessary, with the ingredients divided equally between them), heat half the olive oil just short of the smoking point. Add the steaks in batches and sear 1½ minutes on each side. Set the steaks aside, and pour off any excess oil from the pan, retaining the other drippings.

Add the remaining oil to the pan and bring to moderate heat. Add and lightly brown the garlic. Add the butter, salt and pepper to taste, and cook until the fats blend, then add the beef stock and stir to deglaze the pan. Simmer until the sauce thickens, about 3 minutes. Add the parsley and steaks and cook until the meat is lightly coated and heated through.

Remove the steaks to a warm serving platter. If sauce seems thin, reduce it over high heat until syrupy. Pour the sauce over the steaks and serve.

Recommended wine—The nature of the occasion, even the time of day, sometimes can determine which wine is indicated for a particular dish. If I were serving this steak for lunch, I'd choose an up-front, full wine like Merlot. At dinner, however, I'd want a good Brunello for a more laid-back, longer experience.

SUINO E SALUMERIA
(PORK, HAM, AND SAUSAGES)

◆

INTERLUDE — "COMING BEAUTIFUL"

Although a relative handful of Italian restaurants in the United States cure their own pork products, only an infinitesimal fraction of those that do so cured their own prosciutto until recently. Felidia was one, and, to the best of my knowledge, the only one whose in-house *salumiere* was born and trained in the very heart of Italy's most celebrated prosciutto-producing province. This account of the procedure originally appeared early in 1985 in *Gourmet* magazine.   —J.J.

Although prosciutto is cured elsewhere in Italy, the cured hams of the province of Parma—and more specifically the town of Langhirano—are by far the most highly esteemed that Italy, and arguably the world, produces. As the late Waverley Root noted in *The Food of Italy,* "The ingredient which gives Parma ham its particular quality is not readily duplicable elsewhere—the air. The town of Langhirano, south of [the city of] Parma, has proved to have the ideal atmosphere for the curing of these hams. Nobody has ever been able to work out exactly what conditions are best for ham, but empirical observation has located Langhirano as the place where they exist."

Of the nearly 6.5 million Parma hams produced in 1982 (the last year for which I have statistical data), 20 percent was exported—primarily to France, Germany, Belgium, Switzerland, and Great Britain—and the remainder accounted for 53 percent of all the ham consumed that year throughout Italy. None was, or legally can be, exported to the United States.

Until such time as this country permits importation of Parma hams, (an eventuality considered imminent around Langhirano, where the complexities of American bu-

reaucracy are perhaps less fully understood than is the curing of prosciutto), the nearest approximation to the genuine article likely to be found at this side of the Atlantic is served at Felidia Ristorante.

The prosciutto served at Felidia is cured exclusively for the restaurant's use by Dante Laurenti, one of the duplex establishment's two maîtres d'hôtel, the other being his brother Nino. It is easily the finest prosciutto I've ever eaten in this country, and it is cured in the central Long Island community of Ronkonkoma, where both Dante and Nino own small leisure-time bungalows and where the quality of the air, according to Dante, is not too dissimilar from that of the air around Langhirano. On its face this assertion seems unlikely; the topography around Langhirano is hilly and the climate, soft but relatively dry, whereas central Long Island is pancake-flat, lapped by the sea, and often fog-shrouded. Nonetheless, a taste of Ronkonkoma prosciutto lends considerable credence to Dante's assessment. So do the circumstances of his birth and upbringing.

To quote Waverley Root once more, "Langhirano's whole existence is based on the care and curing of hams, which are sent here for finishing from all over the province of Parma, and even from Lombardy [even, in fact, from outside Italy]. During the dry season . . . private homes are pressed into service. In every room of every house, even the bedrooms, hams hang thickly, suspended from the ceilings three or four layers deep. The inhabitants sleep beneath a ceiling of ham and breathe a ham-flavored atmosphere. What Langhirano cannot accommodate goes as overflow to neighboring villages. . . ."

Root's description was published in 1971 and may not apply to today's rigorously monitored Parma ham industry but accurately reflects the situation that obtained during Dante Laurenti's infancy and formative years. He was born fifty-six years ago in the town of Berceto, twenty-five miles from Langhirano, and grew up among people whose understanding of ham seems more a product of genetics than learning—people who absorb all there is to know about the care and treatment of prosciutto as naturally and with as little effort as they breathe the ham-perfumed air of Langhirano and its environs. When he waxes lyrical about the air of Ronkonkoma, he knows whereof he speaks.

As is my wont, I was blissfully absorbing a dry Martini at Felidia one evening the summer before last when Dante joined me at the bar to confide that he intended to step up his prosciutto production for the following year. He'd be happy, he added, to have me observe the process from start to finish, a process that would occupy nine or ten months, depending on variables that then could not be foreseen. I accepted his invitation at once.

By a happy coincidence an organization called Gruppo Ristoratori Italiani was scheduled to hold its 1984 convention in Parma, and I had been invited to travel there with the American contingent as one of several press observers. The Gruppo, an association of Italian and Italian-American restauraateurs devoted to the furtherance of Italian cuisine on both sides of the Atlantic, also had scheduled tours of a couple of the largest of the 250-odd factories devoted to the production of Parma ham. Thus I'd be able to compare curing techniques in their region of origin and as Dante adapts them to American hams on Long Island.

As is the case with such appellations as Champagne, Cognac, Chianti, and the like, use of the term "Parma ham" is subject to strict control. By Italian law any hams so designated must come from absolutely healthy adult swine, "excluding boars and sows," weighing at least 150 kilograms. (Unless boned after curing, a finished Parma ham must weigh at least seven kilograms, which is to say about fifteen pounds.) To

D'Osvaldo Lorenzo curing prosciutto in Gorizia. The region is famed throughout Italy for its air-cured San Daniele hams.

bear the identifying brand of the genuine article (a five-pointed ducal crown stamped into the rind), the ham must come from a pig raised either in Emilia-Romagna, Lombardy, Veneto, or Piedmont. (Hams from elsewhere may be cured in the province of Parma but not marketed as Parma hams.) Additionally, each pig must have been nourished on a high-protein diet (in most cases made up in large part of the whey left over from the manufacture of Parmigiano), subjected to several inspections for fitness during its lifetime (a little less than a year), slaughtered in "excellent sanitary conditions," and "perfectly bled."

Prior to the onset of the actual curing process the ham cannot be subjected to "any treatment of conservation" other than chilling. The curing process itself must take place within a strictly delimited geographical zone of no great size: an area situated slightly south of the city of Parma, bounded on the east by the River Enza, on the west by the Torrente Stirone, and on the south by the communes of Tizzano and Traversitolo—an area of some four hundred square kilometers.

Despite the foregoing and additional controls, specifications, definitions, and regulations too numerous to mention, the curing of prosciutto remains as much an art as a science, as Italian law makes abundantly clear. In a valiant but ultimately futile effort to standardize a product that, after all, derives from human manipulation of, and variable climatic effects on, the individualized hindquarters of a pig, the legal regulations governing the production of Parma ham resort to a lot of anatomical argle-bargle (". . . limitations to the bare muscular part beyond the head of the femur . . . at a distance of not more than 2 cm"), only to reach the somewhat subjective conclusion that the proper finished ham is "rounded like the leg of a chicken." In its opening paragraph, Law No. 506, enacted in 1970, decrees that "the denomination 'Parma ham' is reserved ex-clusively to ham having characteristic qualities related to its geographical situation—comprehensive of . . . natural and human factors . . ." This is a bit like decreeing a sculpture by Donatello to have qualities characteristic of the zeitgeist of fifteenth-century Florence, comprehensive of its author's personality.

Dante Laurenti originally had planned to begin curing the restaurant's prosciutto in early December for use in the latter part of the following year. The procedure was deferred for several weeks, however, in accordance with variable natural and human factors. Night after night I'd drop into the restaurant in a state of high expectation, only to be told that conditions weren't yet right, that the weather was too warm, and that Dante did not yet sense that the propitious moment was at hand. "The air doesn't feel right yet," he'd say. "In New York it comes later than Parma. Especially this year." He telephoned me at last on January 6 to announce that forty hams would be delivered to the restaurant the following morning and that the actual curing process would begin in Ronkonkoma two days later.

As delivered to a prosciutto factory in Parma—or to the only New York restaurant I'm aware of that cures its own Parma-style prosciutto—a fresh ham is a bit more than what is sold as such in the average American supermarket. It is the entire hind leg of the pig, from the trotter to the upper knob of the femur. The forty hams delivered to the restaurant on the appointed day weighed between twenty and twenty-five pounds each and had been handpicked by Dante, both as insurance of generally high quality and as a precaution against delivery of any lacerated specimens. "The skin cannot be broken the least bit," said Dante. "Not even scratched."

Forty hardly would be a significant number of hams in the Province of Parma, where they are rushed from the slaughterers to the factories by the thousands in immaculate refrigerated trucks the size of cross-country moving vans. In the restaurant's narrow basement prep kitchen, though, forty hams looked like all the hams in the world—some nine hundred pounds of meat, fat, rind, and bone. When I got there, six or eight pork legs lay on the steel-topped counter where the restaurant's fresh pastas and pastries usually are prepared. The remainder had been hung in a commodious walk-in refrigerator, filling it to capacity.

On the morning in question, Lidia had taken a station alongside Dante, determined to master the art of trimming incipient Parma-style hams under the tutelage of a master. Although he was in no position to object to an arrangement orchestrated by his boss, Dante was clearly less than sanguine about the prospect of having this near-Yugoslav fooling around with the sacred mysteries of his birthright. Although Lidia seemed to my untutored eye to be doing a creditable job as the morning progressed, Dante visibly quailed from time to time as his employer hacked away amain at her consignment of hams.

Although the restaurant's production of finished prosciutto is minuscule compared with that of the smallest Parma ham factories, the techniques whereby Dante and the commercial producers in his native region convert raw pork to cured table ham are precisely the same. Except for the final stages of the preparation of *boned* Parma hams (when the work is facilitated to some degree by mechanical aids and press molds), the process is manual from start to finish and decidedly sculptural in the early stages. And, whereas the casual onlooker might conclude that a single leg of swine is no different from any other, the born prosciuttist, knowing better, quickly but thoroughly sizes up each before setting to work on it, like a Michelangelo divining the hidden form within a rough block of marble.

Unlike its Spanish counterpart, the vaunted *jamón serrano* (mountain ham), a Parma ham does not include the animal's foot. After a brief inspection of the first of the hams, Dante lightly grasped the foot like a pet's paw and wiggled it gently to determine the precise location of the joint beneath the skin. He then made an incision just below the knuckle, wrenched the foot loose from the shank, and cut it free. When I remarked that he might have saved himself the trouble by having his purveyor perform the operation, Dante replied, "Oh, no. No way. I have to cut it my way. These butchers, they know nothing about prosciutto. Let them do it, and you have a wasted ham—a dangerous ham. It must be cut so that it can be sealed completely."

Having subjected the late pig to this drastic pedicure, Dante positioned the haunch so that it lay on the work counter with its inner side upward and its butt end facing him. Probing with his fingers, he located the aitchbone beneath the meat and severed it about halfway along its short length with a sharply angled stroke of his cleaver, bringing the forward point of the blade into play. Working beside him, Lidia followed suit, as a manifestly spooked Dante shot her an alarmed sidelong glance. Apparently she did no irreparable harm to the prosciutto, for the tense hunch of Dante's shoulders relaxed momentarily.

Dante next cut away a considerable portion of the exposed surface of the buttock, tossing the excised hunk of meat into a plastic tray ("for cotechino, zampone, and sausage"), and extracted the socket end of the riven aitchbone, thereby completely exposing the knob of the femur. Trimming and smoothing the meat beside the thighbone, he explained that there must be no opening left on the surface of the meat if the ham is to cure properly, with no infiltration by unwanted organisms. Then, working with a larger knife, he pared away a thick strip of rind-edged fat, beveling off the ham to produce the chicken-leg configuration decreed by ancient custom and, more recently, Italian law. Finally, he located the femoral artery deep beneath the skin and muscle and forced out the residual blood.

Working easily but steadily, Dante and Lidia gave rough shape to all forty hams during the course of the morning, punctuating their activity with occasional bits of byplay. Satisfied, as the morning wore on, that his boss was an uncommonly adept apprentice, Dante reverted to his habitual geniality and worked away in good humor until Lidia suggested with mock seriousness that I get myself an apron and join in the fun. I may have saved him a stroke by declining the invitation.

In relays of a half-dozen-or-so at a time, Dante had transferred the roughed-out hams to the walk-in box, replacing each relay on the work counter with an equal number of whole untreated legs. Tying a short, looped length of stout twine around the knuckle end, he hung each prosciutto butt-end down in the refrigerator, where it would rest for forty-eight hours at a temperature set at about 55 degrees Fahrenheit. "You could hang it in a cellar without refrigeration," he explained, "but the temperature would have to be between fifty and sixty degrees." Anything colder, he said, would inhibit the exudation of unwanted fluids, and anything warmer would tend to induce spoilage.

Late in the morning of the third day I arrived at the restaurant in time to help Dante load his station wagon with the forty hams. The weather was brisk, and the car windows were kept open during the two-hour drive to Ronkonkoma. Two by two the hams were unloaded and carried down into Dante's cellar, which already looked like a well-stocked *salumeria* with homemade coppa, culatello, and cotechino hanging from low rafters. Dante sniffed the pork-redolent air, felt a few of the hanging meats, and proclaimed himself satisfied with the condition of the atmosphere. "Just right," he crowed. "They're coming beautiful. The air

from the lake [Lake Ronkonkoma] is just like the river air around Langhirano."

According to the usually reliable Waverley Root, who obviously never observed the prosciutto-curing process firsthand and garbled some third party's description of it, Parma hams are boned before curing. Root's assertion seemed manifestly absurd to me, but I asked Dante whether such was ever the case. "Never," he replied. "It cannot be. To bone the prosciutto, you have to cut it open, and to open a prosciutto before curing is to destroy it. Later in the year, when these hams are ready for eating, I'll bone some of them but only just before using them." (The boning of prosciutto is merely a convenience for those shop owners and restaurateurs who machine-slice their hams. Purists insist that prosciutto is best when the bone is left in and the meat is sliced by hand. Regrettably, hand-slicing prosciutto is on its way to becoming a lost art these days, and the waiter-captain who can extract long, uniformly paper-thin slices from a cradle-mounted ham belongs to a vanishing breed. A couple of years ago when Dante heard that I was planning a New Year's Eve buffet, he generously presented me with a prosciutto, which one of my guests insisted on slicing. Because the volunteer happened to be a surgeon, I entrusted the knife to him. Heaven help his patients.)

As a preliminary to the actual curing process, Dante gave each of the forty hams a brief but thorough massage to condition the meat and to smooth wrinkles from the rind. "When you massage the [exposed] meat, you rub a little salt into it," he said, suiting the action to the word. As he worked, he told me that he had emigrated from Parma twenty-two years earlier, had purchased his Ronkonkoma bungalow about three years thereafter, and had investigated the potential of his cellar almost as soon as he owned it. "I tried making prosciutto the first couple of years I had the house," he said, "and I see it's coming very good." He has made prosciutto every year since and says it has been consistently good, year in and year out.

Although any inhabitant of his native region acquires prosciutto expertise merely by virtue of being born there, Dante augmented his inheritance by studying informally with "a prosciutto company man in Langhirano." "I became the family prosciutto maker," he added, "and we had a big family with lots of relatives. Some of them would kill a pig every year, or two pigs, or four, and I'd cure about a hundred hams every year."

Having given a vigorous rubdown to each of the forty hams, Dante prepared the actual curing mixture: sea salt blended with fractional quantities of whole and crushed peppercorns, sugar, and saltpeter. In its promotional literature the Consorzio del Prosciutto di Parma (an—or rather, the—association of commercial producers monitored by the Italian ministries of Health, Agriculture, and Forestry, among others) omits mention of pepper, sugar, and saltpeter. Dante insists that all three ingredients have figured in the authentic formula for centuries and are used by all the commercial producers in Parma today. (The origins of today's Parma ham, incidentally, have not been traced with any precision; Hannibal is known to have eaten salt-cured ham of some sort in the city of Parma, after drubbing the Romans at the Trebbia River in 218 B.C., but whether that ham was dry-cured or corned, nobody knows.)

Because it seemed unlikely that I or any readers of this article would attempt to cure forty hams for home use, I asked Dante to quantify the curing mixture for a single leg of pork. "For one prosciutto," he said, "you would mix a pound of salt with a tablespoon each of whole and crushed black peppercorns, a tablespoon of sugar, and, to make the color come beautiful, half a teaspoon of saltpeter." When the color of a whole pro-

sciutto "comes beautiful," the meat is much darker than it appears when served in translucently thin slices. The effect of this translucence is markedly diluent and roughly comparable to an artist's extraction of a thin watercolor wash from a block of solid pigment. What shows up on a white plate as a pale-rose or salmon-pink substance is sliced from flesh nearly the color of oxblood.

After preparing the salt mixture (which he measured out by eye and heft) Dante began to apply it to the hams. "You have to rub it into the [exposed] meat," he explained as he worked. "Sort of pat it in. All of the open [exposed] parts must be covered, and when the ham is salted it must rest with the meat side up." As he salted each ham he positioned it on a sturdy, sawhorse-supported wooden rack: a duckboardlike arrangement of spaced one-by-two slats on a two-by-four frame. "The knuckle end has to be a little lower than the butt end," he explained, "and the air has to circulate all around the prosciutto. The air is nice and dry today, but when it's very humid the salt can melt. If that happens, you have to salt the hams all over again. I'll keep the hams like this for twenty-five to forty days, depending on how the weather comes. If the weather comes dry, twenty-five, thirty days at fifty to sixty degrees [Fahrenheit]. If it comes wet, thirty-five or forty days." Dante's cellar is equipped with a dehumidifier for emergency use during overly damp spells, and the air temperature is thermostatically controlled—two conveniences that were neither known nor needed when he was growing up in Berceto.

Dante, his brother Nino, and I returned to Ronkonkoma a week later to check the progress of the forty hams. It was a clear, bright day, and there was a thin crust of snow on Dante's lawn when we got to the bungalow. In the cellar (accessible via an old-fashioned trapdoor behind the house) I could detect a hint of heightened fragrance in the air—the first faint promise of the

unique bouquet of mature Parma-style prosciutto. Or so I convinced myself. Dante
inspected the hams and beamed. (A ruddy,
rather fleshy, handsome man, he beams in-
candescently.) "They're coming beautiful,"
he said.

"Beautiful," echoed Nino. "Beautiful."

Dante blended a small batch of the curing
mixture and applied it here and there, where
patches of salt had dissolved and dripped
from the surfaces of the hams. As we prepared to leave, I glanced back from the top
of the cellar stairs just before Dante doused
the lights. The forty hams made an oddly
affecting sight as they slumbered through
the beginning of a new life.

During the drive back to Manhattan Nino
and Dante talked mostly of prosciutto. They
would return to Ronkonkoma once a week
for the next three or four weeks, depending
on the weather, to turn the hams on the
salting rack. Then, Dante explained, when
the initial stage of curing was finished, the
hams would be hung butt-end downward.
Gradually the caked salt would drip away
and a coating of mold—a desideratum—
would form during the next ten to twelve
weeks. After hanging another month the
hams would be cleansed of the mold with a
stiff brush and cold running water. Then
they would be taken outdoors, suspended
in a shady spot, and given a day-long airing.
"They must hang in the shade," Dante cau-
tioned. In the evening they'd be returned
to the cellar to hang for another two weeks,
during which time a second coating of mold
probably would form. Again they'd be
washed, aired outdoors on the first fine, dry
day, and left hanging in the cellar for another
month. Under optimal climatic conditions,
the hams would be ready for "sealing"
around mid-April—just about the time I was
scheduled to return from my trip to Parma.

Primavera had come to Emilia-Romagna
a good deal earlier than last year's spring
was to make itself manifest in New York.
The drive from Milan to the city of Parma,
mostly through farmland, was about as po-
etic as a bus ride is likely to be. The terrain
was blanketed with fresh, tender growth of
startling verdancy; the trees in the middle
distance, almost girlish in new leaf, seemed
to pirouette across a carpet of green velvet
as we whizzed past them, and the sunlight
appeared to have been pressed from Trebbiano grapes. Before the week was out I'd
have it to the ears with prosciutto, parmigiano, and tortellini, but our first meal in
Parma, built around these three local ubiq-
uities, amounted to an ingestion of a regional
ethos, and was splendid. After several years
of steady exposure to commercially produced American prosciutto (much of it
quick-processed by methods that would be
deemed hanging offenses in Italy, and much
of it egregiously misrepresented as "*jambon
de Parme*" on French restaurant menus),
the veritable Parma ham, in particular, absolutely sang.

From time immemorial in Europe, pigs and
other domestic meat animals traditionally
were slaughtered in early November for
want of winter fodder. Fresh pork was eaten
at Martinmas (November 11), and what
wasn't consumed then was preserved one
way or another for use during the lean
months to come. As is the case with most
food nowadays, however, Parma ham is no
longer subject to seasonal dictates. When
the representatives of the Gruppo Ristoratori Italiani and their guests arrived at the
G. Tanara prosciutto factory in Langhirano,
it was precisely five months and a day after
Martinmas. Tons of freshly slaughtered
pork legs were being transferred from refrigerated trucks to the factory's loading
dock.

Because both commercial pork and
Parma ham production are no longer gov-
erned by the cycle of the seasons and the
curing process now can be initiated on a
year-round basis, a visit to a prosciutto factory may occupy only an hour or two but

amounts in effect to the better part of a year's work. From fresh meat to finished packaged product, the hams can be observed at every stage of their development—an experience comparable to viewing a time-lapse film in which a natural cycle of some months' duration unfolds in a matter of minutes. Reversing the analogy, ten months or so of observation at Ronkonkoma would amount to a two-hour tour of a Langhirano factory filmed in excruciatingly slow motion. In both cases, however, the process itself would be exactly the same in all its essentials. As a later visit to the Fini factory would reveal, all manner of other regional specialties can be entrusted to machines and produced with bewildering speed (an automated tortellini-maker, for example, eerily replicates the action of the human fingers while twisting thousands of pasta dumplings per minute), but any prosciutto worth the name remains a product of the human hand from start to finish and must mature in its own good time.

The United States Department of Agriculture might be a good deal less leery of the importation of Parma hams were a few of its inspectors packed off on a tour of the factories around Langhirano. As is the case with the other establishments I visited, a near-fanatical concern for antisepsis prevails at the immaculate Tanara plant. Moreover, a surprisingly large number of incoming hams are culled out on delivery and consigned to the sausage and salami makers, although they have been periodically inspected from birth to slaughter at the sources of supply and arrive bearing government attestations to their fitness. (According to both spokesmen for the Parma ham industry and disinterested authorities, even in the highly unlikely event that a less than pristine leg of pork somehow should pass muster, further built-in safeguards ensure that no potentially harmful ham can find its way to anyone's table. As they contend, citing "twenty centuries of steady safety,"

the long curing process itself destroys any and all pathogens that might be resident in the ham. Furthermore, they maintain, any ham suffering from any sort of internal damage that might elude notice during early inspections will not cure evenly and not pass inspection during the later stages of the curing process. As a final precaution, however, hams are inspected not only superficially at maturity, but internally, by means of a needlelike probe that extracts minuscule samples from deep within the prosciutto.)

Waverley Root did not exaggerate when he noted that "Langhirano's whole existence is based on the care and curing of hams," but he hardly could have foreseen that Parma ham production would quadruple during the decade following publication of his book or that some thirty-five hundred workers in and around Langhirano would be producing seven billion lire worth of hams annually by the early 1980s. Impressive as these statistics sounded to a guy accustomed to dealing with prosciutto four ounces at a time, their full impact didn't begin to get home to me until I found myself wandering through rooms almost the size of football fields, all closely hung, ceiling-almost-to-floor, with tier upon tier of curing prosciutto.

The Tanara factory is hog heaven in more ways than one, but, although it ranks among the larger prosciutto processors, its output represents a mere fraction of the region's total production. To me it seemed to house far more hams than the world's entire ham-eating population conceivably could consume. Hams hung by the thousands—in some cases, the tens of thousands—in vast refrigerated rooms, in nonrefrigerated but temperature-controlled rooms, and outdoors on the roof in the sweet, light Langhirano air. Hams were being salted by the hundreds here, scrubbed of their mold there. In one airy, light-flooded room, workers massaged hams. In another, hams were being given a final "manicure" (a purely cosmetic touch-up preparatory to packaging). Hams were being sealed here, stamped with the ducal crown of authenticity there, inspected in various locations at various stages of development, boned, packaged, press-molded, paddled, given their first trimming prior to the initial salting. Of all these operations, only three of any significance—application of the ducal crown, molding after boning, and packaging—would be omitted by Dante in Ronkonkoma.

Eighty percent of the factory's hams are boned before distribution. The boning itself is a hand operation but is accomplished with the negligible aid of a mechanical contrivance that bends ham away from bone as one worker, plying a long-bladed knife shaped like a woodworker's gouge, cuts upward around the femur and dislodges a bone virtually clean of meat. The ham then is slung across a workbench to be folded shut and laced up along its edges by machine—an operation from which it emerges looking like an oversized first baseman's mitt with the thumb closed over the pocket. Finally the ham is compressed in a metal mold, to force all fissures tightly shut as a safeguard against bacterial invasion, and packaged for shipment.

The fresh hams delivered to the prosciutto factories are, of course, roughly circular in lateral cross section. A fully cured Parma ham, on the other hand, is much flatter and yields an oblong shape in cross section. The flattening is accomplished naturally as the ham dries and loses weight during the curing process. As Tanara executives shepherded their guests through the various factory operations, they explained that the average ham undergoes a four percent weight loss during the initial, twenty-five-day-long salting and loses an additional nine percent of its weight during the next forty-five days. Another ten percent is lost during the remainder of the ham's stay at the factory, and a finished prosciutto is twenty-three percent lighter than it was as it underwent the initial salting.

As our guides went on to explain, a Parma ham absorbs about six percent of the salt used in curing it, and the trick is to use as little salt as possible, a procedure greatly facilitated by the quality of the Langhirano air. Aside from its fine, silky texture, distinctive tenderness, "sparkling" character, and the appealing color of both its rosy meat and snowy fat, we were told, the distinguishing characteristic of Parma ham is its unusually mild, relatively salt-free flavor. Half-facetiously, I asked whether either of a given pig's two hams was considered preferable to the other. "Oh, yes," was the solemn reply. "The right side is better than the left."

"How's the prosciutto?" I asked Dante on my return to New York. "It's coming beautiful," he replied, "beautiful. I'll seal them in a few days now." We drove out to Ronkonkoma a few days later. The early greening shrubs and trees, forsythia and weeping willows, were just taking on a vague aura of color and the air was perfumed with the earthy aroma of burgeoning new growth.

Externally, at least, all forty hams certainly were "coming beautiful." Like hams in a comparable state of maturation at Langhirano, they had taken on the deep mellow burnish of well-cared-for-leather and had flattened to the characteristic shape of the finished product. "How do they look?" asked Dante, knowing far better than I how they looked. I replied that they looked good enough to eat, then and there. "You know," he said, "when I started to make prosciutto in this country, I was surprised to see it coming this good. After all these years I'm still surprised how beautiful it comes every time. I've made prosciutto here in this cellar every year for the past eighteen years and never had a problem.

"These commercial companies in America could make beautiful prosciutto, but they take too many shortcuts. They inject the hams with sal ammoniac [sodium chloride] or cure them in tanks. They wet the hams—cook them with salt—instead of curing them naturally in good air. This air here in Ronkonkoma is beautiful, like in Langhirano, but there must be other places all over the country where the air is just as good."

All this smacked just a bit of heresy to me. I asked whether Dante really found the air around Ronkonkoma equal to the vaunted air of Langhirano. "Well, it's not exactly the same," he conceded. "Even the air in other parts of Parma isn't exactly the same. The air here is not the same every day, like in Langhirano, but it's close enough for prosciutto to come beautiful if you make little adjustments." He prepared to begin the sealing process. It was, he explained, a final precaution against formation of *mosca di prosciutto* (literally but inaccurately, "ham-fly"), a bacterium that can thrive in Parma-style hams unless they are air-impermeable during the last five months or so of the curing process.

After giving the hams a final washing and drying them thoroughly, Dante took a knife and scraped them free of whatever mold had formed on the fatty portions and on all discolored meat around the knob of the femur. Then, to my surprise, he kneaded these substances together and packed them in tight around the salient knob of bone. Next, he prepared the sealent: "For one ham," he said, "you'd use a teaspoon each of chilled rendered fresh pork fat, flour, salt, and pepper and two teaspoons of water." He smeared the thick paste liberally over all the exposed meat, and we carried the hams outdoors to hang in the shade. "We'll leave them out there about two and a half hours," Dante said. "Then we'll hang them back in the cellar and just let them rest until they're ready to eat. When the weather comes warmer, I'll set the temperature between fifty and sixty degrees. Otherwise there's nothing to do except clean the hams before using them."

From time to time as the months went by, I'd ask Dante how the hams were progressing, mainly because I derived childish enjoyment from his invariable, beaming response. "They're coming beautiful," he'd say each time, "beautiful." I passed the summer like an expectant father awaiting the arrival of his firstborn, trying somehow to will the long dog days away, insanely preoccupied with pigs' rear ends, salivating in anticipation of the first prosciutto of the season. Spring and early summer had been rainy—a circumstance I equated with disaster—but Dante had assured me that his dehumidifier had the situation under control. Still I fretted.

Early in September I was absorbing another flawless Martini at the restaurant when Dante appeared at the bar and invited me to join him in the kitchen. The first prosciutto of the season lay on a work counter. Beside it lay one of the channel-bladed boning knives I had seen in Parma. (Lidia, who had attended the Italian restaurateurs' convention there, had brought a couple of the knives back to New York as gifts for Dante.) Using a conventional boning knife, the *maestro del prosciutto* made a deep lengthwise incision in the ham parallel to the femur. Then, using the more specialized of the knives, he worked it in close along the edge of the bone and deftly excised the latter (which would be saved for use later in the year, when Lidia prepares *jota* [*yota*], the traditional cold-weather bean-and-cabbage soup of her native region). After allowing me a close, heady whiff of the ham's freshly released bouquet, Dante shut the prosciutto like a book and tied it as though it were a rolled roast. Because it would be consumed in short order, there was no need to lace and press it in the commercial manner.

I returned to the bar. A few minutes later Dante placed a plate of sliced prosciutto before me, along with homemade bread and a crock of butter. In a ridiculously emotional turmoil I first regarded, then sniffed, and

Aragosta in Brodetto
Lobster Stew

Gnocchi di Susine

Plum Gnocchi

Gnocchi di Zucca
Butternut Squash Gnocchi
120

Top: *Polenta*

129

Bottom: *Quaglie in Squazet*

Quail *in Squazet*

211

finally tasted the ham. Images of the soft, sweet Parma countryside floated before me as I drank in the winy air of Langhirano on East Fifty-eighth Street in Manhattan. "Well," said Dante, "what do you think?"

"Dante," I replied, "it has come beautiful."

It really had.

Postscript: The ban on importation of Parma hams finally was lifted in the fall of 1989, five years after the foregoing piece originally appeared. Genuine prosciutto di Parma now is available regularly at Felidia, other fine restaurants, and fancy food shops, but Dante Laurenti continues to cure a quantity of hams at Ronkonkoma, for the delectation of his fortunate kinfolk and friends, and continues to function as the restaurant's resident *salumiere*. As an act of faith, I defer to his assessment of the genuine article, which he finds superior to his own. Allowing for the inherent differences between the whey-fed raw materials as received in Langhirano and their corn-fed counterparts of Midwestern American provenance, both finished products seem equally virtuosic to me. The difference between both and any prosciutto of domestic commercial production that I've tasted, however, are immeasurable. Dante's recipes for prosciutto and several varieties of sausage follow.

Curing Prosciutto

In this country, the process of curing ham in the Parma manner may be initiated at any time between mid-September and mid-January, depending on the regional onset of cooler weather. The procedure should begin as soon as temperatures between 45° and 60° F. can be sustained for several months, preferably without mechanical control and ideally in the neighborhood of a natural body of water. The step-by-step procedure follows.

1. Select a whole fresh hind leg of pork, 20–25 pounds, with absolutely unbroken skin.

2. Bend the foot to determine the exact location of the joint. Make an incision completely around the joint just below the base of the knuckle, twist the foot loose, and cut it free.

3. Position the leg with the inner thigh facing upward and feel beneath the butt end for the aitchbone, which forms a right angle with the femur, or thigh bone. Split the aitchbone halfway along its length with a cleaver or chisel and cut out the part nearest the knob of the femur.

4. Working from the inner part of the thigh downward, trim away and reserve for other uses enough meat and fat (about 2 pounds) from the butt end to produce a smooth, rounded, somewhat beveled shape, with both the knob of the femur and the remainder of the aitchbone exposed.

5. Working the thumbs upward from the base of the leg along the inner side of the femur, press along the length of the femoral artery, squeezing out any residual blood.

6. Hang the ham, butt-end downward, for 48 hours at 45°–60° F.

7. Blend 1 pound sea salt, 1 tablespoon sugar, 1 tablespoon each crushed and whole peppercorns, and ½ teaspoon saltpeter.

8. Using approximately a cupped handful of the salt mixture, massage the entire pork leg thoroughly and vigorously, allowing all exposed flesh to absorb the salt mixture.

9. On a rack that allows free circulation of the air, position the ham with the inner thigh uppermost and the knuckle slightly lower than the butt end.

10. Cover the exposed fleshy portions of the ham with the remainder of the salt mixture and allow the ham to remain on the rack 25–30 days (35–40 in humid weather) at 45°–60° F., reapplying the salt mixture in the original proportions wherever parts of the original application melt away.

11. Turn the ham horizontally on the rack once a week for the next 3 weeks (4 weeks in humid weather), then hang it as is, butt-end downward, for 14–16 weeks, or until a coating of mold has formed.

12. On the morning of the first sunny day thereafter, with a stiff brush and cold running water, remove the mold that has formed on the ham and hang the ham outdoors in a shady spot during the daylight hours.

13. In the evening, rehang the ham indoors and, after 2 weeks, repeat the washing and outdoor airing procedures.

14. Allow the ham to hang indoors another 3 weeks, then wash it thoroughly under cold running water and dry it. With a small knife, scrape off all mold and any meat that may have discolored around the knob of the femur. Knead the scrapings to form a pastelike substance and pack it in tightly around the knob of the femur and the space between the femur and the remainder of the aitchbone.

15. Blend together a teaspoon each of chilled rendered fresh pork fat, flour, salt, and pepper, and 2 teaspoons water. Using a soft brush, paint the mixture over all exposed meat surfaces, "sealing" the ham.

16. Hang the sealed ham outdoors in the shade for 2½ hours, and then rehang it indoors at 50°–60° F. for 12–16 weeks or longer, until ready for use. In all, the ham should cure for at least 8 months, preferably 10.

Cotechino

YIELDS 8 POUNDS

There's no equivalent in English for the term cotechino, which derives from the *cotenna,* or skin, that gives this hefty sausage its distinctive texture and succulence. The Friulani, who cure their pork products much as the Modenese do, call their version of this Modenese specialty *musetto,* or "snout." Our in-house *salumiere,* Dante, who was born in Parma not far from Modena, inherited his mastery of the pork butcher's art from his father and grandfather. This is his recipe, and should be followed closely because it's important to use the proportions he specifies for skin, fat, and lean pork butt: 1:1:2, respectively. The best *cotenna* and fat is from the head of the hog. A small head of about six pounds should provide enough of both. Because cotechino keeps well (two weeks in the refrigerator or up to two months frozen), there's no point in making smaller quantities than this.

½ cup dry white wine

4 cloves garlic, minced

7 bay leaves

¼ teaspoon allspice

4 pounds lean pork butt

2 pounds pork skin (cotenna)

2 pounds face and butt fat

4 tablespoons salt

½ tablespoon freshly ground pepper

½ tablespoon whole peppercorns

½ teaspoon saltpeter (optional, see Note)

Sausage casing, 2" diameter

In a small bowl, mix the wine, garlic, bay leaves, and allspice, and allow the butt, skin, and fat to marinate 30–45 minutes.

Cut the pork skin in strips about ½" × 7" and feed it through a meat grinder fitted with ⅛" openings. Cut the fats into pieces and grind at a ³⁄₁₆" setting. Cut the lean butt in pieces and grind at ½" or have the butcher do the grinding.)

In a large bowl, mix the ground meats with your hands (or use a mixer dough hook), adding the salt, ground pepper, whole peppercorns, and the saltpeter, if desired, and distributing them evenly.

Strain the wine marinade over the meat and mix thoroughly. Cover and refrigerate overnight.

Wash the sausage casing well, pat dry, and stuff with meat mixture, tying off sausages every 6" or 7" and leaving 1" unfilled casing between them. Continue until all the meat has been used. Hang the cotechino overnight in a cold place (50°–55° F.), exposing all sides to the air, then refrigerate until ready to use.

Note: Saltpeter (potassium nitrate) is regarded by some as potentially harmful, although it has been used in the curing of meats for centuries with no reliably documented ill effects. Its use, as a preservative of color, is purely cosmetic, and its omission won't otherwise affect your cotechino.

Set the cotechino in lightly salted cold water with 6 bay leaves. Bring to a boil, reduce to a simmer, and cook 1 hour. Remove and drain the cotechino, slice it ½″ thick, and, after removing the casing, serve with good mustard and *mostarda di Cremona* (available at Italian groceries and specialty food shops). The best accompaniment for cotechino is lentils.

Recommended wine—In Reggio Emilia, Lambrusco would be the wine to drink with cotechino, but I also enjoy a good Montepulciano d'Abruzzo. This is a wine with complexity of flavor and plenty of palatal stimulation. It complements the cotechino's gelatinous texture.

With any of the other sausages in the following recipes, I'd drink either a fresh red from Friuli, such as Cabernet, Merlot, or Refosco, or a spunky Barbera or Nebbiolo.

Salsiccia Mantovana

Mantuan Sausage

YIELDS 5 POUNDS

The cooking of Mantova, heavily reliant on spices, tends toward sweetness. It's the cuisine of the nobility appropriated by the middle class. This sausage marries well with pasta and *broccoli di rape,* vegetable soups, and tomato sauce. It's also good just grilled and served as is.

5 pounds pork butt, fat to lean ratio 1:5	¼ teaspoon cinnamon
3 tablespoons salt	¼ teaspoon ground cloves
1 teaspoon coarsely ground pepper	½ cup dry white wine
	Sausage casing, 1" diameter

The pork should be ground at a ½" setting.

In a bowl, blend all ingredients well except the sausage casing and refrigerate overnight. Stuff the washed and dried casing, tying the sausages off at 4" intervals. Refrigerate until ready to use.

Salsiccia Trevisana
Trevisan Sausage

Y I E L D S   6   P O U N D S

Radicchio, for which Treviso is renowned, makes a fine accompaniment to this less well-known Trevisan specialty and can be grilled together with it. The vegetable's slightly bitter undertaste sets off the sweetness of the sausage wonderfully. It's also excellent with polenta (recipe page 129). *Salsiccia Trevisana* will keep for two weeks under refrigeration or if air-dried in a well-ventilated place at a fairly constant temperature in the high 30s or low 40s. It can be kept in the freezer up to two months.

6 pounds pork butt, fat to lean ratio 1:5

3 tablespoons salt

1 teaspoon ground coriander

¼ teaspoon cinnamon

1 cup dry white wine

½ teaspoon coarsely ground or crushed pepper

Sausage casing, 1″ diameter

Pork should be ground at a ½″ setting. In a large bowl, thoroughly blend all ingredients except the casing and refrigerate overnight. Stuff the washed and dried casing, tying the sausage at 4″–5″ intervals.

Luganega, or *Salsiccia al Metro*
Luganega, or Sausage by the Yard

———

YIELDS 6 POUNDS

In other times, this specialty of Lombardia and the Veneto was sold by length, rather than weight. Extremely versatile, it can be used in ragoûts and sauces, with pasta or risotto, or grilled as a breakfast sausage.

Luganega will keep up to three weeks in the refrigerator, if first air-cooled overnight, and up to two months in the freezer.

6 pounds pork butt, fat to lean ratio 1:5

1½ tablespoons salt

1 cup light basic stock (recipe page 69)

Freshly ground pepper to taste (optional)

¾ cup grated Parmigiano

½ teaspoon allspice

½ cup white wine

Sausage casing, ½" diameter

Pork should be ground at a ³⁄₁₆″ setting.

In a bowl, mix all ingredients except casing well, cover, and refrigerate overnight. Stuff the washed and dried casing, knotted at the end, either letting the sausage run in an uninterrupted coil or tying it off at 1′ intervals.

Cappucci Guarniti
Sauerkraut with Pork

SERVES 6

This dish, with its Slavic and Germanic characteristics, always was served on special occasions when I was a child. No wedding or holiday or celebration of any kind was complete without it. Even when something else was served as a main course, *cappucci guarniti* would turn up later, if people lingered into the evening. During the postwar years of my childhood, there may have been little other meat available, but every family with a little ground kept a pig or two and, after the slaughter, cured various parts for later use.

1 pound smoked pork butt, halved

1 pound kielbasa sausage

1 pound smoked pork ribs

2 tablespoons olive oil

4 pounds sauerkraut, washed twice and drained

2 cloves garlic, sliced

6 bay leaves

Salt and freshly ground pepper to taste

Before proceeding further, boil the meats 10 minutes in plenty of water and drain.

Pour the olive oil into a large straight-sided skillet, a large saucepan, or a Dutch oven. Add half the sauerkraut and strew with the garlic, bay leaves, salt and pepper. Arrange the meats over the sauerkraut, cover with the remaining sauerkraut, and add 2 cups of water. Bring to a boil, lower the heat to medium, and simmer, covered, 45 minutes, occasionally stirring from the bottom up.

With a slotted spoon, remove the kielbasa and ribs to a warm oven. Cook the remaining ingredients over medium heat 20 minutes longer, until the liquids have almost completely evaporated. Return the kielbasa and ribs to the pan, cover, and let stand 15 minutes off the heat. Slice the meats and arrange them on a serving platter, with the sauerkraut at the center.

Recommended wine—As with *sarma* (following recipe), Schioppettino by Ronchi di Cialla or Ronco dei Roseti by Abbazia di Rosazzo, although beer may be more appropriate than either with this dish.

Sarma
Istrian Stuffed Cabbage

SERVES 8

When Istria became part of Yugoslavia after the Second World War, there was a sudden influx of Slavs in my family's region. Among them was an aunt of mine from Zagreb who cooked the first stuffed cabbage I ever tasted. Stuffed cabbage, of course, is emblematic of Eastern European cookery, but this version is an Istrian adaptation.

1 large head cabbage, about 4½ pounds	2½ teaspoons salt
1 cup white wine vinegar	¾ teaspoon freshly ground pepper
2½ cups minced onion (2 large)	1 pound ground beef
7 tablespoons olive oil	1 pound ground pork
¾ cup long-grain rice	1 egg, beaten
6 cups chicken stock (recipe page 69)	1 cup bread crumbs
One 35-ounce can Italian peeled tomatoes	⅓ cup minced Italian parsley

With a paring knife, core the cabbage. Bring a large pot of water to boil, add the vinegar, and place the cabbage in the pot, weighted with a heavy heatproof plate to keep it submerged. Cook until the leaves soften, about 12 minutes, remove the cabbage, and cool under running water. Carefully remove 16 whole leaves from the cabbage, saving the remainder for other uses, and set them aside to drain on paper towels.

In a saucepan, sauté ½ cup of the onion in 3 tablespoons of the olive oil until translucent. Stir in the rice, add 1 cup of the chicken stock, and bring to a simmer. Cover and cook over low heat 7 minutes. Set aside to cool.

In a large heavy casserole (preferably enameled cast iron), sauté the remaining onion in the remaining olive oil until translucent. Crush the tomatoes and add to the casserole with all liquid from the can. Add ½ teaspoon of the salt, ¼ teaspoon of the pepper, and the remaining chicken stock, and simmer gently while you prepare the stuffing.

In a mixing bowl, combine the ground meats, egg, bread crumbs, reserved rice, parsley, and the remaining salt and pepper, mixing well. Divide the mixture into sixteen equal portions and roll each into a sausagelike cylinder about 2½ inches long.

Working with one reserved cabbage leaf at a time, place a cylinder of stuffing perpendicular to the stem. Roll the leaf around the stuffing, forming a snug fit, and tuck in both ends of the leaf to enclose the stuffing completely. Repeat with the remaining cabbage leaves and stuffing.

Arrange the cabbage rolls side by side in two layers in the casserole containing the tomato sauce and return to a simmer. Gently lift cabbage rolls from time to time to prevent them from sticking to the bottom of the pan and scorching. Reduce the heat to low and simmer gently 1½ hours. Cover partially during the last 30 minutes.

To serve, spoon the tomato sauce over the cabbage rolls.

Note: This dish benefits from an overnight rest in the refrigerator and may be gently reheated the next day.

Recommended wine—A Schioppettino by Ronchi di Cialla or Ronco dei Roseti by Abbazia di Rosazzo. Both are full-bodied, intensely flavorful wines with a good acidic backbone, which is what this complex dish requires.

6

Cacciagione e Selvaggina

Game

INTERLUDE — THE ANATOMY OF A DINNER

ABOUT SGUAZET

WINES WITH GAME DISHES

Quaglie in Sguazet

Quaglie al Mattone

Faraona in Cartoccio

Fagiano Arrosto

Piccione con Bigoli o Polenta

Anitra in Umido con Crauti

Anitra in Sguazet

Coniglio in Sguazet

Coniglio alla Salvia

Filetto di Capriolo

Capriolo in Sguazet

Cinghiale Brasato al Barolo

INTERLUDE — THE ANATOMY OF A DINNER

A few years ago, Thomas Hoving, then editor-in-chief of *Connoisseur* magazine and former director of the Metropolitan Museum of Art, proposed that a dinner prepared by Lidia and consisting entirely of wild foods be the subject of an article for his magazine. Lidia agreed to the proposal on condition that I write the piece. Hoving drew up the guest list, Lidia put together a six-course menu for *"una cena stagionale d'autunno,"* and I equipped myself with a blank notepad. What follows has been excerpted from the *Connoisseur* article, and is included here for the insights Lidia provides into her thinking as she orchestrates both individual dishes and an entire meal.

—J.J.

Except to say that the *cena stagionale* was superb from start to finish, I'll not subject the seasonal meal itself to any more adjectival effusions than are unavoidable. Black tie had been specified, and the participants assembled at a single long table in a sedate, wood-paneled private dining room on the restaurant's second floor. There were a dozen or so of us present, selected by and including Thomas Hoving, whose sworn, thumb-biting enmity I'd incurred years earlier but who turns out to be a charming guy, really, once the Berlucchi spumante (the evening's *aperitivo*) gets flowing.

The meal opened with portions of venison Carpaccio, blanketed in shavings of Piedmontese white truffle, and *insalata di coniglio:* a salad of steamed rabbit, cut in julienne strips, disposed on a bed of white chicory, garnished with raisins and walnut meats, dressed with Tuscan olive oil and Modenese balsamic vinegar. Writing of that last ingredient, one native Modenese out-Prousted Proust's *madeleine* evocations while sparing his readers Proust's stupefying prolixity by describing how the merest whiff of *aceto balsamico* enabled him to reenter the world of his childhood, ". . . a whole world, peaceful and slow-moving . . ." Just how peaceful and slow-moving is the world of balsamic vinegar was brought home to me a couple of years ago, when a prominent Modenese winegrower invited a group of dinner guests to inspect a small barn where his personal supply of the dark sludge was aging in a chronological succession of twelve oak casks. Asked when the most mature stage of the sequence would be ready for use, our host, then well into his sixties, replied, "In another thirty years."

The next two courses, served together, were truffled risotto and pappardelle with porcini—the fleshy, cepelike wild mushrooms named for their supposed resemblance to fat piglets. Redundant as the pungency of white truffles in successive courses may have been, the nearest thing to articulated criticism to be heard was a collective sigh of rapture. The two meatless offerings were succeeded by cotechino sausage. This, the handiwork of Dante Laurenti, the resident prosciuttist and general *salumiere,* had been made with duck, pork, and free-range Texas boar, and was served with *mostarda di Cremona,* the chutneylike fruit relish that impels some of its fanciers to place the violin second among Cremona's civilizing influences. The evening's *pièce de résistance* was a fillet of elk, which had been subjected to five days of juniper-sharpened marination, then had been sliced, panseared, and simmered in an intense Barololaced sauce derived from the beast's browned bones and spare parts. Dessert was a quince tart, accompanied by Malvasia delle Lipari from Stromboli. Reluctant to put an end to our revels, we all lingered on for some time, conversing animatedly, telling raunchy stories, nibbling *biscotti* as we sipped the heel taps of the Malvasia, greeting Lidia's postprandial appearance with a heartfelt round of applause.

Lidia and I later got together for the analytic postmortem she had promised me. "The courses were planned first," she said, "and the wines were matched to them. This wasn't a wine-tasting, but a dinner of wild foods, and I didn't want them to be submissive to the wines. I chose the Berlucchi spumante as the *aperitivo* for several reasons. Most Americans still think of the sweet Astis in connection with spumante, but Italy is now producing some fantastic *brut* spumantes—*dosage zero* wines, with no sugar at all. The Berlucchi is fresh, with a bit of acidity. It starts the gastric juices flowing, and the oxygen clears the taste buds.

"Cooking and eating are all memory; you recall specific experiences and sensations in general terms geared to the circumstances of the moment. Rabbits here, for example, don't eat as much grass or get as much exercise as in Europe, so you make adjustments to compensate for the difference. The chicory in the salad gave the rabbit some of the grassy flavor I remember. In Italy, there'd be pomegranate seeds in the dish, but Americans won't eat seeds and, anyway, pomegranates weren't in season, so I used raisins.

"The venison [raised and supplied by Joseph von Kerckerink, one of the dinner guests] was so fine that I wanted to serve it as simply as possible. Also, I didn't want to upstage the truffles or too closely foreshadow the elk, which was to be the crescendo of the whole orchestration. The wine for the first courses, Lacrymosa di Hirpinia, a rosé from Mastroberardino, was a compromise between the demands of the venison and the rabbit. It wouldn't stand up to the venison in more robust form but was well matched to the Carpaccio treatment and to the delicacy of the rabbit.

"For the risotto, I wanted as little complication as possible, because the rice was just a background support for the truffles; a play of one texture against another that reversed the play of the soft pappardelle against the meatier porcini. The risotto was Arborio rice, cooked with shallots, butter, and chicken consommé, and finished with grated Parmigiano and lots of fresh-ground pepper. Why pepper? Because your taste buds have a threshold of receptivity which diminishes with successive tastings. The pepper sensitizes the nerve endings, making them receptive to whatever follows. The pappardelle was homemade in the Istrian style, which is only half as eggy as most fresh Italian pastas and doesn't conflict with the unique flavor of porcini which has a heavy richness of its own. The elements of the rice and pasta dishes complement each other. The insubstantial truffle shavings need the harder, more defined texture of the rice, but the mushrooms, with more texture, need a less-defined base. I chose a '71 Lodali Barbaresco for both dishes and the next course, too, because too many wines would have created confusion. It's one of the fine vintages, with a finish like worsted [whereas] a Barolo would have been too woolly in context; a finish that brings out the truffles and the porcini, but stands up to the big flavor and density of the cotechino. White truffles, by the way, can be found in Istria. They don't compare with the Piedmont truffles we use in the restaurant and have a limited commercial market, but we ate them at home in season.

"The '77 Amarone served with the elk is a round, full-textured wine that stands up well to the dish. [My own, possibly idiosyncratic impression of the dish was that it tasted like the color purple.] It hasn't much complexity, but it's much fruitier than the others we served. I wanted that fruitiness because of the high mineral content of elk, and the wine's simplicity, so that the food could be the focus of attention. The meat was served with turnips, chestnut and carrot purees, Savoy cabbage, and lady apples—all seasonal accompaniments with climatic and geographical affinities to the elk.

"The quince tart makes use of a winter fruit that has special, nostalgic associations for me. I remember picking up green [windfall] quinces as a little girl in Istria, and putting them in dark closets, where they'd perfume our clothes while they ripened. The Malvasia delle Lipari served with the tart grows in very mineral soil under an intense sun, and has a very lovely apricot aroma that complements the unique subtle flavor and pulpy texture of the quince. With its golden color, it looks syrupy in the bottle, but it's not, because the minerals in the soil cut the sugar produced by the sun."

Lidia concluded with a question: Had everyone enjoyed the dinner? I assured her that everyone had indeed. Seeking further assurance, she asked whether it could have been improved in any way. "Only by taking the same risks in public that you take at home," I replied. An impish grin spread over her face. Among the wild foods she and Felice favor most are the mushrooms they gather on weekends in the woods and fields of Long Island and upstate New York. I had dined *chez* Bastianich on a couple of occasions, sharing a number of hauntingly aromatic dishes made with various esoteric harvests, and often had urged Lidia to put them on her restaurant menu. "I can't take those chances with my customers," she always had replied. "Only with my friends."

ABOUT SGUAZET

Sguazet, an Istrian idiom with no ready English translation, denotes a preparation, usually served with pasta or polenta, that transcends but maintains some of the characteristics of a mere sauce. *Quaglie in sguazet,* for example, one of the most popular dishes we serve at Felidia, is a way of presenting whole quail, in a sort of ragoût, on a pasta base or with polenta. The term *sguazet* applies to the whole culinary procedure, not just the saucing agent, and connotes a relatively long, gentle cooking process usually involving an onion-and-shallot base, tomato, rosemary, bay leaves, and wine, slowly reduced to their essences. This process can't be applied to quickly cooked organ meats or to the better cuts of beef, veal, or lamb, which would be wasted if subjected to the *sguazet* treatment. *Sguazet* is the essence of cooking as I knew it as a small child in Istria immediately after World War II, in a deprived time when the family cook had to make the most of what little she had to work with. Today, in altogether different circumstances, it remains the basic technique on which many of our restaurant's best-selling dishes are based.

WINES WITH GAME DISHES

Most game is intensely flavorful and requires a big round red wine to harmonize with its mineral content—a wine such as Barolo, Barbaresco, or Brunello di Montalcino. When game is paired with polenta, any such wine would be appropriate, but the neutrality of the cornmeal also admits of such lighter reds as Chianti, Cabernet, or Merlot.

Most game is more complex, chemically, than domestic meats, so pairing wines with game can be tricky. Don't look for a wine that coincides perfectly with every characteristic of a given game dish; you probably won't find one. Instead, choose a wine that complements the salient qualities of the dish and matches the mood of the occasion.

Quaglie in Sguazet
Quail *in Sguazet*

SERVES 4

Although this recipe calls for quail, we often had squab the same way at Busoler, where I have a cousin, Renato, who'd stand in the courtyard and just whistle the pigeons down. They'd land all over him, and he'd walk into the house with our dinner perched on his head and shoulders. Even the youngest squabs found in the market will be somewhat larger than commercially farmed quail, so the number of birds should be adjusted accordingly if you substitute squab. If there's a hunter in your family, wild quail or dove would, of course, be much closer to what we ate in Istria than anything to be found at your local butcher's. See "About Sguazet," page 210.

8 quail, about 7 ounces each

⅓ cup olive oil

1 large onion, diced

¼ cup chicken livers, minced

2 slices bacon, diced

3 bay leaves

1 teaspoon fresh rosemary,
or ½ teaspoon dried

4 whole cloves

Salt and freshly ground pepper to taste

4 teaspoons tomato paste

1 cup dry white wine

1½ cups chicken stock (recipe page 69)

1 recipe basic or fried polenta (page 129)

Remove any traces of viscera from the quail cavities. With the tip of a small knife, make a small slit in one thigh of each bird and tuck the end of the other leg into it. Pat the birds dry and set aside.

In a large nonreactive skillet, heat the olive oil over medium flame. Add the onion, chicken livers, bacon, bay leaves, rosemary, and cloves, and sauté about 5 minutes, until the onion is wilted. Push the mixture to the side of the pan farthest from the center of the burner.

Season the quail with salt and pepper, add them to the pan, and brown them on both sides, turning once, about 4 minutes on each side. If necessary, re-duce the heat to prevent the onion from burning.

Add the tomato paste, wine, and chicken stock, and bring to a simmer, shaking the skillet and scraping the bottom with a wooden spoon. Cook 5 minutes, turning the quail once. Remove the quail to an ovenproof platter, cover with foil, and keep warm in a low oven. Bring the contents of the skillet to a boil and cook until thick enough to coat a spoon, about 10 or 15 minutes. Pass the sauce through a very fine sieve, pressing down hard on the solids, and pour over the quail. Serve immediately on beds of basic polenta or flanked with lozenges of fried polenta.

Quaglie al Mattone
Bricked Quail

SERVES 4

Throughout Italy and western Istria, small birds traditionally were sautéed beneath the weight of a brick (*mattone*), to keep them in complete, even contact with the pan. These days a clean-bottomed heavy skillet usually is substituted for the brick. At Busoler, my brother Franco would take me hunting for quail and other small birds. We had two ways of catching them. One was to find a certain type of bush (*vench*), from which we'd cut green shoots, anoint them with *vischio,* a gluelike sap, and scatter them around a puddle where the birds came to drink. As the birds got their feet stuck to the shoots, we'd just gather them up. Our other method involved a big washboard, a long string, and a few handfuls of grain. We'd prop the board up at a slight tilt, scatter the grain on the ground under it, and stretch the string, which was attached to the top of the board, to a hiding place in the bushes. When the birds gathered to eat the grain, we'd tug the string, the washboard would fall on the birds, and my brother would run out and jump on the washboard. The washboard had a two-inch lip so the birds were not squashed. They would sometimes crawl out from the sides, but we would be waiting for them with a burlap bag.

8 quail, about 2½ pounds, eviscerated and cleaned

¾ cup plus 1 tablespoon olive oil

1 tablespoon fresh rosemary leaves

4 bay leaves

6 cloves garlic, crushed

½ teaspoon salt

¼ teaspoon pepper

2 tablespoons chopped Italian parsley

With a small sharp knife, make parallel incisions on each side of birds' spines working as close to the bone as possible, and cut out the spines. Open the birds with your fingers, loosen the breastbones with the point of the knife, taking care not to damage the meat, and pull them away from the flesh. Remove all other bones except thigh and leg bones.

In a mixing bowl, prepare a marinade by blending the ¾ cup olive oil, the rosemary, bay leaves, garlic, and salt and pepper. Dip each quail in the marinade, coating it thoroughly, and arrange the birds in a deep 6″ × 10″ roasting pan.

Pour the remaining marinade over the birds, distributing the garlic and herbs evenly, and refrigerate 4 hours. Heat the remaining 1 tablespoon olive oil in a 14″ skillet. When the oil is hot but not smoking, arrange the quail skin side down in the skillet, leaving 1″ clear space between the birds and the sides of the pan. Place a heavy, clean-bottomed 12″ skillet atop the birds and cook 2 minutes. Lift the smaller skillet, turn the quail, reapply the weight, and cook 2 minutes longer. Transfer the birds to warmed plates, sprinkle thoroughly with the parsley, and serve.

Faraona in Cartoccio
Guinea Hen Roasted in Parchment

SERVES 4 (SEE NOTE)

Some of the finest meals of my life have been served in the homes of Italian wine producers. This dish was the highlight of a dinner given by Alfredo Corrado Vietti, who makes wonderful Barolos and Barbarescos in Castiglione Falletto.

1 guinea hen (2¾–3 pounds)

1½ teaspoons salt

1 teaspoon freshly ground pepper

4 leaves fresh sage

1 tablespoon fresh rosemary

2 bay leaves

2 sheets parchment paper, about 17" × 25"

1 tablespoon unsalted butter, melted

2 tablespoons olive oil

2 tablespoons Grand Marnier

Preheat the oven to 400° F. Remove all visible fat from the hen. Rinse the bird under cold water and pat dry with paper towels. Blend the salt and pepper, and powder the bird thoroughly with the mixture, inside and out. Distribute the sage, rosemary, and bay leaves inside the cavity, and truss the hen.

Center the bird breast up on a double thickness of parchment paper. In a bowl, combine the melted butter, olive oil, and Grand Marnier, and generously brush the mixture over the bird. Draw the parchment up around the bird as tightly as possible and tuck the longer edges together in a tight double fold that lies snugly along the bird's breastbone. Crimp each end of the parchment tightly and fold inward, to make a completely airtight package.

Transfer the wrapped hen to a heavy ovenproof skillet and roast 1 hour. Then reduce the oven temperature to 375° F. and roast 30 minutes longer.

Remove the bird from the oven and allow it to rest for 10 minutes. Cut away the top portion of the parchment with scissors and gently lift the bird from its wrapper, allowing the juices to drain back into the wrapper. Set the bird on a cutting board and divide it into serving pieces, or slice and carve as you would a turkey.

Strain and pour all juices from the parchment into a small saucepan and bring to a boil. Lower the heat immediately, skim off the excess fat, and spoon the sauce over the meat.

Note: Preceded by appetizers, one bird will be ample for four portions.

Fagiano Arrosto

Roast Pheasant

SERVES 4

Pheasant always was a special treat at Busoler. When we were lucky enough to get one, the bird would be hung in the *cantina* (wine cellar) for several days, gradually losing its feathers as we kids used them to tickle one another, or to make Indian war bonnets. For this dish, the sauce should be made first.

FOR THE SAUCE

¼ cup dried porcini mushrooms

3 tablespoons olive oil

Gizzard and neck from the pheasant

½ pound chicken gizzards or wings

1 small onion, coarsely chopped

1 rib celery, chopped

1 carrot, sliced in ¼" rounds

1 tablespoon flour

2 bay leaves, preferably fresh

1 tablespoon fresh rosemary

1 tablespoon unsalted butter

6 juniper berries

2 cups chicken stock (recipe page 69)

1 cup dry white wine

Salt and pepper to taste

Preheat the oven to 425° F. Soak the porcini in 1 cup hot water and set aside. In a small heatproof roasting pan or a large nonreactive ovenproof skillet, heat the olive oil, add all the gizzards, the neck, and chicken wings, and roast 5 minutes. Add the onion, celery, and carrot, and roast 15 minutes longer, stirring occasionally and taking care not to let the onion burn. Sprinkle the flour over contents of pan and add bay leaves and rosemary. Stir well and roast until nicely browned, 10–15 minutes.

Remove the porcini from their soaking liquid, cutting off and discarding any tough bits. Strain the soaking liquid through cloth or paper toweling, to eliminate any residual grit. Add the liquid to the roasting pan along with the porcini, butter, juniper berries, chicken stock, and wine, and simmer over low-to-moderate heat until the sauce has thickened and the flavors are concentrated, about 45 minutes. Strain sauce through a fine sieve, pressing hard on the solids to extract all liquid, and season with salt and pepper to taste.

One 3- to 4-pound pheasant, dressed
Salt and freshly ground pepper
3 tablespoons olive oil

3 sprigs fresh rosemary
3 bay leaves

Preheat the oven to 425° F. Season the pheasant inside and out with salt and pepper. Rub the pheasant with 2 tablespoons of the olive oil and stuff the cavity with rosemary and bay leaves. In a heavy ovenproof skillet, heat the remaining oil over high flame and brown the pheasant on all sides until deeply colored. Cover with aluminum foil and roast 1 hour. Remove the bird from the oven and allow it to rest for 10 minutes. Carve and serve with the reheated sauce.

Piccione con Bigoli o Polenta
Squab with Bigoli or Polenta

Squab goes equally well with either bigoli or polenta, although it's seldom served with the pasta outside Venice, where bigoli originated, and nearby Trieste. Bigoli is an interesting, dense, spaghetti-shaped pasta that always remains "alive." It is so popular among its fanciers that it even figures in a courtship song in which a suitor serenades his prospective bride: "I like bigoli with luganega [sausage], Maria; serve it with the appetizer, Maria, serve it please."

4 medium squab	2 tablespoons unsalted butter
½ cup olive oil	Salt and freshly ground pepper
1 large onion, chopped	1½ tablespoons tomato paste
2 slices lean bacon, diced	1 cup dry white wine
3 bay leaves	2 cups chicken stock (recipe page 69)
1 teaspoon fresh rosemary	1 recipe bigoli (page 110) or fried polenta (page 129)
4 whole cloves	

Have the butcher remove the backbones from the squab and quarter each bird. Wash each squab, removing any traces of viscera, and pat dry with paper towels.

In a large, nonreactive skillet, heat the oil over moderate flame, and add the onion, bacon, bay leaves, rosemary, and cloves. Sauté until the onion is wilted, 3 minutes. Transfer half the mixture to a second skillet of the same size and add half the butter to each pan. Divide the squab between the pans and brown on both sides, turning once, about 5 minutes, reducing the heat as necessary to prevent burning the onion. Add salt and pepper to taste.

Transfer the squab to a casserole. In a bowl, whisk together the tomato paste, wine, and stock. Pour half the mixture into each skillet and bring to a boil, scraping the bottoms of the pans well. Boil 1 minute, then pour into the casserole, over the squab. Cook at a gentle simmer until the squab is tender when pierced with a fork or skewer, 30–45 minutes, depending on the quality of the birds.

Remove squab to a heated platter and cover with foil to keep warm. Strain the sauce through a fine sieve into a saucepan and skim off as much fat as possible. Boil to reduce the sauce until thickened and very flavorful, about 30 minutes, skimming frequently. Season to taste. Return the squab to the sauce and heat.

To serve, arrange four pieces of squab on each plate, flanked with bigoli or two pieces of fried polenta, and pour sauce over and around the squab.

Anitra in Umido con Crauti
Duck Roasted with Sauerkraut

SERVES 4

My grandmother always had a barrel of sauerkraut in her *cantina* (wine cellar) at Busoler. After the year's wine was pressed in the fall, Nonna harvested her first frost cabbages, which were sliced, after pickling, on a wooden frame fitted with a blade. Both the cabbage and the year's supply of turnips were pickled in leftover wine must. We'd usually have this dish on Sunday. When the duck was killed, we'd have the innards with a *frittata* for *merenda,* and we'd render the bird's fat and bake the cracklings in our bread. Later in the day, the main meal would be duck with sauerkraut, which, incidentally, along with *crauti guarniti,* is a dish common to both Istrian and Alsatian cookery. *Anitra con crauti* is a logical combination; the sauerkraut breaks the fattiness of the duck and sets off the richness of the meat. Plain boiled potatoes will mediate nicely between the sauerkraut and the duck.

1 Long Island duck, about 3 pounds	5 cloves garlic, crushed
Salt and freshly ground pepper to taste	2 tablespoons olive oil
5 bay leaves	3 pounds sauerkraut (see Note)
1 sprig fresh rosemary	10 whole peppercorns
¼ cup vegetable oil	2 cups water
3 cups chicken stock (recipe page 69)	

Preheat the oven to 500° F. Meanwhile, remove the duck gizzard, liver, and excess fat, and reserve for other uses. Season the duck inside and out with salt and pepper, and place 2 bay leaves and the rosemary in the body cavity. In an ovenproof skillet, heat the vegetable oil and brown the duck on all sides, about 10 minutes.

Discard all oil from the skillet, add the chicken stock, transfer to the oven, and bake 30 minutes. While the duck bakes, in a deep pot large enough to accommodate the bird and sauerkraut with ample headroom, brown the garlic in the olive oil. Add the washed sauerkraut, 3 bay leaves, the peppercorns, 1 teaspoon salt, and 2 cups water, and bring to simmer. Transfer the duck and its juices (after skimming the fat) to the sauerkraut pot and simmer 1 hour, half-covered, stirring occasionally.

To serve, carve the duck into eight parts, remove and discard the bay leaves and garlic, and place two pieces of duck (one lighter, one darker) on each plate, flanking it with sauerkraut.

Note: Packaged or canned sauerkraut may be used. Either one should be washed twice under running water and tasted for sourness. If too sour, wash once more.

Anitra in Sguazet
Duck *in Sguazet*

SERVES 6

My grandmother had one laying duck, and one of my childhood chores at Busoler was to gather its eggs, along with those laid by Nonna's chickens and geese. The duck always hid its eggs in the bushes, where they were hard to find, and sometimes I'd pretend to miss them. Nonna knew exactly how many eggs I should have collected each day and must have known I was swiping a few, but she let me get away with it. Then, when I had accumulated enough of them, we kids would have a picnic of scrambled eggs and field salad. There also was a blind old lady, her name was Fosca, who lived in one of the houses back-to-back to ours. She loved to talk and tell stories. I would tiptoe in at times, to test whether she was really blind, but every time she would call out *"Chi je tamo?"*—who's there. I guess her hearing was so acute that it partially replaced her sight, but I always did wonder if she could see a little. Well, some of those eggs I swiped from my Nonna, I would bring to her. I would also cook them for her. She liked a *frittata*—mind you I had also to swipe a deciliter or two of wine—and she would ask, "Little one, did you bring me something to drink?" She liked that. I think she liked the wine more than the *frittata*. See "About Sguazet," page 210.

At Easter, we made bread with duck eggs pressed into the loaves, but when a duck was killed, it was almost always for *sguazet*.

½ cup (about 1 ounce) dried
porcini mushrooms

1½ pounds duck breasts, or any part,
skin attached

¼ cup olive oil

Salt and freshly ground pepper to taste

3 medium onions, chopped

⅓ cup pancetta or bacon, chopped fine

½ cup chicken livers, coarsely chopped

2 bay leaves

1 sprig rosemary, or 1 teaspoon dried

4 whole cloves

1 cup dry white wine

3 tablespoons tomato paste

3 cups chicken stock (recipe page 69)

Pasta or gnocchi (see Note)

Freshly grated Parmigiano

Presoak the porcini in 2 cups of warm water for 20–30 minutes, until softened. Remove the porcini from the soaking liquid, rinse well, and snip off any tough bits. Chop the porcini coarsely and set aside. Strain the soaking liquid through a sieve lined with cheesecloth or paper toweling and reserve.

Pat the duck breasts dry. In a large, heavy casserole, heat the olive oil over high flame, add the duck breasts skin side down, and sprinkle lightly with salt and pepper. Reduce the heat to moderately high and cook, turning often, until lightly golden, about 10 minutes. Pour off about ¾ of the fat, which can be reserved for other uses.

Add the onions and pancetta or bacon to the casserole, season lightly with salt and pepper, and sauté until golden, about 5 minutes. Add the chicken livers and cook, stirring, 2 minutes. Add the porcini, bay leaves, rosemary, and cloves, and cook, stirring, 5 minutes. Add the wine and cook, stirring, until the wine has nearly evaporated.

Stir in the tomato paste and simmer 2 minutes, stirring to coat all ingredients. Add the reserved mushroom liquid and the chicken stock, and bring to a boil. Lower the heat, partially cover the casserole, and simmer gently until the sauce has thickened, about 1 hour. Remove and discard the cloves, bay leaves, and rosemary stems, if any. Skim off the surface fat, adjust the seasonings, and serve with the pasta of your choice or with gnocchi, and grated Parmigiano.

Note: I usually serve this dish with bigoli (recipe page 110), *fuzi* (recipe page 108), or gnocchi (recipe page 117), and grated Parmigiano to taste.

Coniglio in Sguazet
Rabbit *in Sguazet*

SERVES 4

Every family kept a rabbit pen in Busoler, and rabbit was an integral part of my childhood diet. Because rabbits multiplied fast and prolifically, theirs was the one meat we always had in abundance. The only problem was feeding so many rabbits. Every vegetable leaf and paring we didn't eat ourselves was fed to them, along with the bundles of grass I was sent to gather. Today, when we return to visit our relatives in Istria, we know exactly what our first meals there will be; there's always a goat ready for slaughter—and a rabbit already hanging when we arrive. See "About Sguazet," page 210.

1 young rabbit (2½–3 pounds)	1 teaspoon fresh or dried rosemary
¼ cup olive oil	4 whole cloves
1 large onion, sliced	Salt and freshly ground pepper
2 slices bacon, diced	1½ tablespoons tomato paste
3 bay leaves	1 cup dry white wine
4 sage leaves	2 cups chicken stock (recipe page 69)

Cut (or have your butcher cut) the rabbit into eight pieces.

In a large, nonreactive casserole, heat the olive oil and add the onion, bacon, herbs, and cloves. Sauté over moderately high heat, stirring constantly, until the onion is wilted, about 3 minutes.

Season the rabbit pieces with salt and pepper, add them to the casserole, and cook until lightly browned, about 3 minutes per side. Add the tomato paste and mix to coat the rabbit. Add the wine and scrape the bottom of the casserole. Add the stock and simmer, half-covered, over moderate heat until the sauce is well reduced and the rabbit is cooked through, about 30 minutes.

Remove the rabbit pieces and strain the sauce. Serve the rabbit and its pan sauce with gnocchi (recipe page 117) or pappardelle (recipe page 108).

Coniglio alla Salvia
Rabbit with Sage

SERVES 4

My Aunt Lidia, my mother's sister, kept rabbits of various ages for various uses. The older, more flavorful but tougher, animals were stewed or prepared *in sguazet*. The younger rabbits usually were roasted, braised, or sautéed. This is how my Aunt Lidia cooked rabbit with sage, one of her specialties, except for the inclusion of balsamic vinegar, which she wasn't aware of in Istria. *Verze e Patate*—Savoy Cabbage with Potatoes—(recipe page 87) is an excellent accompaniment to this dish.

4 slices bacon	*One 3-pound rabbit, dressed, in 8 pieces*
3 cloves garlic, peeled	*Salt and pepper to taste*
6 fresh sage leaves, or 1 tablespoon dried	*Flour for dredging*
2 cups chicken stock (recipe page 69)	*1 teaspoon balsamic vinegar*
½ cup vegetable oil	*1 cup dry white wine*

Chop the bacon, garlic, and sage very fine, to paste consistency. (If using a blender or processor, add 1 or 2 tablespoons of the stock.) Heat the vegetable oil in a large casserole, meanwhile seasoning the rabbit parts with salt and pepper and dredging them lightly in flour, shaking off the excess. Add the rabbit to the casserole and cook over high heat, turning it until browned, about 3 minutes per side.

Discard the oil from the casserole. Add the bacon mixture, and return to the heat, cooking 3 minutes and stirring occasionally. Add the balsamic vinegar and white wine, and simmer 5 minutes. Add 1 cup of the stock, salt and pepper to taste, and cover the casserole. Simmer until the rabbit is tender, about 45 minutes, stirring occasionally and adding the remaining stock gradually, as needed, to keep the meat moist. Transfer the rabbit pieces to a large serving dish and strain the sauce, which should be thick, over them. If the sauce is thin, quickly reduce it over high heat.

Filetto di Capriolo
Fillet of Venison

SERVES 6 – 8

We seldom had the better cuts of meat or large game animals during my childhood, when scarcity dictated widespread sharing of whatever was killed. We tried to bring out the best of whatever came our way, though, and this is my adaptation of my family's treatment of venison, applied to medallions cut from the fillet.

2 pounds venison fillet	*2 pounds venison bones and scraps (see Note)*

FOR THE MARINADE

3 cups dry red wine, such as Barolo, Barbaresco, or Chianti	*6 bay leaves*
2 cups dry white wine	*2 teaspoons rosemary*
2 medium carrots, sliced	*1 teaspoon crushed peppercorns*
2 ribs celery, sliced	*1 teaspoon juniper berries*
2 medium onions, chopped	

In a deep, nonreactive dish arrange the fillet, bones, and meat scraps. Cover the meat completely with the wines, add all the other ingredients, distributing them evenly, and marinate, refrigerated, 2 days. Strain marinade and reserve the liquid, vegetables, and bones and trimmings. Keep the fillet refrigerated.

Note: If your butcher is unable to supply them, beef bones and trimmings will do.

Salt and freshly ground pepper to taste
½ cup (approximately) olive oil
2 tablespoons flour
½ cup minced shallots

¼ cup brandy
¼ cup dry Marsala
8 cups boiling beef or basic stock (recipes page 69)

Preheat the oven to 500° F. Salt and pepper the reserved bones and meat scraps, set in a roasting pan with 2 tablespoons of the olive oil, and roast 20 minutes, turning them occasionally. Sprinkle the flour over the bones and return them to the oven for 15 minutes longer.

Meanwhile, in a large skillet, sauté the shallots in 3 tablespoons of the olive oil until translucent. Add the reserved marinade vegetables and sauté until softened, 15–20 minutes. At the same time, in a large nonreactive saucepan, bring the reserved marinade liquid to a simmer. Add the contents of the skillet to the roasting pan, along with the brandy, Marsala, and simmering marinade liquid. Stir well, scraping the bottom of the pan, and return to the oven for 30 minutes.

Transfer the contents of the roasting pan to a heavy stockpot and simmer on top of the stove, uncovered, 2 hours, gradually adding the 8 cups boiling stock, stirring occasionally and skimming often. Strain the sauce into a medium saucepan, pressing hard on the solids, and boil sauce until reduced to 1½ cups, about 20 minutes. Season to taste.

Slice the reserved venison fillet into medallions ½″ thick and salt lightly. Heat a wide, heavy skillet well, swirl 2 tablespoons of the olive oil around the bottom of the pan, and sear the medallions for about 1 minute on each side. Arrange the medallions on warmed serving plates and spoon the sauce over them.

Capriolo in Sguazet
Venison *in Sguazet*

SERVES 4

As with most *sguazet* preparations, this venison treatment normally would be reserved for the tougher, more flavorful cuts, whereas the legs, fillets, chops, and the like would be roasted, grilled, or sautéed. At our restaurant, however, our customers expect choice cuts and are served accordingly. This is one of Felice's favorite dishes and a popular seller at Felidia. See "About Sguazet," page 210.

2 pounds venison leg or shoulder

½ cup dried porcini mushrooms

1 medium onion, minced

¼ cup minced pancetta or bacon

¼ cup olive oil

Salt and freshly ground pepper to taste

2 bay leaves

1 sprig fresh rosemary, or
1 teaspoon dried

2 whole cloves

½ cup dry red wine (preferably Barolo)

2 tablespoons tomato paste

3½ cups chicken stock (recipe page 69)

Cut the venison into 1″ cubes.

Soak the porcini in 2 cups of hot water about 20 minutes. While the porcini are soaking, in a large casserole, over moderately high heat, sauté the onion and pancetta or bacon in the olive oil until golden, about 8 minutes. Season lightly with salt and pepper, add the venison, and cook until all the meat liquids have evaporated, about 15 minutes.

Pick out the porcini and chop them coarsely, reserving the liquid (except for the last 2 tablespoons of gritty sediment).

Add the porcini to the casserole, along with the bay leaves, rosemary, cloves, and wine, and cook, stirring, 5 minutes, until the wine is nearly evaporated.

Stir in the tomato paste and season lightly with salt and pepper. Add the chicken stock and reserved mushroom liquid, bring to a boil, reduce the heat to moderately low, and simmer, partially covered, until the meat is tender and the sauce is thickened, about 1½ hours.

Remove the bay leaves and rosemary, adjust the seasoning, and serve with gnocchi (recipe page 117) or polenta (recipe page 129).

Gamberoni alla Griglia
Broiled Shrimp

Trippa con Patate

Tripe with Potatoes

175

Red Snapper alla Griglia
Grilled Red Snapper
136

Top: *Focaccia*

Flat Bread

229

Bottom: *Calamari al Forno*

Oven-baked Squid

159

Cinghiale Brasato al Barolo
Wild Boar Braised in Barolo Wine

SERVES 8

During the years of my childhood, we had wild boar only once or twice a year, and it was always a memorable event. One of my cousins was a hunter, and my grandfather was the community butcher. In hunting season, the *bora* blew down across the Adriatic. The wind howled, everyone was cold, and we cooked polenta for warmth. And when my cousin was in luck, we ate it with *cinghiale*.

1½ cups minced onion

2 tablespoons pancetta or bacon

½ cup olive oil

Salt and freshly ground pepper to taste

1 cup shredded carrot

6 bay leaves

6 whole cloves

1 teaspoon fresh rosemary leaves

3½ pounds wild boar (see Note)

3 tablespoons tomato paste

2 bottles Barolo wine (see Note)

1 cup peeled Italian plum tomatoes, drained*

6–8 cups beef stock (recipe page 69)

In a large, deep, nonreactive casserole or stockpot, sauté the onion and pancetta or bacon in the olive oil until golden. Season with salt and pepper to taste. Add the carrot, bay leaves, cloves, and rosemary. Stir well and push the mixture to one side of the pot.

Season the meat with salt and pepper, add it to the pot, and lightly brown on all sides, sautéeing about 15 minutes. Add the tomato paste and stir. Then add the wine and simmer 30 minutes. Add the tomatoes* and stock, and simmer, skimming frequently and stirring occasionally, until the meat is tender, about 3½ hours.

Remove the meat from the pot and set aside. Pass the sauce through a sieve, pressing the solids to extract as much liquid as possible. Discard the solids, return the meat and strained sauce to the pot and simmer until the liquid reduces to about 3½ cups, about 45 minutes, skimming any foam from the surface as it forms.

Slice meat, arrange it on a serving platter, and top with the sauce.

Note: Wild boar can be found in season at specialty butcher shops. Use either a boneless roast or a shoulder roast with bone. Barolo wine is costly, but makes a difference. We use it in this dish at Felidia, but substitute our house red when we cook at home.

*Use fresh tomatoes if perfectly ripe. Otherwise use canned Italian plum tomatoes.

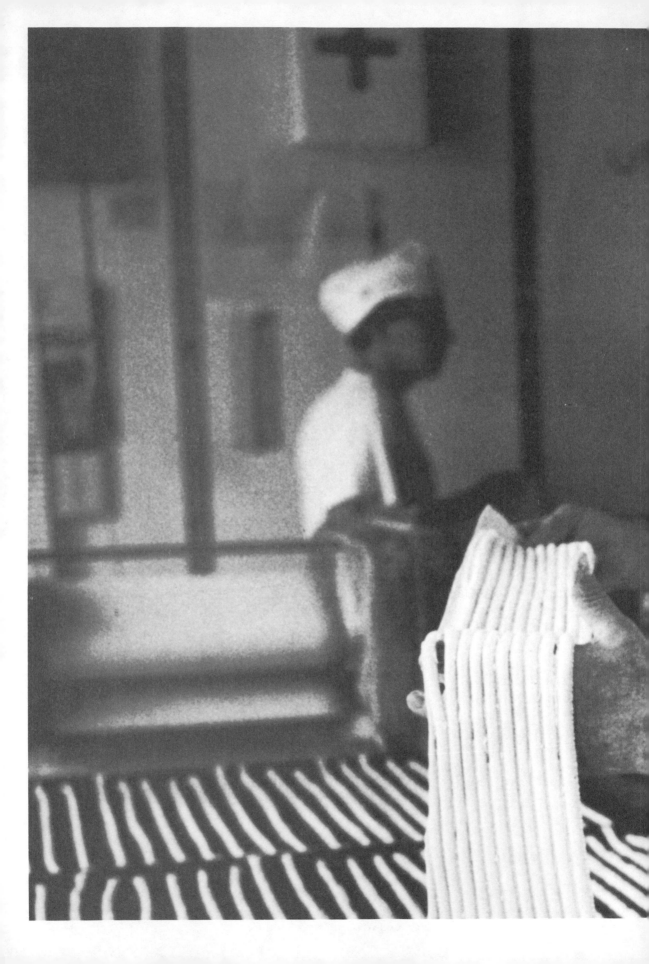

7

Pane e Pasticceria
Bread and Desserts

Focaccia
Flat Bread

SERVES 12

This savory bread is the direct ancestor of pizza and the descendant of the hearth cakes eaten throughout Europe during the early Middle Ages.

2 envelopes (½ ounce) active dry yeast

2 cups warm water (105°–115° F.)

1 tablespoon sugar

5½ cups flour

1 tablespoon coarse or kosher salt

3 tablespoons olive oil

1 small onion, thinly sliced

¾ teaspoon crumbled dried rosemary

Freshly ground pepper to taste

In a medium-size bowl, mix the yeast, warm water, and sugar, and allow it to stand 10 minutes, until foamy.

In a large bowl, mix 5 cups of the flour and 1½ teaspoons of the salt, forming a well in the center. Pour the yeast mixture into the well, along with 2 tablespoons of the oil. Stir with a wooden spoon, gradually incorporating the ingredients to form a soft dough. Use floured hands to mix the dough when it becomes too stiff to work with a spoon.

Dust a work surface with about ¼ cup of the remaining flour, turn the dough out onto it, and knead 10 minutes, adding flour if the dough gets sticky. (Alternatively, this step can be accomplished with the dough hook of an electric mixer.) When the dough is smooth and elastic, shape it into a small ball and place it in a greased bowl, turning it once to bring the greased side up. Cover with a damp dish towel or plastic wrap, and allow it to rise until doubled in volume,

about 30 minutes. Punch down the dough, cover, and allow it to rise as before.

With your hands, spread and press the dough into a greased 11″ × 15″ jelly-roll pan, forcing up the edges to form a 1″-high wall. With your knuckles, press the surface of the dough all over, making a pattern of indentations. Cover and let rise 15 minutes, while the oven preheats to 450° F.

In a bowl, blend the remaining olive oil and salt, the onion, rosemary, and pepper. Press down the dough with your knuckles, exactly as before. Spread the onion mixture over the dough, leaving the edges bare, and brush the edges with whatever oil remains in the mixing bowl.

Bake for 30–35 minutes. When golden, after approximately 20 minutes, cover with foil and continue baking 15 minutes longer. To serve, cut the focaccia into rectangles.

Treccia di Pane all'Uovo
Istrian Wedding Bread

SERVES 8

This egg-rich bread—actually a cake—is baked for weddings and other special occasions. In its most festive form, sugar almonds are embedded in the dough.

½ cup sugar

1 cup warm milk (body temperature)

3 tablespoons fresh yeast or 1 envelope active dry yeast

2 pounds unbleached flour, sifted

1 tablespoon salt

3 whole eggs, lightly beaten

Grated zest of 1 orange

Grated zest of 1 lemon

1 cup raisins (optional)

2 tablespoons (approximately) warm water

Olive oil

Dissolve 3 tablespoons of the sugar in the warm milk, then add and dissolve the yeast. Add ¾ cup of the flour and stir to make a loose mixture. Allow the mixture to rise in a warm place for 20 minutes. You should have a spongy mixture which has doubled in volume.

In a bowl, blend the remaining flour, the remaining sugar, and the salt. Add the yeast mixture, then the eggs, and mix well. Add the citrus zests and, if desired, the raisins, and enough warm water to bind all ingredients. Hand-knead the dough for 10 minutes (or 5 minutes by machine with a dough hook) and set it in a lightly buttered, nonreactive bowl. Allow it to rise, covered with a towel, 45–60 minutes, until doubled in volume.

Divide the risen dough into 3 parts, roll each into a 15"-long cylinder, and braid the cylinders together, pressing the ends together firmly. Set the braid on a lightly greased baking sheet, cover loosely with a towel, and allow to rise in a warm place, about 30 minutes. (A gas oven with just the pilot light on will do the job.)

Preheat the oven to 375° F. and bake bread 40 minutes. Test for doneness by inserting a wooden toothpick in the center of the loaf and brush lightly with olive oil before serving.

Crostoli

Sweet Bows

ABOUT 36 PIECES

These simple fried pastries, with minor variations on the basic theme, are eaten all over Italy. They also are called "women's sweet lies." This has been my family's version for generations.

6 tablespoons unsalted butter
¼ cup plus 2 tablespoons sugar
¼ cup milk
½ teaspoon salt
2¼ cups flour
1 whole egg plus 1 yolk

3 tablespoons dark rum
Grated zest of 1 lemon
Juice of ½ lemon
Vegetable oil for deep-frying
Confectioners' sugar

In the top of a double boiler, melt the butter, then add the sugar, milk, and salt.

In the bowl of an electric mixer, combine the flour, butter-milk-sugar mixture, whole egg and egg yolk, rum, lemon zest and juice. Mix until the dough is soft but not sticky, 10–15 minutes.

On a lightly floured surface, cut the dough in half and roll out each piece to form a rectangle ⅛" thick. With a fluted cutter, cut the dough in to 1" × 6" strips and form each one into a very loosely knotted bow.

In a deep fryer or deep, wide skillet, heat the vegetable oil just short of the smoking point and fry the bows in batches, turning them once, until golden brown. Transfer to paper towels to drain, allow them to cool, and sprinkle with confectioners' sugar.

Frittole allo Yogurt
Sweet Yogurt Fritters

ABOUT 30 PIECES

I picked up this recipe in the Istrian town of Castelnuovo (now Rakalj), where my brother-in-law Romano took us to a party for which somebody named Vera made these fritters. I don't remember Vera very well, but her *frittole* were memorable.

1 cup golden raisins
¼ cup dark rum
1 ounce fresh yeast or ½ envelope active dry yeast
½ cup warm milk (body temperature)
4 tablespoons sugar
2 cups flour
1 egg
¼ teaspoon salt

¼ teaspoon vanilla extract
6 ounces plain yogurt
½ tablespoon baking powder
Grated zest of 1 lemon
Grated zest of 1 orange
¼ pound pignoli (pine nuts)
3 cups vegetable oil
Confectioners' sugar to taste

Soak the raisins in the rum. Dissolve the yeast in the warm milk together with half the sugar and ½ cup of the flour. Mix well (the mixture will resemble lumpy pancake batter), cover, and set aside in a warm place to activate the yeast. The mass should double in volume within 15–20 minutes.

In the meantime, beat the egg with the remaining sugar, the salt, vanilla extract, and yogurt. Combine the baking powder with the remaining flour and add it to the yogurt mixture. Blend well and add the yeast mixture. Beat 10–15 minutes, until the dough is soft and sticky. Drain the raisins and add them to the dough, together with the citrus zests and pignoli, distributing the fruit and nuts evenly. Cover the dough with a dry cloth and let it rise in a warm place until the volume doubles, about 40 minutes.

In a deep skillet, heat the vegetable oil just short of smoking point (see Note). Dip a teaspoon into the hot oil, then scoop up as much dough as the spoon will hold, and slide it into the hot oil. Repeat the process until skillet is full. Fry the fritters, turning them with a slotted spoon, until honey-brown on all sides. Repeat with the remaining dough, draining the fritters on paper towels as they are done. When the fritters are cool, sprinkle them with confectioners' sugar.

Serve at room temperature.

Note: It's essential that the frying oil be kept at an even temperature, very hot but not smoking. If not hot enough, the oil will be absorbed by the fritters; if too hot, it will scorch them.

Putizza
Yeast Cake Roll

SERVES 16

Traditionally, we Italians don't finish our meals with cakes or pastries, except on special occasions, and even then we prefer to keep them simple and not too rich. *Putizza* is a dialect term used in Istria and the surrounding provinces. The cake, which is served mostly at wedding parties, derives from Hungarian cookery.

FOR THE DOUGH

1 envelope (¼ ounce) active dry yeast

½ cup sugar

¾ cup warm milk (body temperature)

3 egg yolks (whites reserved for the filling)

4 tablespoons unsalted butter, softened

3½ cups flour

Grated zest of 1 lemon

¼ teaspoon salt

2 tablespoons dark rum

Beaten yolk of 1 egg, for brushing

To make the dough, dissolve the yeast and 1 tablespoon of the sugar in 4 tablespoons of warm milk. In the bowl of an electric mixer, beat the egg yolks with the remaining sugar and the butter. Add 3 cups of the flour and incorporate well. Add the lemon zest, salt, rum, and the yeast-milk mixture. Add remaining milk, a little at a time, until the dough is smooth but not dry. Work well with a dough hook or knead by hand on a lightly floured surface, about 10 minutes. Transfer the dough to a large bowl, cover with a cloth, and keep in a warm place until almost doubled in volume, about 30 minutes. (I usually keep it in the oven, where the heat from the pilot light is enough to raise the dough.)

2 teaspoons sugar	*½ teaspoon vanilla*
4 tablespoons dark rum	*1 teaspoon finely ground espresso coffee beans*
16 vanilla wafers, crushed fine	
½ cup minced walnuts	*⅓ cup milk*
⅓ cup raisins	*3 reserved egg whites*
2 oz. semisweet chocolate, shaved	

While the dough rises, make the filling: blend the sugar and rum, add all the remaining ingredients except the milk and egg whites, and mix well. Add enough of the milk to obtain a moist paste. (It may not be necessary to use all the milk.)

TO ASSEMBLE PUTIZZA

Preheat the oven to 375° F. (Remove the risen dough first.)

Roll out the risen dough on a lightly floured surface, forming a 12″ × 14″ rectangle. Beat the reserved egg whites until they form stiff peaks. Spread the filling evenly over the entire surface of the dough and then evenly spread the beaten egg whites over the filling. Working from one of the longer sides of the rectangle, roll it up, jelly-roll fashion, then curl in a spiral to form a snail-like shape. Butter a baking sheet or line it with parchment paper, transfer the roll to the baking sheet, and bake 20 minutes. Remove from the oven, brush with the beaten egg yolk, and return roll to the oven. Bake until nicely browned, about 30 minutes longer, and cool on a rack. To serve, slice the *putizza* crosswise ¾″ thick.

Puff Pastry

YIELDS ABOUT 2 ½ POUNDS

In France, debate has raged for centuries about the origins of puff pastry, the only point of common agreement (among the French) being that it was a French invention. It wasn't. The Saracens introduced puff pastry into Europe during the eighth century, and all existing evidence suggests that it was naturalized in Italy and Sicily earlier than it was in France. In Sicily, it was termed *millefoglie,* and in Naples, it was known as *sfogliatelle* for some time before the French applied the derivative *mille-feuilles* to the expatriated delicacy and it became known as *strudel* in *Mitteleuropa.* To their credit, the French (among others) have added more refinements and made more inventive use of puff pastry than have the Italians in general, but this lightest and most elegant product of the baker's art has played a role, albeit somewhat subdued in Italy since early medieval times, in both sweet and savory treatments. Regional variations on the basic theme abound, some oil– and some butter–based. This is how we make puff pastry at Felidia.

FOR THE DOUGH MIXTURE

1 stick (¼ pound) unsalted butter

2½ cups flour

1¾ teaspoons salt

½ cup cold water

Cut the butter into several small pieces and allow it to come to room temperature. In a bowl, combine the flour and salt and, using a pastry blender or scraper, cut the butter into the flour until the mixture takes on a coarse mealy texture. Add the cold water and mix until the dough begins to cohere. Gather it into a ball and pat it out to form an 8″ × 11″ rectangle. Wrap it in floured waxed paper or foil and refrigerate about 30 minutes. Meanwhile, prepare the butter mixture.

FOR THE BUTTER MIXTURE

1 cup flour

3 sticks (¾ pound) unsalted butter, firm but not hard

In a bowl or on a work surface, work the flour into the butter with a pastry blender or scraper until blended, working quickly so that the butter doesn't become too soft. Shape the mixture into a 4½″ square. When the dough and butter mixtures are similar in consistency and texture, set the dough on a well-floured surface (preferably marble or stainless steel). Place the butter mixture on the center of the dough rectangle and fold the dough over it on four sides, completely enclosing the butter. Press the seams with your fingers to seal.

Using a rolling pin, flatten the dough slightly, then gradually roll it out evenly, frequently flouring both sides and forming a 10″ × 20″ rectangle, with a short side facing you. Fold over ⅓ the length of the rectangle from the top and bottom so that the folded portions meet at the middle, then fold dough once more, like a book, to form a fourth layer. Roll the dough lightly so that the folds cohere.

Shift the dough, positioning the seam at your left. Roll it out again into a 10″ × 20″ rectangle. Should the butter break through the surface at any point, flour the spot heavily and proceed. Fold the dough again as before, rolling it lightly to effect cohesion. Cover with a damp cloth and refrigerate 1 hour.

Repeat the foregoing rolling procedures three more times, with a 1 hour rest period in the refrigerator after each repetition. The dough will then be ready for use and will keep, tightly sealed in plastic wrap and refrigerated, up to 1 week.

Gubana in Pasta Sfoglia
Rolled Pastry for Company

SERVES 12–14

This filled puff pastry roll is a specialty of Friuli. Because it keeps well, many families prepare it in advance, to have on hand if visitors should drop in.

½ cup dessert wine (Verduzzo or Vin Santo)

2 tablespoons Marsala

¼ cup grappa

2 tablespoons dark rum

2 tablespoons amaretto liqueur

1 cup raisins

2 eggs, one separated

4 tablespoons bread crumbs

2 tablespoons unsalted butter, softened

Grated rind of 1 lemon

Grated rind of 1 orange

½ cup coarsely chopped hazelnuts

1 cup finely chopped walnuts

½ cup finely chopped almonds

1 tablespoon chopped candied fruit

1 tablespoon unsweetened cocoa

2 tablespoons grated dark semisweet chocolate

3 tablespoons sugar plus 1 tablespoon for sprinkling

1 pound puff pastry dough (recipe page 235)

Blend all the cordials, wines, rum, and grappa, and divide in half. Reserve one half and steep the raisins in the other for about 1 hour.

Beat the separated yolk and reserve it for brushing the pastry. Beat the separated white stiff. Beat the whole egg separately and reserve.

Toast the bread crumbs lightly in the butter. In a mixing bowl, combine the citrus rinds, nuts, candied fruit, cocoa, chocolate, 3 tablespoons of sugar, the toasted crumbs, and the raisins with their liquid. When the ingredients are well blended, fold in the beaten egg white.

Roll out the puff pastry dough, forming a rectangle 12″ × 16″, with the longer side facing you. With a spatula, spread the filling mixture evenly over the dough, leaving a 1″ border uncovered on all sides. Brush the border lightly with the beaten egg yolk. Roll the dough up from the side facing you, like a jelly roll, then curl the roll in a loose spiral resembling a coiled rope. Place the pastry in a lightly greased and floured 10″ round baking pan.

Preheat the oven to 375° F. Brush the exposed pastry surface with the beaten whole egg and sprinkle it evenly with the remaining 1 tablespoon sugar. Bake 45 minutes and cool in the oven. Cut into serving wedges and sprinkle lightly with the reserved liquor mixture.

Torta di Fagioli Bianchi
White Bean Cake

SERVES 6 – 8

In Istria, beans were a major staple of our cuisine, and this cake would be baked when the harvest was abundant. Sometimes, when we cooked beans for *pasta e fagioli* we'd add an extra batch to the pot and reserve them for salads and other dishes—or for this cake. It's wonderful served with *crema di caffè* (recipe page 256).

¾ pound Great Northern beans	3 eggs, separated
1 teaspoon active dry yeast	3 tablespoons dark rum
¾ cup sugar	1 pinch salt
3 tablespoons warm milk (body temperature)	Softened sweet butter and bread crumbs for the pan

Soak the beans overnight in cold water to cover generously. Drain, again add water to cover generously, and boil beans 30–40 minutes, until tender. (The cooking time will vary, depending on the size and quality of the beans.) Drain and puree them, and strain to remove the skins.

Preheat the oven to 350° F. Dissolve the yeast and 1 teaspoon of the sugar in the warm milk and set aside. In a bowl, beat the egg yolks with the remaining sugar, add the bean puree, the rum, salt, and yeast-milk mixture, and amalgamate well. Beat the egg whites until they form stiff peaks, and fold them into the mixture.

Brush an 8″ springform pan with softened butter, coat the inner surfaces with bread crumbs, and shake to discard the excess crumbs. Pour the cake batter into the lined pan and bake until a tester inserted into the center of the cake comes out clean, about 50 minutes. Cool before serving.

Pan di Spagna di Polenta

Polenta Sponge Cake

SERVES 8

During the early postwar years in Istria, wheat flour sometimes was in short supply, but cornmeal was relatively abundant. Sometimes the two were combined for cakes, and sometimes only cornmeal was used. Serve this with *zabaglione al Barolo* (recipe page 254).

2 tablespoons milk	Grated zest of 1 orange
⅔ cup sugar	Juice of ½ lemon
½ envelope active dry yeast	½ teaspoon vanilla extract
4 eggs, separated	3 tablespoons dark rum
Grated zest of 1 lemon	⅔ cup instant polenta°

Preheat the oven to 350° F. Butter and lightly flour an 8″ cake pan.

In a small saucepan, warm the milk and remove it from the heat. Add 1 tablespoon of the sugar and the yeast, and stir until the yeast dissolves.

In a large bowl, beat the egg yolks with the remaining sugar until the mixture is pale yellow. Add the grated citrus zests, the lemon juice, vanilla, and rum, blending them thoroughly. Sift the polenta into the egg mixture, stirring. Add the milk-yeast mixture and combine well.

Beat the egg whites until they form stiff peaks, and fold them into the polenta batter. Pour the batter into the cake pan and bake until lightly browned and a tester inserted into the center comes out clean, about 24–30 minutes.

*Instant polenta is available in grocery stores and supermarkets.

Torta di Ricotta
Ricotta Cheesecake

SERVES 6

This is my region's version of the universal Italian cheesecake. We made it in Busoler with our own goat's milk ricotta, and whenever we did, the goats would be fed stale market bread soaked in the whey produced during the cheese-making process. The egg whites folded into the cake mixture give it a texture I like very much.

1 pound ricotta cheese
⅓ cup raisins
2 tablespoons dark rum
3 eggs, separated
½ cup sugar
1 pinch salt

Grated zest of 1 lemon
Grated zest of 1 orange
⅓ cup pignoli (pine nuts)
Softened butter and bread crumbs, for the pan

Drain the ricotta overnight in a cheesecloth-lined sieve.

Soak the raisins in the rum. Preheat the oven to 375° F. Beat the egg yolks with the sugar until pale yellow. Add the drained ricotta, salt, and citrus zests, and blend thoroughly. Add the pignoli and the raisins and rum, blending well. Beat the egg whites until they form stiff peaks and fold them into the cake mixture. Brush a 6″ springform pan with softened butter, coat the inner surfaces with bread crumbs, and shake out the excess.

Pour the cake mixture into the prepared pan, bake 30 minutes, and cool before serving.

Crostata di Pesche
Peach Tart

SERVES 8 – 10

Our two headwaiters, Nino and Dante Laurenti, were born near Passo della Cisa, outside Parma, a region world-famous for its prosciutto and Parmigiano. Dante's in-laws operate the Molinari Inn at Passo della Cisa, where they serve such wonderful fruit tarts that the inn has become a popular tourist attraction in its own right. This is their recipe. Apples, pears, or plums can be substituted in the same amount for the peaches.

3 large ripe peaches

1 tablespoon lemon juice

¾ cup plus 1 tablespoon sugar

2 eggs

2 tablespoons milk

2½ teaspoons baking powder

¼ teaspoon salt

2 cups unbleached flour

3 tablespoons butter, softened

2 tablespoons smooth apricot jam, heated in 1 tablespoon water (optional)

Slice the unpeeled peaches in eighths; there should be 2 cups of sliced fruit, so add or subtract accordingly.

In a bowl, mix the peaches, lemon juice, and 1 tablespoon of the sugar, coating the peaches well, and marinate 10 minutes.

Preheat the oven to 350° F.

Beat the eggs with the milk. Mix the remaining dry ingredients and incorporate them into the egg-milk mixture. Then add the softened butter. This process can be done in the mixer with a dough hook, with a wooden spoon, or by hand.

Lightly butter a 10″ springform tart pan and line it with the dough, pressing down with your fingers to make it even. Arrange the peaches, skin-side down, in a radiating pattern and press them lightly into the dough. Bake 30–40 minutes. Serve tart at room temperature as is or, if you like, while still warm, brush the surface with apricot glaze.

Crostata
Fruit Tart Shell

YIELDS THREE 10″ SHELLS

This is a cookielike dough, and rolling it out can be a bit tricky. If it tears, patch it with your fingers, adding additional scraps of dough.

4½ cups flour	*3 eggs, beaten*
1½ cups sugar	*3 sticks (¾ pound) unsalted butter, softened*
2 teaspoons baking powder	
1 pinch salt	*¼ teaspoon almond extract*

In a large bowl, combine the flour, sugar, baking powder, and salt. Add the eggs and stir with a wooden spoon or mix with your hands until the mixture looks crumbly. Work in the softened butter and almond extract until no traces of butter are visible. Divide the dough into three equal portions, roll each into a ball, and flatten to form thick disks. Wrap separately in plastic wrap and refrigerate until firm, or freeze for later use.

To prebake a tart shell, preheat the oven to 350° F. On a floured surface, roll out the dough to a thickness of ⅛″. (Allow the dough to soften slightly if it is too cold to work easily.) Transfer the rolled dough to a 10″ tart pan with a removable bottom. Prick the bottom of the tart freely with a fork. Trim off any excess or overhang, crimp the border with the tines of a fork, and put shell in the freezer 10 minutes. Bake shell 30 minutes and cool before filling.

Crostata di Prugne
Plum Tart

We grew lots of plums at Busoler and could eat only so many in season. We distilled them for an off-season plum brandy similar to slivovitz, used them in jams, in gnocchi (recipe page 117), and, at the height of the season, in this plum tart.

¼ cup smooth apricot jam

one 10" tart shell, (recipe page 242), prebaked 15 minutes

14 firm, ripe purple plums, halved and pitted

2 tablespoons sugar

½ teaspoon water

¼ teaspoon lemon juice

Preheat the oven to 350° F. Brush 3 tablespoons of the apricot jam over the bottom of the prebaked tart shell. Starting from the outside edge of the shell, arrange the plums in concentric circles until the shell is filled. Bake the tart 10 minutes, sprinkle the sugar over the plums, and return to the oven for an additional 25–35 minutes or longer, depending on the texture of the plums, until the pastry is nicely browned and the plums are well cooked. Remove from the oven and cool.

In a small saucepan, melt the remaining apricot jam in the water and lemon juice. (Strain if the jam is lumpy.) When the tart has cooled somewhat, brush the plums with apricot glaze. Serve at room temperature.

Crema Pasticcera
Pastry Cream

FOR TWO 10" TARTS

1⅔ cups milk

1 whole egg plus 2 yolks

2 tablespoons plus 1 teaspoon cornstarch

3 tablespoons sugar

1 teaspoon vanilla extract

In a medium saucepan, scald the milk. Meanwhile, in a bowl, whisk together the whole egg, egg yolks, cornstarch, and sugar until smoothly blended. When the milk boils, add a little bit to the egg mixture and whisk well. Add this mixture to the saucepan with the remaining milk and whisk to blend.

Cook over moderate heat, whisking constantly, until the pastry cream thickens and loses its raw taste, about 5 minutes. Off the heat, beat in the vanilla. With a spatula, scrape the cream into a bowl and press plastic wrap directly onto the surface to prevent a skin from forming. Chill well before using.

Crostata di Fragole

Strawberry Tart

SERVES 8 – 10

We had a strawberry patch at Busoler, and we have one today at home in Douglaston, where my mother, Erminia, delights in tending our gardens. We use this recipe for strawberry tart at Felidia.

½ recipe pastry cream (page 244)

1 prebaked 10" tart shell, cooled (recipe page 242)

2 pints firm ripe strawberries, washed, hulled, and halved

¼ cup smooth apricot jam

1 teaspoon lemon juice

1 teaspoon water

Spread the pastry cream evenly over the cooled prebaked tart shell. Starting from the outside, arrange the strawberries, cut side down, in tight concentric circles, trimming them to fit as necessary, until the shell is filled.

In a small saucepan, heat the apricot jam, lemon juice, and water until the jam is melted. Brush the mixture over the strawberries. Serve at room temperature.

Palacinke
Sweet Crêpes

SERVES ABOUT 10

There were evenings when *palacinke* with fresh goat's milk were the whole meal. I remember being impatient, waiting for all of them to be fried while my friends were playing outside. So, while they were still hot, I would roll them with sugar or marmalade and wrap the bottom part with a piece of brown paper bag so as not to scorch my hands. *Palacinke* in hand, I ran out to play: jump rope, hide-and-seek, or whatever the game of the day was. Sometimes I was so intensely involved in the game that I would bite paper and all. "What can you say about *palacinke?*" Jay asks. What can I say? This is the common Eastern European dessert, with minor regional variations, the Slavic progenitor of the elegant French *crêpes Suzettes,* introduced to international hotel cookery via Istria and eventually naturalized in French Canada, where savory pancakes are sweetened with maple syrup. Every culture on earth has its own version, sweet or savory. The Mexicans have their tortillas; the Ethiopians, their stew-filled *injera.*

2 eggs	*1 teaspoon vanilla extract*
2 cups milk	*2 cups flour*
½ cup club soda	*6 tablespoons melted butter*
¼ cup sugar	*Grated zest of 1 lemon*
¼ teaspoon salt	*Grated zest of 1 orange*
1 tablespoon dark rum	*Vegetable oil, for frying*

In a bowl, whisk the eggs. Add the milk, club soda, sugar, salt, rum, and vanilla, and blend well until the sugar has dissolved. Gradually sift in the flour to form a batter; then stir in the melted butter. (The consistency should be that of melted ice cream). Add the citrus zests.

In a 6"–7" crêpe pan, heat 1 tablespoon vegetable oil over moderately high flame, pouring off the excess. Tilt the heated and oiled pan at a 45° angle to the floor and pour batter in small batches into the pan, allowing it to run down from the highest point. (Usually, ½ ladleful of batter will cover the pan adequately.) The secret is to flex your wrist, distributing the batter as thinly as possible.

Return the pan to the heat, reduce the flame to moderate, and cook the crêpe until lightly browned, 30–40 seconds. Flip it carefully with a spatula and cook the second side until brown spots appear. Remove from the pan and repeat the process with the remaining bat-ter, re-oiling the pan only as necessary. (Each crêpe should take about ½ minute per side.)

The finished crêpes can be sprinkled with sugar or spread with marmalade, folded into quarters, drizzled with a little Grand Marnier, sprinkled with confectioners' sugar, or served hot with a spoonful of whipped cream and some fresh berries.

Alija Kljuco, a Busoler neighbor, with Lidia's cousin Dinco, and one of the many Busoler goats.

Crostata di Mele alla Crema
Apple-Custard Tart

Any pastry chef worth his or her flour and sugar puts a personal "signature," however unobtrusive it may be, on the standard recipe for this dessert, which has been in the public domain almost since God made little green apples. This is how our own *pasticciere*, Michael Colon, interprets a perennial classic.

1 unbaked 10" tart shell (recipe page 242)
2 medium Granny Smith apples
2 eggs
1/4 cup sugar

1 cup heavy cream
1/2 teaspoon vanilla extract
1/4 cup smooth apricot jam
3 tablespoons hot water

Preheat the oven to 350° F. Bake the tart shell 15 minutes, remove it from the oven, and cool slightly on a rack.

Meanwhile, peel and core the apples and slice each into sixteen thin wedges. Beat the eggs and sugar together. Add the cream and vanilla extract, and mix well until the sugar is completely dissolved.

Spread 2 tablespoons of the apricot jam inside the tart shell and arrange the apple slices over it in two concentric, overlapping circles. Transfer the tart to a baking sheet and pour the custard mixture over the apples. Return the tart to the oven and bake until the apples are tender and the custard is set, about 40 minutes.

Allow the tart to cool on a rack while melting the remaining apricot jam in 3 tablespoons hot water. Brush the jam mixture over the surface of the tart, and serve either at room temperature or lightly chilled.

Pesche in Vino Bianco
Peaches in White Wine

SERVES 4

This is just my own version of macedonia, or, as the French say, *macédoine*. A simple, refreshing summer dessert, it should be prepared 3 hours ahead of time. Blueberries or strawberries can be substituted for the cherries.

16 mint leaves
3 ripe peaches, peeled and sliced
1 cup pitted cherries
1 cup dry Spumante wine

1 cup dry white wine
1 tablespoon Peachtree Schnapps
2 tablespoons sugar

Reserve 4 of the mint leaves, combine all other ingredients in a wide, deep dish, stir lightly until the sugar dissolves, and refrigerate 3 hours.

Serve in stemmed glasses, topped with the reserved mint leaves.

Pesche con Mascarpone
Peaches with Mascarpone

SERVES 4

This is an old dish, a good marriage of fruit and cheese, and a nice light way to finish a meal.

1 cup fresh mascarpone cheese
2 tablespoons heavy cream
4 ripe peaches, halved and pitted

2 tablespoons chopped walnuts
8 strawberries
4 mint sprigs

In a bowl, blend the cheese and cream. With a pastry bag, pipe the cheese mixture into the peach cavities (or use a spoon if you prefer). Sprinkle the walnuts over the cheese filling and serve two peach halves per portion, flanked by a pair of strawberries and a sprig of mint.

Fragole al Balsamico
Strawberries with Balsamic Vinegar

SERVES 6 – 8

It was in Modena, the home of balsamic vinegar, that I discovered the many uses to which that marvelous substance can be put. One of my teachers, Franco Colombani, owner of Ristorante il Sole in Maleo, introduced me to this simple, sprightly dessert. The orange juice is my own addition to his recipe and may be omitted if you prefer.

3 pints ripe strawberries
2 tablespoons traditional balsamic vinegar

2 tablespoons superfine sugar
2 tablespoons fresh-squeezed orange juice (optional)

Wash and hull the berries, and slice them into a bowl. Add the balsamic vinegar, mix well, and marinate 15–20 minutes. Add the sugar and, if desired, the orange juice, mix thoroughly, and serve.

ABOUT ZABAGLIONE

Zabaglione is an unset custard laced with a fortified wine—most commonly Marsala. To make it properly requires an understanding of its chemistry. As the egg yolks are heated and whisked, their fat molecules expand, and it's into these stretched fatty molecules that the evaporating wine and sugar are absorbed, thereby imparting a fluffy creaminess to the custard.

The proper ratio of ingredients is all-important to the success of the dessert and works out to 1 egg yolk to 1 tablespoon sugar to 1 tablespoon Marsala. These ingredients must be thoroughly blended before being subjected to heat, and once the heating has begun, temperature must remain constant and moderate. If the heat is too high, the evaporating alcohol will escape, leaving the fat molecules empty and the custard unable to rise. Moreover, the zaba- glione mixture scorches easily; what happens is that the proteins in the egg yolk coagulate over excessive heat, and when coagulation takes place your zabaglione becomes an unwanted dish of scrambled eggs.

Although other wines of comparable alcoholic content can be blended with or substituted for Marsala, cordials or liquors of higher alcoholic content are too volatile: Their alcohol will escape immediately, leaving a flat zabaglione in the mixing bowl. Overly rapid alcohol loss can be avoided when stronger spirits are used, but not without more experience and dexterity than most home cooks are likely to have. The procedure entails a reduction of the ratio of sugar to egg yolks, a lower starting temperature, and a very gradual, minutely calibrated heat increase.

Torta di Zabaglione al Cioccolato
Chocolate Zabaglione Cake

SERVES 8 – 10

When our gifted young pastry chef, Michael Colon, joined the Felidia family, he brought us a recipe for chocolate zabaglione cake. Working together, Michael and I refined it somewhat, and this is the ultimate result, the version we serve at the restaurant. It's not a simple production, but it's worth the time and effort. The cake should cool for two or three hours before it's assembled, and refrigerated overnight before it's served. Also it's important that a fairly constant, warm temperature be maintained at every step of each procedure, so that all ingredients combine properly.

FOR THE SPONGE CAKE (GENOISE)

1 cup flour	*⅛ teaspoon baking soda*
¼ cup unsweetened cocoa	*3 large eggs*
⅛ teaspoon baking powder	*¾ cup sugar*

Preheat the oven to 375° F. Grease and lightly flour a 10″ cake pan with sides 3″ high.

Sift together the flour, cocoa, baking powder, and baking soda. In a medium bowl set over a pan of simmering water, beat the eggs and sugar together until the mixture has warmed and most of the sugar has dissolved, about 3 minutes. Using a hand-held electric mixer, beat the egg-sugar mixture at high speed until doubled in volume, about 5 minutes. Off heat, fold in the sifted dry ingredients, pour the batter into the prepared cake pan, and bake about 25 minutes, until a tester inserted into the center of the cake comes out clean and the cake's surface springs back when lightly pressed. Cool completely for 2–3 hours.

FOR THE SYRUP

½ cup Marsala	*2 tablespoons confectioners' sugar*

Warm the Marsala in a saucepan and whisk in the sugar until dissolved.

1 teaspoon unflavored gelatin	½ pound semisweet chocolate, chopped
¼ cup plus 1½ tablespoons cold water	½ cup Marsala
⅓ cup plus 1 tablespoon sugar	1½ cups heavy cream, whipped until stiff
7 egg yolks (at room temperature)	3 tablespoons unsweetened cocoa

In a small saucepan, soften the gelatin in the 1½ tablespoons cold water. In a medium-size heavy saucepan, combine the sugar with the ¼ cup of water and bring to a boil over moderately high heat. Cook until the resultant syrup registers 250° F. on a candy thermometer, or forms a ball when dropped into cold water, about 5 minutes.

Meanwhile, beat the egg yolks in a stainless-steel bowl. Set the bowl over a pan of lightly simmering water and beat until warmed through but not cooked. Beat in the sugar syrup until well blended, and remove from the heat.

Melt the softened gelatin over low heat until completely dissolved. In a small bowl set over a pan of gently simmering water, melt the chocolate until smooth but not hot. Beat the chocolate into the egg-sugar mixture, then beat in the dissolved gelatin and the Marsala. Fold in the whipped cream until no traces of white are visible.

ASSEMBLING THE CAKE

Using a long, serrated cake knife, slice the chocolate sponge cake horizontally to form three layers of equal thickness. Set the bottom layer into a 10″ spring-form pan and brush the surface with Marsala syrup, moistening it well. Spoon ⅓ of the filling over the surface, and repeat all steps with the remaining two layers of sponge cake, ending with filling to cover the surface of the top layer. Smooth with a spatula, cover, and refrigerate overnight.

Remove the cake from the spring-form pan and sift the unsweetened cocoa over the top. Serve in slices with hot Chocolate Zabaglione Sauce (recipe follows).

Chocolate Zabaglione Sauce

YIELDS ABOUT 2 CUPS

6 egg yolks (at room temperature)

1/4 cup dry Marsala

1/4 cup sugar

3 ounces semisweet chocolate, chopped and melted

In a large saucepan, bring 3″ of water to a simmer. In a large copper or stainless-steel bowl, whisk together the egg yolks, Marsala, and sugar. Set the bowl over the simmering water and whisk constantly until the mixture is fluffy, light, and hot, 3–4 minutes. Off the heat, very slowly and thoroughly fold in the melted chocolate. Spoon hot sauce over cake.

Note: This sauce must be made just before it is served.

Zabaglione al Barolo

SERVES 8

Barolo is the noblest of Italy's Nebbiolo red wines—big, rounded, and robust, full of complex nuances. For this simple but grand dessert, I recommend a well-aged vintage from a dependable winery, and not some flimsy substitute for a wine truly deserving of its name.

6 egg yolks

3/4 cup superior Barolo wine

6 tablespoons sugar

In a copper or stainless-steel bowl, whisk all three ingredients together.

Set the bowl over gently simmering water and whisk mixture constantly $2\frac{1}{2}$–$3\frac{1}{2}$ minutes, until it is very light, frothy, and warmed through. Serve immediately in parfait glasses.

Semifreddo alle Mandorle
Soft Ice Cream with Almonds

SERVES 8–10

In naming this dessert, someone used an adjective as a noun, but the literal translation, "half-cold," remains stubbornly adjectival and altogether unsatisfactory. Semifreddo isn't really ice cream, nor can it properly be termed frozen custard. For the sake of convenience, I've settled on "soft ice cream" here. This is one case when eating your words is sweeter than quibbling over them.

½ cup whole almonds	*5 eggs, separated*
½ cup grated semisweet chocolate	*1 cup superfine sugar*
6 amaretto cookies, crumbled	*2 cups heavy cream*
1 tablespoon brandy	

On a baking sheet or aluminum foil, toast the almonds a few inches beneath the broiler, turning them frequently until golden, about 2 minutes. When cooled, chop the almonds fine (the food processor will do the job in seconds). In a bowl, blend the chocolate, crumbled amaretto cookies, almonds, and the brandy.

In a larger bowl, beat the egg whites until foamy. Add ½ cup of the sugar and beat until stiff, but not dry. In a third bowl, beat the egg yolks with the remaining sugar until pale yellow and thick.

In another bowl (if you haven't run out of bowls), whip the heavy cream until stiff. In either the second or the third bowl, gently fold the beaten yolks and whites together until evenly combined. Then gently fold in the whipped cream.

Line a 9-cup loaf pan snugly with plastic wrap. Spoon ⅓ of the egg mixture into it and tap the bottom of the pan on a hard surface to settle the mixture in a level layer. Sprinkle half the chocolate-almond mixture over the surface in an even layer, and repeat the sequence, finishing with the last ⅓ of the egg-cream mixture. Smooth the surface with a spatula, cover with plastic wrap, and freeze until hard (overnight).

To serve, invert the pan and tap the bottom sharply to loosen the frozen mixture. Remove the plastic wrap and slice semifreddo ¾" thick.

Semifreddo will keep in plastic wrap about 1 week in the freezer.

Crema di Caffè
Espresso Mousse

SERVES 8

Italians in general are passionate about coffee in almost any form and make particularly good use of it in all sorts of desserts. I wish I could remember where I picked up this recipe, but I can't. I think you'll like the flavor of the dish as much as I do.

1 tablespoon unflavored gelatin
½ cup cold water
1 cup sugar
3 drops fresh lemon juice
1 cup milk
1¾ cups heavy cream

3 eggs, separated
½ cup strong espresso coffee (see Note)
¼ teaspoon vanilla extract
Coffee beans or shaved chocolate for garnish

Sprinkle the gelatin over ¼ cup of the cold water and allow it to soften.

In a medium-size heavy saucepan, combine the sugar with ¼ cup of water and the lemon juice. Bring to a boil and cook until the sugar caramelizes to a rich dark brown, about 7 minutes. (Do not stir as it cooks.)

Meanwhile, in a second pan, scald the milk. When the caramel is ready, remove it from the heat and immediately add ¾ cup of the heavy cream. (Stand back because it may splatter.) Whisk the cream and caramel together, blending thoroughly, then whisk in the scalded milk.

In a bowl, beat the egg yolks. Add some of the caramel mixture and whisk well, then pour the contents of the bowl into the saucepan and whisk to blend. Return to moderately low heat and cook, stirring with a wooden spoon, until the custard coats the back of a spoon, about 9 minutes.

Off the heat, blend in the softened gelatin and stir well until thoroughly dissolved. Add the coffee and vanilla extract and combine well. Transfer the mixture to a bowl and refrigerate 30 minutes, stirring occasionally, until it begins to thicken.

Meanwhile, whip the remaining 1 cup heavy cream until stiff and keep chilled. When the mousse mixture has thickened, beat the egg whites until stiff. Fold them into the espresso custard, then fold in the whipped cream, lightly but thoroughly.

Pour into individual serving dishes or a large serving bowl and chill 3–4 hours. To serve, allow the mousse to rest about 10 minutes at room temperature to develop flavor, and decorate with coffee beans or shaved chocolate.

Note: 2 tablespoons instant espresso dissolved in ½ cup water can be substituted.

Fagiano Arrosto
Roast Pheasant
214

Crostata di Agnello
Rack of Lamb

178

Top to Bottom:
Crostata di Prugne
Plum Tart

243

Crostata di Fragole
Strawberry Tart

245

Crostata di Mele alla Crema
Apple-Custard Tart

248

ABOUT GRANITA

Granita is the rough-hewn older Italian cousin of the suave French sorbet and reflects an underlying difference between the two nations' approaches to cookery in general. Whereas the French tend to prize smoothness in everything from soups and sauces to cheeses, forcemeats, and desserts, we Italians favor coarser textures that we can get our teeth into. Granita is a case in point. Its name derives from *grano*, a kernel of grain, and the graininess of its texture is considered its distinguishing and most refreshing feature.

In its earliest form, granita was simply flavored mountain snow and appears to have originated in southern Italy or Sicily, where the citrus drinks and coffees of the Arabs were combined with snow or crushed ice. Later, around the middle of the nineteenth century, granitas were sold by Sicilian street vendors whose horse-drawn carts were equipped with freezers of a sort—copper drums that produced a semifrozen slush with which various flavoring agents were combined. The Italian ices—shaved ice and fruit syrup—and snow cones sold on the streets of some American cities today are rudimentary granitas, but those served in the better restaurants are as elegant as the most refined of the French sorbets and, to the Italian taste, have more character.

Granita di Caffè
Coffee Granita

SERVES 6

½ cup sugar

1 cup water

2 cups strong espresso coffee, cooled

½ pt. heavy cream, whipped with
1 tablespoon sugar

Roasted or chocolate-covered coffee beans
for garnish

In a medium saucepan, combine the sugar and water, bring to a simmer, and cook 5 minutes. Allow the sugar syrup to cool. Add the espresso and stir well. Pour the mixture into a 9″ × 13″ metal baking pan and place in the freezer. Stir every 8–10 minutes, to break up the ice crystals as they form around the edges of the pan, stirring them into the center of the mixture. The whole process should take about 1 hour.

To serve, scoop the granita into chilled serving glasses, top with whipped cream, and garnish with 2–3 coffee beans.

Granita di Pesca
Peach Granita

SERVES 4

2 cups water

1 pound unpeeled ripe peaches

⅓ cup sugar

2 tablespoons fresh lemon juice

1 drop vanilla extract

Mint leaves for garnish

Bring the water to a boil in a medium saucepan. Add the peaches and sugar, and simmer gently 30 minutes. Allow the peaches to cool thoroughly in the liquid, and pass the contents of the pan through a fine-mesh strainer, scraping the solids to extract as much pulp as possible. Add the lemon juice and vanilla extract, and freeze 45 minutes to 1 hour, scraping the ice crystals that form around the edges into the center every 10 minutes with a spatula. The mixture should be of an even, grainy consistency when ready.

To serve, scoop the granita into chilled serving glasses and garnish with mint leaves.

8

Spiriti e Infusioni
Spirits and Infusions

ABOUT GRAPPA

One of the most vivid of my early child-hood memories is of the *vendemmia,* or grape harvest, and the wine making that followed it—one of the most exciting events of the year. The *vendemmia* started early in the morning, before the sun was high enough to warm the grapes to be harvested. Everyone would go to the vineyards armed with pruning shears, except for the youngest kids: We had ordinary household scissors, which were tied to our belts with strings, so we wouldn't lose them among the clusters of grapes. Regard-less of age, everyone who could walk took part in the harvest, because the grapes had to be picked quickly once the sugar levels were right, and there were only a few days in which to get the job done.

Each adult carried the harvested grapes in a *brenta,* a big heavy hod strapped to a shoulder, but we kids had lighter, woven baskets. The gathered grapes were loaded into big barrels and taken to the *cantina,* or wine cellar, in tractor- or horse-drawn carts. Along the way, we kids would climb into the bar-rels barefoot, hold onto their rims, and begin the crushing of the grapes by jumping up and down on them. When we reached the *cantina,* we raced to the water hose to wash away the sweet juice, which was a great attraction for the swarms of bees that hung around there. There were lots of close calls, but somehow we rarely were stung.

We kids weren't really involved with the vinification of the grapes, but we hung around while the big barrels bub-bled during the fermentation process and waited excitedly for the first sweet taste of the year's new wine. After a week or two of quietude, the *svinatura* took place—the separation of the must, or vinifiable liquid, and the *vinacce,* or skins, residual pulp, and solids. It's the *vinacce* from which grappa is distilled, and the excitement began all over again when the process got under way. One of our neighbors had built the communal still, and everyone took part in the con-stant vigil that began once the fire was lighted under it. The fire had to be kept at an even, unvarying temperature and stoked with precise timing as the grappa slowly dripped, drop by drop, down a string suspended from the end of the recondensing coil, into the *damigiane*

Ivan Grabar distilling grappa, Busoler.

(demijohn). Grappa is powerful stuff, and the whole *cantina* reeked of its fumes; after ten minutes in there a kid could get woozy just by breathing.

Grappa was an integral part of our lives. We made infusions of it with fruits and herbs, used it to alleviate tooth-aches and stomach disorders, to cure hiccups and sneezing fits, and as a rub-down when we were feverish. When I had an aching tooth, I was given a tea-spoon of grappa, which I held in my mouth while I turned my head this way and that, until the elixir found the tender spot and anesthetized it somewhat. I still don't know whether the medicinal properties of grappa or the lighthead-edness induced by its alcoholic content did the trick.

The grappa produced commercially today is a far cry from the countrified home brew (the equivalent of American "moonshine" or, more precisely, the *marc* of rural France) of my childhood. My good friends, the Nonino family in Percoto, in Friuli, among others, have made a state-of-the-art science of grappa distillation. From single varietal grapes, such as Picolit, Fragolino, and Verduzzo, they now distill the juice, thereby retaining much more bouquet and flavor, eliminating the once-characteristic choking harshness of country grappa, and reducing the alco-holic content, which formerly was ex-cessive. This distillation is called *uve*. Today's grappas have taken their place among the world's finest brandies. Some of the other great grappa produc-ers are Bruno Ceretto, Angelo Gaja, and Bruno Giacosa.

Cherries or Grapes in Grappa

———

Various fruits have been macerated in grappa for centuries. The relationship is symbiotic: The fruits temper the harshness of the grappa while the grappa both preserves the fruits and intensifies their flavors. Proportions of fruit to grappa are variable. The intensity of the fruit flavor in the grappa will vary with the quantity of fruit you choose to macerate. Here is a rule-of-thumb recipe:

Select the largest, firmest cherries or grapes available, in the desired quantity. Clip the stems with scissors, leaving ⅛″ attached. Fill quart-size glass jars with the fruit of choice, add 4 tablespoons sugar to each, and add grappa to cover.

Leave the jars on a sunny windowsill, loosely covered, for 1 week. Seal tightly and allow to steep 3 months, away from strong light, before use.

Serve grappa and fruit together in a brandy snifter as an after-dinner *digestif*.

Figs in Grappa

———

Fill a wide-mouthed jar with loosely packed dried figs. Fill with grappa, cover tightly, allow to steep 2 months, and serve grappa and fruit together.

Food is my primary interest, but wine—itself technically a food—is a close runner-up. Wine has been an integral part of my life for as long as I can remember. I recall vividly the excitement that built up around Busoler in late September, when the barrels were washed and the *cantina* was readied to receive the sun-ripened varietal grapes of the region: Malvasia, Merlot, Terran, and Cabernet-Franc. Everyone, regardless of age, took part in the harvest, and the children were rewarded with tastes of the first, unfermented grape juice. We kids also were served real wine with our meals, although it was diluted with water and called *bevanda*. Significantly, the countries of the Mediterranean basin, where wine has been accepted as a natural component of a proper meal since ancient times, consistently have had the lowest rate of alcoholism anywhere in the non-Islamic world.

In my experience, there are three ways of pairing wines with nonvinous foods. If the food is to be dominant, the accompanying wines should be submissive. For example, if you serve a risotto with white truffles, or a wonderful *foie gras,* the character of the food should take precedence, with the wines you serve playing supporting roles. They should be of the finest quality, but of a character that doesn't upstage the meal's starring players. Wines strong in tannins, acidity, bouquet, or fruitiness should not be permitted to contend for dominance with richly flavorful or subtly aromatic foods. As a general rule, one powerful palatal or olfactory sensation should be clearly experienced and not obscured by another.

On the other hand, if the object of the occasion is to enjoy some great, rare wines, you certainly don't want to overshadow them with assertively flavorful, aromatic, highly acidic, or intensely spiced foods. On such occasions, spicy tomato-based sauces are not appropriate, nor are vegetables like artichokes, fennel, and asparagus—all high in mineral content.

Except on special occasions focused on particular dishes or wines, your goal should be to infuse the meal with harmony and balance. In my view, the menu takes precedence over the wine list unless the object of the occasion clearly and explicitly is to sample a selection of extraordinary wines. In the ordinary course of events, the chosen wines should complement and enhance the foods of choice, not compete with them for attention. When the menu has been determined, analyze the characteristics of the dishes you'll be serving—the intensity and nature of their flavors and aromas, their richness or lack thereof—and match your wines to your foods accordingly. If, for example, the food tends toward fattiness—say, it's smoked salmon or caviar—a wine of relatively high acidity will provide an agreeable counterbalance to the richness of the dish. Conversely, if the dish is a light preparation like broiled chicken, a full-bodied, fruity white or a light red will set it off nicely. As the complexity and intensity of the food increases, so should the complexity and amplitude of the wine.

If, for whatever reason, you choose to match foods to wines, the same principles should be your guide, with the foods, rather than the wines, playing supporting roles against which the wines can resonate. Have confidence in your choice of wines; you don't have to be a world-class oenologist with encyclopedic knowledge of the subject to make sound, logical selections. (As a general rule, the wines and foods of a particular region are well matched.) Within certain broad categories, wines share common characteristics; family traits that make them all compatible with correspondingly broad categories of foods and inappropriate for others. It isn't necessary to have tasted, or to be able to identify with pinpoint precision, every member of a particular family of wines. Any Barolo, say, of a good vintage and producer won't be so dissimilar from any other that it would be unacceptable in any context that calls for a big, round red. Nor will any other wine, whatever its origin and vintage, of comparable quality and character.

Above all, let your own taste be your guide. I've provided wine suggestions for most of the dishes in this book, but they reflect my own taste, which may not coincide with yours, and they necessarily fail to take into account the composition of an entire meal. Ultimately, it's your orchestration of that meal that determines its character and effect. You are the composer of a symphony and must determine its rhythms and harmonies, the placement of its crescendi and diminuendi, its syncopated passages and its passages of mellow resonance. Between them, foods and wines allow you a lot more scope than the musical composer's eight notes of the scale.

The tradition of making wine from grapes is older in Italy than anywhere else in Europe except Greece. It doesn't necessarily follow that Italian wines are superior to all others (the Greeks having abdicated any claims to preëminence by the second century B.C.), but the traditional affinity between a given culture's wines and foods has been established longer in Italy than in any other wine-producing nation.

If I were French or Spanish, I'm sure I'd mostly drink and cook with French or Spanish wines, which complement their respective cuisines better than any others. Because I'm an Italian cook, I naturally gravitate toward the wines of my own heritage, just as the people of other wine-growing cultures gravitate toward theirs. Who would deny the traditional excellence of the great Bordeaux and Burgundies, or the more recent emergence of superior wines in Spain, California, and elsewhere? It's more a matter of accent and idiom: A particular culture's wines, grown in the same soil and under the same sun as its foods, on the same terrain and in the same climate that nurtured its language and its ethos, harmonize more readily with its own style of cooking and its own way of living.

Because all the recipes in this book are for Italian dishes, all the wines I've recommended for use in conjunction with them are Italian. Admittedly, distinctions that seem quite obvious to those born speaking, eating, and thinking Italian may be lost on those who don't share the same heritage. I don't insist that you use exclusively Italian wines if your preferences lie elsewhere, but I hope that any non-Italian wines you select at least will share the basic qualities and characteristics of those I've specifically recommended.

THE NEBBIOLO GRAPE: BAROLO AND BARBARESCO

The Nebbiolo is a grape grown in the Langhe region of Piemonte, where the hills have a high limestone and clay content. This is the grape from which the great Italian reds, Barolo and Barbaresco, are made, along with such scattered regional wines as Nebbiolo, Ghemme, Carema, and Gattinara, among others.

The differences between Barolo and Barbaresco derive from their respective regions of growth: the DOCG (Denominazione di Origine Controllata e Garantita) zones surrounding the towns of Barolo and Barbaresco. The major technical difference between the two is that by law Barolo must be aged a year longer than Barbaresco.

Barolo is a garnet-colored wine with mingled aromas of summer poppies, violets, and freshly picked fruit, with hints of roses and tar, a somewhat licoricelike flavor, and a full, dry body. It ages exceptionally well for upward of thirty years.

At present, two styles of Barolo are produced: old and new. The major differences are provided by the vinification process used and the dominant tannins.

Tannins are proteins, amino acids, that are the backbone of wine. They are found in the skin and outer layer of the grape's flesh, or at the core, around the seeds. The outer tannins are considered the softer tannins, and are dominant in the new-style Barolos, while the old-style product is dominated by the inner, harder. In both cases, the style of the wine is largely determined by the interaction of its dominant tannins with the wood of the barrels in which it is aged. New-style Barolo generally can be drunk younger than old-style.

A fine Barolo is a big, robust wine that marries well with deeply flavorful foods, such as roasts and game.

Barbaresco's garnet color is somewhat brighter than Barolo's. Fewer tannins make it a lighter wine with a silky finish, whereas Barolo is rounder and more satiny. Its bouquet combines vanilla, cinnamon, green pepper, and dried peaches. It ages extemely well and marries beautifully with earthy foods like truffles, mushrooms, and game.

LEADING BAROLO PRODUCERS

F.lli Barale
F.lli Borgogno
Giacomo Borgogno
Gianfranco Bovio
F.lli Brovia
Cantina Mascarello di Bartolo Mascarello
F.lli Cavallotto
Azienda Agricola Ceretto
Clerico
Cogno-Marcarini di Elvio Cogno
Aldo Conterno
Giacomo Conterno
Giuseppe Contratto
Paolo Cordero di Montezemolo
Luigi Einaudi
Fiorina Franco
Fontanafredda
Bruon Giacosa
F.lli Giacosa
"Granduca" Cantine Duca d'Asti
Azienda Agricola di Elio Grasso
Giovanni Lodali
Marchesi di Barolo
Marchese Spinola
Giuseppe Mascarello
Giuseppe Massolino, Azienda Agricola "Vigna Rionda"
F.lli Oddero
Palladino
Pio Cesare
Luigi Pira
Podere Rocche dei Manzoni
Alfredo Prunotto
Renato Ratti
Francesco Rinaldi
Giuseppe Rinaldi
"Rocche" Costamagna
Paolo Scavino
Filippo Sobrero
Vietti di Alfredo Currado
Giacomo Voerzio

LEADING BARBARESCO PRODUCERS

F.lli Barale
Giacomo Borgogno
F.lli Serio & Battista Borgogno
Cantina Glicine
Castello di Neive
F.lli Cigliuti
Giacomo Conterno
Giuseppe Contratto
Franco Fiorina
Fontanafredda
Gaja
Bruno Giacosa
Enrico Giovannini–Moresco
"La Spinona" Azienda Agricola di Pietro Berutti
Martinenga dei Marchesi di Gresy
Giuseppe Mascarello
F.lli Oddero
Parroco di Neive
Elia Pasquero Secondo
Pio Cesare
Produttori del Barbaresco
Alfredo Prunotto
Renato Ratti
Francesco Rinaldi
Vietti di Alfredo Currado

BRUNELLO DI MONTALCINO

Brunello di Montalcino is produced in the area of Montalcino, south of Siena, in Toscana. It is made from a subvariety of the Sangiovese grape called Sangiovese Grasso or Brunello (for its dark color). The cultivation of wine grapes in the region dates back to Etruscan times.

A big wine that needs time to develop, Brunello is ready after seven years of aging and at its best after ten to fifteen years. It has a deep, shadowy garnet color and a bouquet of cherries and wild blueberries, with undertones of spices and nuts. Its texture should be velvety, rather than silky, and other sensations it produces should linger in the mouth. It's an elegant, noble wine, to be savored with robustly sauced pastas, polenta, red meats, roasts, and game.

LEADING BRUNELLO PRODUCERS

Altesino	Il Poggione (Franceschi)
Biondi-Santi	
Capanna (G. Cencioni)	Lisini
	Mastrojanni
Case Basse	Tenuta di Caparzo
Castelgiocondo	Tenuta Col D'Orcia
Luigi Cecchi	Val di Suga
Colle al Matrichese (Costanti)	Villa Banfi
Fattoria dei Barbi (Colombini)	

CHIANTI

The region of Toscana where Chianti is produced comprises the provinces of Arezzo, Pisa, Pistoia, and Siena. Chianti is made from a blend of grapes combined in varying proportions: Sangiovese, 70–90 percent; Canaiolo, 5–10 percent; the remainder, Trebbiano, Malvasia, and others.

The blending, called *uvaggio,* varies from producer to producer, giving each label its own individuality within recognizable parameters. Characteristically, Chiantis are excellent medium-bodied wines with balanced tannins and acidity and elegant style. Among the most versatile of the Italian reds, they complement a wide range of dishes, age well, and also can be drunk young. They are best after five to eight years of aging, but an exceptionally fine bottle can be laid down for twenty years or more.

A good Chianti is characterized by a satisfying fullness of varied flavors, myriad aromas, and a silky texture.

LEADING CHIANTI PRODUCERS

Badia a Coltibuono
Brolio
Capannelle
Giovanni Cappelli
Carbaiola di
    Barfede-Certaldo
Castellare
Castell'In Villa
Castello dei Ram-
    polla
Castello di Ama
Castello di Quer-
    ceto
Castello di S. Paolo
    In Rosso
Castello di Volpaia
Fattoria Monta-
    gliari, Giovanni
    Cappelli
Fontodi
Fortilizio il Colom-
    baio
Fossi
Isole e Olena

La Pagliaia Riserva
    Granduca Ferdi-
    nando III
La Ripa
Le Bocce
Le Masse di San
    Leolino
Lilliano
Melini Riserva
Monte Vertine
Nozzole
Pagliarese
Palazzo al Bosco
Poggio al Sole
Quercia al Poggio
Ruffino
San Felice
Signoria di Barfede-
    Certaldo
Tenuta la Colom-
    baia
Tenuta Villa Rosa
Villa Antinori
Villa Banfi
Villa Cerna
Villa Colombaio

AMARONE

Amarone wine is made from Recioto grapes, which are spread on bamboo trays after the harvest, and turned over a period of four to six months, during which time they dehydrate and concentrate their sugars. By the time they are ready for vinification, they have lost about three-quarters of their original weight.

Their fermentation is a long, slow process, and the wine may be aged from three to six years in the barrel, depending on the producer.

Amarone characteristically combines a full body with concentrated flavors. Its color is deep purple-red. Its bouquet suggests dried fruits and flowers. It's quite a dry wine as it's sipped, with a slight after-sensation of sweetness. It's a great companion for stewed, braised, and roast meats, and for nose-intense cheeses.

LEADING AMARONE PRODUCERS

Allegrini
Bertani
Bolla
Boscaini & Figli
Gasparini
Guerrier-Rizzard
Le Ragose
Maculan
Masi

Pierobon
Pieropan
Scamperle
Speri
Venegazzù
Zenato
Zeni
Zonin

VINO NOBILE DI MONTEPULCIANO

Montepulciano is an area near Siena, in southern Toscana. The grapes used in the production of Vino Nobile are approximately 50 percent Sangiovese Grasso; 10–20 percent Canarolo Nero; 10–20 percent Trebbiano, and 10 percent Grechetto Bianco.

The interesting light complexity of this wine derives from the use of white grapes, which may account for 25 percent of the overall blend. The wine requires at least five years of aging and will tolerate several more.

With age, it takes on a velvety finish, complex aroma, and full flavor. It matches very well with rich soups, beef, lamb, and roast fowl.

LEADING PRODUCERS OF VINO NOBILE DI MONTEPULCIANO

Avignonesi	Fassati
Bologna Bonsignori	Fattoria del Cerro
Boscarelli	(Saiagricola)
Cantine Baiocchi	Fattoria Fognano
(Saiagricola)	Melini
Casalte	Poliziano
Fanetti	

MONTEPULCIANO D'ABRUZZO

Montepulciano is a place name that occurs in at least three scattered parts of Italy, and this wine, from Abruzzo, shouldn't be confused with the foregoing wine from Toscana. To further complicate matters, the grape used for Montepulciano d'Abruzzo is named for the place.

This is a light, fruity red that can be excellent with various pastas, fowl, stewed lamb, and roasts.

LEADING PRODUCERS OF MONTEPULCIANO D'ABRUZZO

Barone Cornacchia	Emidio Pepe
Casal Thaulero	Edoardo Valentini

FRIULI, VENEZIA GIULIA

Friuli has a venerable wine-making history, but has undergone many vicissitudes at the hands of the Romans, Huns, Byzantines, Venetians, Austro-Hungarians, Slavs, and Italians, none of which was conducive to uninterrupted oenological progress.

It wasn't until 1960 that programs were instituted and funds invested to realize the full potential of what since has become the best white wine region of Italy. Then, old Friulian varietals and selected imported varietals were planted, and six DOCG zones were established: Aquileia, Collio, Colli Orientali del Friuli, Grave del Friuli, Isonzo, and Latisana.

Old Friulian varietals include white Picolit, Ribolla, Tocai Friulano, Verduzzo Friulano, red Pignolo, Refosco, Schioppettino, Tacelenghe, and Terrano.

Imported varietals are white Chardonnay, Malvasia Istriana, Müller-Thurgau, Pinot Bianco, Pinot Grigio, Riesling, Sangiovese, Traminer, red Cabernet Franc, Cabernet Sauvignon, Merlot, and Pinot Nero.

Many Friulian wines have been discussed in some detail elsewhere in the book, in connection with specific dishes, and I won't belabor the subject here, except to note that the technique of *uvaggio* (grape blending), enhanced by wood aging, has been used in recent years with exceptional results. Some of the mavericks of the *uvaggio* are Silvio Jermann, Ronco del Gnemiz, Abbazia di Rosazzo, Livio Felluga, Marco Felluga, and Volpe Pasini. Their wines are notable for complexities, balance between their several varietals, and longevity. To generalize broadly, Friulian wines are characterized by crispness, vivaciousness, and a fresh fruitiness. Between the whites and the reds, they complement the whole spectrum of foods, from the most delicate freshwater fish to the most intensely flavorful game.

LEADING FRIULIAN PRODUCERS

Abbazia di Rosazzo
Casa Vinicola Tenuta Angoris
Borgo Conventi
Collavini
Girolamo Dorigo
Giovanni Dri
Enofriulia
Livio Felluga
Marco Felluga
Formentini
Gian Franco Furlan
Gradnik, Azienda Agricola
Jermann
Azienda Agricola F.lli Pighin

Boris Pintar
Azienda Agricola Plozner
Azienda Agricola Ronchi di Ciallia
Azienda Agricola Ronco del Gnemiz
Azienda Agricola Pietro Rubini & Figli
Azienda Agricola Mario Schioppetto
Azienda Agricola Vigne Dal Leon

TORCOLATO

This is a delightful dessert wine, especially as rendered by my dear friend Fausto Maculan, who achieves a delicate balance between sweetness and just enough acidity to keep the palate clean while providing myriad sensations of flowers, apricots, peaches, and apples. It is vinified from semidried Vespaiolo, Garganega, and Tocai grapes. It can be served as an *aperitivo,* as an accompaniment to light, somewhat sweet antipasti (such as prosciutto), and, of course, most desserts.

RECIOTO

This desert wine might be described as Amarone in an early stage of development. Fermentation is not completed, so that residual sugars render it full-bodied and sweet. It's deep red-purple, with subtle hints of prunes, violets, and dried fruits. It goes well with fresh fruits and chocolate desserts.

MOSCATO D'ASTI

A light, fizzy Muscat wine, low in alcohol, fresh, delicate, and redolent of fruits and flowers. Refreshing after a meal, it is well suited to fresh fruit desserts, as a table accompaniment or macerating agent. My favorite producers are Giacomo Bologna and Paolo Saracco.

BRACHETTO D'ACQUI

A sprightly sparkling red, this is a fresh, grapey wine to be drunk young. Serve it with fruits or as a simple summertime drink. Good producers are Giacomo Bologna, G. Carnevale, and Villa Banfi.

VIN SANTO

This "holy" wine traditionally was made as a by-product in most wine-producing homes in Toscana. Originally semi-smoked in kitchens, the grapes used are Malvasia and Trebbiano. It is vinified between December and March, then aged in small barrels for three to five years. Changing temperatures during the aging, a desirable process, can produce wide variations of color within the yellow-gold range. Its natural sugars balance its acidity well. Traditionally served with hard Tuscan cookies (as a dunking medium), it complements other pastries or can be served alone.

BUKKARAM

The name of this wonderful dessert wine derives from the Arabic, although the Arabs don't drink (which didn't prevent them from supplying us with the word "alcohol"). This is a product of the island of Pantelleria, halfway between Sicilia and the North African coast, and is vinified from sun-dried Moscato grapes. Its nose is intense, almost Sherrylike; its flavor fresh but full of ripe grape. Serve it unaccompanied or with spicy cheeses or somewhat dry pastries. A leading producer is Azienda Vecchio Sampieri di Marco De Bartoli, also famed for aged Marsalas in the old Solera tradition.

Photo Captions
Part Titles and Chapter Openings

Lidia's maternal grandmother Nonna Rosa (right), great-aunt Santola Maria, and cousins at Busoler. Santola Maria was the village's reigning mushroom forager. pp. 16–17

A gathering in the Istrian seaport of Rakalj (formerly Castelnuovo). pp. 46–47

Bruno Visenauer slicing mortadella at Da Giovanni, his immensely popular trattoria in Trieste. pp. 48–49

The Mercato Centrale, the chief produce market of Trieste. pp. 78–79

Pasta making at an Italian "macaroni" factory. (Courtesy of the Bettman Archives) pp. 94–95

Fisherman mending nets on the island of Grado, in the Gulf of Trieste. Settled by refugees from Aquileia during the time of Attila, Grado is a popular summer resort celebrated about equally for its splendid cathedral and splendid seafood. pp. 132–33

Gathering lambs, Rakalj. pp. 160–61

In Busoler, pheasant was hung in the wine cellar before roasting for a special treat. pp. 204–5

Making *grissini* (breadsticks) at a bakery in Udine, about forty miles northwest of Trieste. pp. 226–27

Lidia's cousin Renato tastes his wine in the *cantina* at Busoler. pp. 260–61

INDEX